Surviving the Future

CHANDOS
INFORMATION PROFESSIONAL SERIES

Series Editor: Ruth Rikowski
(email: Rikowskigr@aol.com)

Chandos' new series of books are aimed at the busy information professional. They have been specially commissioned to provide the reader with an authoritative view of current thinking. They are designed to provide easy-to-read and (most importantly) practical coverage of topics that are of interest to librarians and other information professionals. If you would like a full listing of current and forthcoming titles, please visit our web site www.chandospublishing.com or email info@chandospublishing.com or telephone +44 (0) 1223 891358.

New authors: we are always pleased to receive ideas for new titles; if you would like to write a book for Chandos, please contact Dr Glyn Jones on email gjones@chandospublishing.com or telephone number +44 (0) 1993 848726.

Bulk orders: some organisations buy a number of copies of our books. If you are interested in doing this, we would be pleased to discuss a discount. Please info@chandospublishing.com or telephone +44 (0) 1223 891358.

Surviving the Future

Academic Libraries, Quality, and Assessment

GAIL MUNDE AND KENNETH MARKS

Chandos Publishing

Oxford · Cambridge · New Delhi

Chandos Publishing
TBAC Business Centre
Avenue 4
Station Lane
Witney
Oxford OX28 4BN
UK
Tel: +44 (0) 1993 848726
Email: info@chandospublishing.com
www.chandospublishing.com

Chandos Publishing is an imprint of Woodhead Publishing Limited

Woodhead Publishing Limited
Abington Hall
Granta Park
Great Abington
Cambridge CB21 6AH
UK
www.woodheadpublishing.com

First published in 2009

ISBN:
978 1 84334 477 3

British Library Cataloguing-in-Publication Data.
A catalogue record for this book is available from the British Library.

Typeset by Domex e-Data Pvt.Ltd.
Printed in the UK and USA.

Printed in the UK by 4edge Limited - www.4edge.co.uk

Contents

List of figures and tables		ix
List of abbreviations		xi
About the authors		xiii
Preface		xv
1	**Quality, assessment and evaluation**	**1**
	Defining quality	1
	Measurement	6
	Assessment	8
	The challenges of self-assessment	9
	Notes	12
	Bibliography	12
2	**Creating a culture of assessment**	**19**
	Introduction	19
	Evaluating your library's culture	22
	Notes	28
	Bibliography	29
3	**Frameworks for quality improvement**	**31**
	Malcolm Baldrige National Quality Award	32
	Academic Quality Improvement Project (AQIP)	37
	European Foundation for Quality Management (EFQM)	39
	Australian Business Excellence Framework (ABEF)	45
	Notes	49
	Bibliography	50

4	**Strategic planning, the Balanced Scorecard and benchmarking**	**55**
	Strategic planning	55
	Measurement systems and the Balanced Scorecard	59
	Benchmarking	67
	Notes	73
	Bibliography	74
5	**Performance indicators**	**81**
	Introduction	81
	Establishing library performance indicators	83
	Impacts and outcomes	96
	Notes	103
	Bibliography	104
6	**The library's role in successful faculty research and teaching**	**111**
	A framework for faculty success	111
	Faculty and the current academic environment	112
	Critical factors in faculty research success	113
	Critical factors in faculty teaching success	117
	Desirable faculty outcomes of library engagement	121
	Notes	122
	Bibliography	123
7	**The library's role in successful postgraduate and professional education**	**127**
	A framework for postgraduate and professional student success	127
	Postgraduate students and the current academic environment	130
	Information literacy as the critical factor in postgraduate student success	132
	Desirable outcomes of library engagement	137
	Notes	138
	Bibliography	138

8	**The library's role in the success of undergraduate students**	**141**
	A framework for undergraduate student success	141
	Undergraduate students and the current academic environment	142
	Critical factors in undergraduate student success	146
	Desirable outcomes of library engagement	166
	Notes	167
	Bibliography	169
9	**User satisfaction as a quality indicator**	**173**
	Approaches to satisfaction research	174
	User-centered research	176
	Analyzing qualitative data from user-centered research	182
	Bibliography	183
10	**Using group norms and peer comparisons as contexts for quality**	**185**
	Why compare your library to other libraries?	186
	Peer and cohort comparisons	187
	Accreditation and quality audits	188
	Communicating the results	189
	Notes	189
	Bibliography	190
11	**Toward surviving the future**	**191**
Index		197

List of figures and tables

Figures

2.1 Evaluation questionnaire "Do you have a culture of assessment?" 24–5

3.1 The seven criteria of the Baldrige Education Excellence framework 34

3.2 The EFQM Excellence Model® 41

4.1 Kaplan and Norton's Balanced Scorecard 61

4.2 The Balanced Scorecard reoriented for library use 64

Tables

1.1 Criteria by which library quality is judged 5

3.1 The EFQM Excellence Model® definitions and their interpretations for further and higher education 42–3

3.2 Australian Business Excellence Framework categories and supporting items 47

3.3 The Australian Business Excellence Framework learning cycle 48

5.1 Performance indicator by adapted Balanced Scorecard perspective 88

5.2 Comparison of IFLA and OIS performance indicators 89–95

List of abbreviations

ABEF	Australian Business Excellence Framework
ACRL	Association of College and Research Libraries
AQIP	Academic Quality Improvement Project
ARL	Association of Research Libraries
ARWU	Academic World Ranking of Universities
ASIBU	Annuaire Statistique Interactif des Bibliothèques Universitaires
BIX	Bibliotheksindex
CAUL	Council of Australian University Librarians
CNI	Center for Networked Information
CRM	customer relationship management
CSEQ	College Student Experiences Questionnaire
DEEP	Documenting Effective Educational Practices, or Project DEEP
EFQM	European Foundation for Quality Management
HE	higher education
HEFCE	Higher Education Funding Council for England
ICT	information and communication technology
IFLA	International Federation of Library Associations and Institutions
IGERT	Integrative Graduate Education and Research Traineeship
ILI	information literacy instruction
IPEDS	Integrated Postsecondary Education Data System
ISCED	International Standard Classification of Education
NCES	National Center for Education Statistics

NSSE	National Survey of Student Engagement
OCLC	Online Computer Library Center
OECD	Organisation for Economic Cooperation and Development
OIS	International Organization for Standardization
ROI	return on investment
SCONUL	Society of College, National and University Librarians
SIMALTO	Simultaneous Multi Attribute Level Trade Offs
SMART	specific, measurable, achievable, realistic, and timely
STEM	science, technology, engineering, and mathematics
SWOT	strengths, weaknesses, opportunities, and threats

About the authors

Gail Munde is currently Assistant Professor of Library Science at East Carolina University in Greenville, North Carolina. Prior to teaching, she worked in academic libraries for 25 years as a department chair and associate director/dean, holding positions at the University of Kansas, East Carolina University, and the University of Nevada, Las Vegas. Her research interests are in library human resources management, professional development, and library finance.

Dr. Munde was a partner in two successful IMLS Laura Bush 21st Century Librarian Program grants to recruit and train diverse librarians to serve the western United States. She is a certified Professional in Human Resources and has an MLS from Emporia State University and a PhD in Library Science from the University of North Texas. She has co-authored two books and written numerous journal articles, book chapters and film and book reviews.

Kenneth Marks is the retired Dean of Libraries, University of Nevada, Las Vegas. He served as the Dean/Director of the East Carolina University Library and the Merrill Library and Learning Resources Program, Utah State University. He held positions at the University of Tennessee, Knoxville and Iowa State University. Dr. Marks was involved in the programming, planning, and construction of new libraries for East Carolina University and the University of Nevada, Las Vegas. The University of Nevada, Las Vegas library featured the first deployment of RFID (Radio Frequency Identification Detection) technology in an academic library as well as one of the first automated storage and retrieval systems in the United States.

Dr. Marks has authored two books and many articles, and made many presentations related to technology in libraries, library facility planning, and academic library marketing. He has been the trainer for the Association of College and Research Libraries' Marketing @ Your Academic Library program, and has delivered this training in the United States, Europe, and Asia. Dr. Marks has a BS in History and a PhD in Education from Iowa State University, and an MLS from the University of California, Berkeley.

Preface

In 2007 we set out to prepare a workshop for academic librarians on the general topic of library quality improvement and assessment. Our hope was to distill some basic principles of library quality improvement and assessment, provide a few examples of best practices, *and* to present this overview in a single workshop day. From our mutual interest in the topic and our professional experience working both together and separately in multiple academic libraries, we thought the task would be relatively straightforward. We are still laughing at our ambition and our naivety.

As we began the literature review, we were quickly overwhelmed by the depth and breadth of the scholarship and, to be frank, surprised by its international scope. Borrowing from business and higher education excellence models, academic librarians around the world had published their ideas and their research on efforts to measure library quality, to devise metrics and methods for control, and to make continuous improvements in library quality in response to a universal demand for greater accountability in higher education. Much of the best and most interesting work was reported in journal articles and conference proceedings. The nature of these venues gives the impression that the literature is fragmented, making it difficult to grasp as a coherent whole. We wished there were a few books, or better yet, a single book that would provide a thorough, logical, and integrated view of academic library assessment, evaluation, and quality improvement—a book that would draw together and relate the essential information and understandings necessary for academic librarians to work toward quality improvement in the context of their own institutions. This book is an attempt to fulfill our own wish.

We would like to thank the many, many authors upon whose work we have drawn for this book—for their scholarship and creativity, and for having shared information and ideas with the profession through their publications. Without them, there would have been no basis for this book. We would also like to thank our spouses, Chuck Twardy and Karen Marks, for their endless patience and support.

Gail Munde
Ken Marks
November 2008

Quality, assessment and evaluation

Defining quality

What is quality? Most of us believe that we know quality when we see it. Whether this is actually the case is another matter. We bring so many assumptions to our view of the world that our biases automatically color our assessment of reality. Are there varying levels of quality? Does quality depend on circumstances? If quality is essential, under what circumstances will "good enough" be an adequate and acceptable level of quality? Does quality change over time? Will today's high quality fail to meet future quality standards? How does the library world's concept of quality match up with the views of quality of other segments of society?

How quality is defined will depend on the environment and the observer. The International Federation of Library Associations and Institutions (IFLA) publication *Measuring Quality* states:

> The definition of quality has developed from the product-oriented aspect of control and inspection to a broader service-oriented concept that involves the whole organizational structure. Quality in this sense is fitness for purpose, that is to say, a service or product should supply or perform as it is intended to. The "purpose" of a service or product is defined by the customers. Quality in this sense is neither an isolated standard nor the highest standard; it is defined by the needs of the clientele of the individual institution.[1]

The International Organization for Standardization (OIS) Standard 11620 defines quality as the "totality of features and characteristics of a product or service that bear on the library's ability to satisfy stated or implied needs."[2]

Green has identified a number of concepts of quality:

The traditional concept of quality is associated with the notion of providing a product or service that is distinctive and special, and which confers status on the owner or user ... The notion of exclusivity is implied. Second, there is the notion of quality as conformance to a specification or standard. The definition of quality adopted by most analysts and policy makers in higher education is that of fitness for purpose. Exponents of this approach argue that quality has no meaning except in relation to the purpose of the product or service. Quality is judged in terms of the extent to which a product or service meets its stated purpose(s).

One version of the "fitness for purpose" model concentrates on evaluating quality in higher education at the institutional level. A high quality institution is one that clearly states its mission (or purpose) and is efficient and effective in meeting the goals it has set itself. During the last 20 years, the definition of quality most often used in industry has evolved and is no longer given solely in terms of conformance to a specification but in terms of meeting customers' needs. High priority is placed on identifying customers' needs as a crucial factor in the design of a product or service.[3]

No wonder that defining, and then applying, quality is so difficult for academic librarians. They are faced with concepts that are not only drawn largely from business and industry, but are then cast in terms of higher education in general, and finally applied to academic libraries. The reality is that to a large extent library quality will be defined by the parent institution. In writing about Monash University, Pernat affirms this belief with the following observation:

Fitness of purpose means that the university must create its own agenda for its own unique situation and that purpose at all levels needs to be agreed. Fitness of purpose applied to the library involves examination of the alignment of the library's mission with that of the university.[4]

How can libraries confirm that the library's and university's mission statements are in alignment? Often, librarians view the institutional mission simply as another statement filled with glittering generalities to be given lip service or ignored. Many times the library mission statement is written without any attention to the university's mission. It is the responsibility of the library director to ensure alignment between the two mission statements.

A dramatic international shift in the perspective of librarians toward quality has occurred in the past 10 to 20 years. Historically, academic library quality was thought to be determined by the size of the collection and the size of the budget. It was a numbers game. The shift has been to the concept of the customer-centered library. Hiller and Jilovsky name seven fundamental changes in the library environment that are responsible for this shift:

- explosive growth in networked electronic information and consortial purchasing
- noticeable changes in library use patterns
- new library organizational structures and strategic planning
- instability of library and institutional funding
- increased complexity of navigating the information environment
- moves towards outcomes-based assessment in higher education
- accountability for library expenditures.[5]

The shift has been inevitable as parent institutions have become concerned about outcomes, and the contributions that units make to the achievement of those outcomes. If quality is defined by the customer, then the library should focus on that reality. Hiller and Jilovsky identify the following characteristics of a customer-centered library:

- All services and activities are viewed through the eyes of customers.
- Customers determine quality.
- Library services and resources add value to the customer.
- Data-based decision making is a cornerstone of the customer-centered library in which:
  - decisions are based on facts, research and analysis
  - services are planned and delivered to maximize positive customer outcomes.[6]

According to Hiller and Jilovsky, North American academic libraries continue to have difficulties in implementing the steps that would lead to a customer-centered library. This also appears to be a challenge internationally. One of the reasons for this may be that librarians historically have had difficulty listening to their customers. This is changing, but not quickly enough. A second reason may be that librarians have not been trained to work in an environment where decisions are based on the analysis of data and integrated into a regular planning cycle.

Another reason for the difficulties may be the fact that each stakeholder group has a different concept of what quality means to it. Poll has identified three stakeholder groups: the users (actual and potential), the financing authorities (university, community, commercial firm, etc.), the library's staff, and goes on to say:

> Their view of the library's quality will always differ. While users judge on the quality of services they use, authorities will be interested in the library's benefit to the institution it has been set up to serve and in the library's cost effectiveness. Staff, on their part, look to the quality of their working conditions, to further education and to the library's organization.[7]

The challenge for librarians is how to reconcile these potentially conflicting views of quality. This becomes more difficult if librarians determine that the relative importance of the stakeholder groups will shift from time to time.

Although each stakeholder group has its own concept of quality, an unanswered question remains: what are the characteristics or criteria that make up quality? Poll has adapted work done by Peter Brophy to construct a chart of criteria as shown in Table 1.1.[8]

The characteristics noted in the chart are appropriate for users, but hardly seem relevant to the other two groups of stakeholders—authorities and staff. Authorities will have criteria that include financial control; effective use of resources; outcomes and impacts; planning; and internal and external cooperation. Staff will have criteria that relate to both their physical and organizational working conditions; opportunities for professional development; involvement in planning; involvement in governance; and reputation of their library. Balancing the achievement of these disparate stakeholder criteria is a challenge for library administrators. It is important for a director to remember the following statement by Barrionuevo.

> Quality is a relative concept, closely linked to the level of user expectation and requirements. The relative nature of quality leads ultimately to excellence, a mobile, unattainable concept, the achievement of which requires effort, the assimilation of change, and a forward-looking and positive approach.[9]

| Table 1.1 | Criteria by which library quality is judged |

Criterion	Definition	Example
Performance	A service meets its most basic purpose	Making key information resources available on demand
Features	Secondary characteristics which add to the service but are beyond the essential core	Alerting services
Reliability	Consistency of the service's performance in use	No broken web links
Conformance	The service meets the agreed standard	Dublin Core
Durability	Sustainability of the service over a period of time	Document delivery within 2 days
Currency	Up-to-dateness of information	Online catalog
Serviceability	Level of help available to users	Complaint service
Aesthetics	Visual attractiveness	Physical library, website
Usability, accessibility	Ease of access and use	Opening hours, website structure
Assurance/ competence/ credibility	Good experience with staff's knowledgability	Correct reference answers
Courtesy/ responsiveness/ empathy	Accessibility, flexibility and friendliness of staff	Reference service
Communication	Clear explanation of services and options in jargon-free language	Website, signposting in the library
Speed	Quick delivery of services	Interlibrary lending
Variety of services offered	May clash with quality, if resources are not sufficient for maintaining quality in all services offered	Broad collection, reference service in walk-in, mail, and chat forms
Perceived quality	The user's view of the service	Assessment by satisfaction survey

All librarians want their libraries to achieve excellence, but few understand the linkage between quality and the consequences of accepting and internalizing change, and planning for the future.

Leadership from the director is essential if a library is to be committed to achieving and maintaining quality and, ultimately, excellence. The library administrator is properly placed to monitor the institution's evolving commitment to and definition of quality, thereby ensuring that the library maintains effective alignment of its own efforts to embed quality. As a director considers the issue of quality, the question of how to pursue quality arises. Does the library use total quality management, quality assurance, quality control, quality enhancement, or quality management philosophies, processes and techniques? Each of these has its own proponents and disciples who argue their particular philosophy represents the only "true" way to quality. Many of these approaches rely on the existence of some type of standard against which library activities, resources, services, and programs might be measured. An important question is whether the standard against which measurement occurs is externally imposed or established internally by the library. Another absolutely critical question is: what do we really mean when we use the word "measurement"?

Measurement

Measurement has been the downfall of many academic libraries. They have collected many data on every facet of the library's activities and environment, but have had no plan for processing the information. It seems that while data collection should be useful, quite often the data found in a library is

- gathered but has little relevance in the decision-making process;
- gathered for a specific purpose, but then not used;
- used to justify a decision (and sometimes gathered after the decision is made);
- requested even though sufficient information is available to make a decision (some data manipulation and analysis may be required);
- not used even though some people will complain about the lack of information; and
- not in itself as important as just having it.[10]

Most librarians can remember an experience involving data collection when the staff opinion was that the activity was "busy work." When that opinion becomes the prevailing view, then measurement will be flawed and assessment is doomed.

An often-overlooked fact is that measurement is more than collecting numbers; it is the process of gauging a library's performance. Data collection is often considered to be routine reporting, and performed without any thought as to how those activities being measured are performed, or their effect on library stakeholders. Cullen presents another aspect of performance measurement:

> Performance measurement is a highly political activity, and must be seen as such, at the macro and micro level. We must look outwards to social and political expectations made of our institutions and ensure that they meet the needs and expectations of our significant client or stakeholder groups; we must use our planning and goal-setting activities in a services meaningful way, incorporating appropriate measures, to demonstrate our response to this external environment, and our willingness to align our aspirations to broader corporate goals. But we must also look within and seek to promote an organisational culture which acknowledges the political nature of measurement. This means using performance measurement to:
>
> - indicate the library or information service's alignment with broader organisational goals
> - demonstrate the integration of information with the key activities of the organisation, or of the community
> - support the library's position as the organisation's primary information manager and service provider.[11]

Because academic libraries have traditionally been viewed as a common good and an essential part of any university, the idea that all library activities now have political implications may be unsettling to many librarians. Librarians have been reluctant to play the political game required to garner the budgetary resources necessary to keep their libraries competitive. Also, they have been reluctant to market themselves and their organizations, perhaps based on the assumption that it is somehow unprofessional. Librarians are learning, but it has been a painfully slow process.

Assessment

What is the relationship between measurement and assessment? Often, assessment, evaluation and accountability are used interchangeably, which confuses the individuals trying to understand what a library is doing. Frye states that

> when we assess our own performance, it's assessment, when others assess our performance, it's accountability. That is, assessment is a set of initiatives we take to monitor the results of our actions and improve ourselves; accountability is a set of initiatives others take to monitor the results of our actions, and penalize or reward us based on the outcomes.[12]

A decade ago, Dow offered the following interpretations of assessment:

> Today assessment is the word most often associated with the measurement of educational outcomes. When asked what that means, responses normally have fallen into three categories. The first category relates to evaluation of student learning prior to admission to college ... A second commonly understood meaning of assessment is the measurement of student performance taken while he or she is enrolled in course work ... The third interpretation of assessment places emphasis on the outputs of the educational experience, measuring what students have learned by the time they graduate ...[13]

The third definition is the ultimate challenge to libraries as they become increasingly required to present information delineating their contributions to student development. The critical departure from past measurement efforts is in the focus of measurement. The institution and the library are no longer the focus; the focus is now on the student and what is gained from time in the university and the library. Dugan expressed it as:

> Assessment measures changes in library users as a result of their contact with an academic library's programs, resources and services, such as student known content, developed skills and abilities, and acquired attitudes and values. Therefore, assessment is comprised of statements about what students will know/think/be able to do as a result of their contact with library programs, not statements about what the library should/could do to bring about desired outcomes.[14]

One matter to be clarified at this point is the use of the word "assessment." It actually refers to "self-assessment." Assessment imposed by an external entity is an audit; assessment conducted by the library on its own initiative is a self-assessment. Evans provides a detailed and useful discussion of the stages of self-assessment, in which she identifies seven distinct stages:

1. Identify the role of self-assessment

2. Commit to the process

3. Identify the self-assessment team

4. Choose the self-assessment model/approach

5. Piloting/training/planning

6. Undertake the self-assessment: manage the process

7. Identify priorities for improvement/plan actions/implement actions

8. Review. The final stage is a review of what has been achieved, i.e.:

   - whether the objectives have been reached

   - whether the performance targets have been met

   - whether the planned timescales have been achieved.[15]

The challenges of self-assessment

Troll Covey identified five challenges related to assessment that can assist libraries that are struggling to collect data that will help to confirm their contributions to positive student outcomes:

1. Gathering meaningful, purposeful, comparable data.

2. Acquiring methodological guidance and requisite skills to plan and conduct assessment.

3. Managing assessment data.

4. Organizing assessment as a core activity.

5. Interpreting library trend data in the larger environmental context of user behavior and constraints.[16]

Hiller, Kyrillidou, and Self identified a series of issues that augment Troll Covey's challenges. They note "these issues were likely to fall into the following areas: library leadership, organizational culture, library priorities, sufficiency of resources, data infrastructure, assessment skills and expertise, sustainability, presentation of results, and the ability to use the results to improve libraries."[17]

Typically, librarians have collected statistics as required by institutional authorities, governmental agencies, or professional associations. Sometimes the requests overlapped, and sometimes the requests were in conflict. Making the activity more challenging was the fact that data definitions might change from year to year and any opportunity for longitudinal analysis was lost. The result was an assortment of statistics that reflected the resources, services, and activities that could be most easily counted. In one sense, this might not have been a bad situation for the library, as the likelihood of having library staff with the requisite analytical skills and comfort level to work with data was minimal. This remains the situation in many libraries today. Even when library staff did have the requisite skills and aptitude, it often didn't matter because there was an overwhelming flood of data to be managed, manipulated, and stored. Managing data continues to be challenging, even today. Responsibility for data collection and management can be delegated by the library administrator, but one thing that cannot be delegated is the leadership role, the essential responsibility to instill throughout the library the importance of accurate data collection and to make self-assessment an integral part of the library's existence. It is the library administrator's responsibility to be certain that analysis and interpretation are done within the context of the parent institution and the community of users. It is the library administrator's responsibility to manage the establishment of an effective organizational culture. This can be a persistent challenge for library administrators, as it takes so long to change cultures, and cultures can fail without constant attention. Given all of the challenges and issues surrounding the prospect of conducting a self-assessment, it is no surprise to find the vast majority of libraries doing only marginal self-assessment.

The challenges noted above beg questions of how to avoid or minimize, and eventually to meet them. Creating a self-assessment plan, or outlining a self-assessment process, is a logical place to begin. In a study of library directors' thoughts about assessment and decision making, Beck outlined some of the beginning questions as:

- How do you manage assessment?
- What do you want to learn from assessment?
- What do you want to accomplish once you understand the assessment data?

- How will you use your data in your planning process to establish priorities?
- Will creating a data farm support decision making?
- How do you develop collaborative partnerships with campus units in the development of instrument design and administration, data analysis, data validity and reliability issues?[18]

Myriad sub-questions could fall under each of the bulleted items. Is this a formative or summative assessment? Does the assessment focus on individuals or groups? When assessing undergraduate students, is the focus on skills, knowledge, retention, attitudes, or behavior? Will the library be using a management information system (MIS) to manage its data farm? Will it create its own MIS or will it purchase one? (There are only a handful of libraries that have taken this step, as it involves a significant commitment of funds and skilled staff to maintain.) What is the status of relationships with campus units that could collaborate with the library and offset the absence of needed skills in instrument design, and management and analysis of data collected? Collaboration with other campus units may be the only viable option for many libraries.

It is the library administrator's responsibility to lead the library to answers to Beck's questions and related sub-questions. Until these questions have been answered, the library should not embark on establishing a self-assessment plan or process. If the requisite preparatory work has been done and has involved the library staff and relevant units on campus, then the library should have positive responses to these questions posed by Matthews:

- Are student learning goals identified?
- Will the library's contribution to helping students achieve their goals be addressed by the assessment procedure?
- Are multiple assessment measures used?
- Are the measures understood and valued by all stakeholders?
- Does the plan identify the people (committees) involved and the processes that will be used?
- Are the results of assessment having an impact on the planning process so that changes are made to improve the impact of the library on students, faculty and researchers ...?[19]

Preparatory work involves using a number of existing tools and processes available in the management and public sector planning fields.

Many libraries have employed some of these resources, but most have never used them in an integrated or consistent manner. The resources include a survey for determining whether a culture of assessment exists in a library; a number of excellence frameworks for creating a baseline of information about the library and for creating a strategic plan; the Balanced Scorecard to monitor a limited number of performance measures; benchmarking tools; and finally, assistance in identifying a limited set of performance indicators to provide data related to the desired outcomes identified by the library. In further chapters, these resources are addressed in detail, along with information on the academic library's role in the success of major user groups, user satisfaction measurement methods, and comparative library analyses.

Notes

1. Poll and te Boekhorst, *Measuring Quality*, 11.
2. OIS, *Information and Documentation*, 3.
3. Green, "What is Quality in Higher Education," 13–16.
4. Pernat, "From Planning to Improvement," 1.
5. Hiller and Jilovsky, "Measuring Value," 10.
6. *Ibid.*, 2–3.
7. Poll, "Quality and Quality Systems in Libraries," 2–3.
8. *Ibid.*, 2.
9. Barrionuevo, "Searching Excellence in the Library System," 1.
10. Matthews, *Library Assessment in Higher Education*, 5.
11. Cullen, "Measure for Measure," 12.
12. Frye, "Assessment, Accountability, and Student Learning Outcomes."
13. Dow, "Using Assessment Criteria to Determine Library Quality," 277–8.
14. Dugan and Hernon, "Outcomes Assessment," 378.
15. Evans, "Quality Management and Self Assessment Tools."
16. Troll Covey, *Usage and Usability Assessment*, 53.
17. Hiller et al, "Assessment in North American Research Libraries," 102.
18. Beck, "Making Informed Decisions," 6.
19. Matthews, *Library Assessment in Higher Education*, 127.

Bibliography

Ackermann, Eric. "Program Assessment in Academic Libraries: An Introduction for Assessment Practitioners." *Research & Practice in Assessment* 1, no. 2 (June 2007): 1–9.

Ambrozic, Melita, Vilenka Jakac-Bizjak and Helena Pecko Mlekus. "Performance Evaluation in European National Libraries: State-of-the-Art."

In *Proceedings of the World Library and Information Congress: 69th IFLA General Conference and Council*. The Hague, Netherlands: IFLA, 2003. www.ifla.org/IV/ifla69/papers/024e-Ambrozic_Jakac-Bizjak_Mlekus.pdf

Barrionuevo, Miguel Duarte. "Searching Excellence in the Library System of the University of Cadiz." In *Proceedings of the International Conference on Quality Management in Academic Libraries*. Warsaw: The Polish Librarians Association, 2000. http://ebib.oss.wroc.pl/matkonf/atr/miquel.html [retrieved July 9, 2008]

Beck, Susan J. "Making Informed Decisions: The Implications of Assessment." In *Proceedings of the 11th ACRL National Conference*. Chicago: ALA-Association of College and Research Libraries, 2003. www.ala.org/ala/acrl/acrlevents/beck.PDF [retrieved July 9, 2008]

Belanger, Yvonne. "Tools for Creating a Culture of Assessment: The CIPP Model and Utilization-Focused Evaluation." In *Proceedings of the Library Assessment Conference: Building Effective, Sustainable, Practical Assessment (2006)*, edited by Francine DeFalco et al., 381–5. Washington, DC: Association of Research Libraries, 2007.

Bertot, John Carlo. "Assessing Digital Library Services: Approaches, Issues, and Considerations." In *Electronic Proceedings of the International Symposium on Digital Libraries and Knowledge Communities in Networked Information Society*. Tsukuba, Ibaraki, Japan: University of Tsukuba, 2004. www.kc.tsukuba.ac.jp/dlkc/e-proceedings/papers/dlkc04pp72.pdf

Bertot, John Carlo and Charles R. McClure. "Outcomes Assessment in the Networked Environment: Research Questions, Issues, Considerations, and Moving Forward." *Library Trends* 51, no. 4 (Spring 2003): 590–613.

Brice, Anne, Andrew Booth and Nicola Bexon. "Evidence Based Librarianship: A Case Study in the Social Sciences." In *Proceedings of the World Library and Information Congress: 71st IFLA General Conference and Council*. The Hague, Netherlands: IFLA, 2005. www.ifla.org/IV/ifla71/papers/111e-Brice_Booth_Bexon.pdf

Broady-Preston, Judith and Hugh Preston. "Demonstrating Quality in Academic Libraries." *New Library World* 100, no. 1148 (1999): 124–9.

Brophy, Peter. "Quality Management in Libraries." In *Proceedings of the 1st Northumbria International Conference on Performance Measurement in Libraries and Information Services*. Newcastle upon Tyne: Information North, 1995. http://eric.ed.gov/ERICDocs/data/ericdocs2sql/content_storage_01/0000019b/80/16/69/fe.pdf

Brophy, Peter. "The Quality of Libraries." In *The Effective Library*, edited by Klaus Hilgermann and Peter te Boekhorst, 30–46. Munchen: K.G. Saur, 2004.

Bundy, Alan. "Beyond Information: The Academic Library as Educational Change Agent." Paper presented at the 7th International Bielefeld Conference, Bielefeld, Germany, February 2004. http://conference.ub.uni-bielefeld.de/proceedings/bundy_rev.pdf

Bunzel, Jürgen and Roswitha Poll. "German Academic Libraries: Tradition and Change." *Journal of Academic Librarianship* 28, no. 6 (November 2002): 418–25.

Calvert, Philip J. "International Variations in Measuring Customer Expectations." *Library Trends* 49, no. 4 (Spring 2001): 732–57.

Chen, Tser-Yieth. "An Evaluation of the Relative Performance of University Libraries in Taipei." *Asian Libraries* 6, no. 1/1 (1997): 39–46.

Chim, Winnie. "The Quest for Excellence: One Library's Experience." *Library Management* 28, no. 6/7 (2007): 323–36.

Chua, Clare. "Perceptions of Quality in Higher Education." In *Proceedings of the Australian Universities Quality Forum.* Melbourne: Australian University Quality Agency, 2004. www.auqa.edu.au/auqf/2004/program/papers/Chua .pdf.

Cullen, Rowena. "Does Performance Measurement Improve Organisational Effectiveness? A Post-Modern Analysis." In *Proceedings of the 2nd Northumbria International Conference on Performance Measurement in Libraries and Information Services*, 3–20. Newcastle upon Tyne: Information North, 1997.

—. "Measure for Measure: A Post Modern Critique of Performance Measurement in Libraries and Information Services." In *Proceedings of the 19th Conference of the International Association of Technological University Libraries.* Auckland: International Association of Technological University Libraries, 1998. www.iatul.org/conferences/pastconferences/1998proceedings .asp

Derfert-Wolf, Lidia, Marek M. Górski, and Marzena Marcinek. "Quality of Academic Libraries—Funding Bodies, Librarians and Users [*sic*] Perspectives." In *Proceedings of the World Library and Information Congress: 71st IFLA General Conference and Council.* The Hague, Netherlands: IFLA, 2005. www.ifla.org/IV/ifla71/papers/080e-Derfert-Wolf.pdf

Diaz, Carmen Baena et al. "Excellence and Quality in Andalusia University Library System." In *Proceedings of the World Library and Information Congress: 71st IFLA General Conference and Council.* The Hague, Netherlands: IFLA, 2005. www.ifla.org/IV/ifla71/papers/091e-Diaz.pdf

Dow, Ronald E. "Using Assessment Criteria to Determine Library Quality." *Journal of Academic Librarianship* 24, no. 4 (July 1998): 277–81.

Dugan, Robert E. and Peter Hernon. "Outcomes Assessment: Not Synonymous with Inputs and Outputs." *The Journal of Academic Librarianship* 28, no. 6 (November 2002): 376–80.

Evans, Margaret Kinnell. "Quality Management and Self Assessment Tools for Public Libraries." In *Proceedings of the World Library and Information Congress: 66th IFLA General Conference and Council.* The Hague, Netherlands: IFLA, 2000. www.ifla.org/IV/ifla66/papers/112-126e.htm [retrieved July 9, 2008]

Fontana, Antonia Ida and Alessandro Sardelli. "Managing Quality in a National Library: The Case of the National Central Library of Florence, Italy." In *Proceedings of the World Library and Information Congress: 71st IFLA General Conference and Council.* The Hague, Netherlands: IFLA, 2005. www.ifla.org/IV/ifla71/papers/077e-Fontana_Sardelli.pdf

Franklin, Brinley. "Organizational Assessment: An Academic Library Case Study." Preprint of paper presented at the *5th Northumbria International Conference on Performance Measurement in Libraries and Information Services.* University of Connecticut Libraries Published Works, 2003.

Frye, Richard. "Assessment, Accountability, and Student Learning Outcomes." Bellingham, WA: Western Washington University, Office of Institutional Assessment and Testing. www.ac.wwu.edu/~dialogue/issue2.html [retrieved July 9, 2008]

Garryts, Egbert and Heila Pienaar. "A Key to the New Library." In *The Future of Libraries in Human Communication: Abstracts and Fulltext Document of Papers and Demos Given at the International Association of Technological University Libraries Conference*, 1999. www.iatul.org/conferences/past conferences/1999proceedings.asp

Glowacka, Ewa. "An Introduction into Quality Assurance and Total Quality Management with Reference to Library and Information Institutions." The Nicholas Copernicus University in Torun (Poland), 2003. http://ebib.oss.wroc .pl/english/grant/glowacka.php

Green, Diana. "What is Quality in Higher Education." In *What is Quality in Higher Education?* Edited by Diana Green. London: Society for Research into Higher Education, Ltd., 1994.

Hammes, Monica. "Report From a Deviating Collaborator: The University of Pretoria's Interaction with the Emerging Integrated System of Quality Assurance in South African Higher Education Libraries." In *Proceedings of the World Library and Information Congress: 73rd IFLA General Conference and Council*. The Hague, Netherlands: IFLA, 2007. www.ifla.org/IV/ifla73/ papers/131-Hammes-en.pdf

Harlan, Brian. "Developing a Quality Service Strategy." In *Proceedings of the World Library and Information Congress: 71st IFLA General Conference and Council*. The Hague, Netherlands: IFLA, 2005. www.ifla.org/ IV/ifla71/papers/076e-Harlan.pdf

Hernon, Peter and Charles R. McClure. *Evaluation and Library Decision Making*. Norwood, NJ: Ablex Publishing Corporation, 1990.

Hiller, Steve and Cathie Jilovsky. "Measuring Value: A Comparison of Performance Quality Measures and Outcomes Identified by Australian and North American Libraries." In *Proceedings of the 3rd International Evidence Based Librarianship Conference*. Kingston, Australia: Australian Library and Information Association, 2005. http://conferences.alia.org.au/ebl2005/Hiller.pdf

Hiller, Steve and James Self. "From Measurement to Management: Using Data Wisely for Planning and Decision Making." *Library Trends* 53, no. 1 (Summer 2004): 129–55.

Hiller, Steve, Martha Kyrillidou, and Jim Self. "Assessment in North American Research Libraries: A Preliminary Report Card." *Performance Measurement and Metrics* 7, no. 2 (2006): 100–6.

Hiller, Steve, Martha Kyrillidou, and Jim Self. "When the Evidence Isn't Enough: Organizational Factors that Influence Effective and Successful Library Assessment." Presented at the 4th Evidence-based Library & Information Practice Conference, May 6–11, 2007, Chapel Hill-Durham, North Carolina. www.libqual.org/documents/admin/eblip4_hiller.ppt.

Jantti, Margie. "Assessing the Service Needs and Expectations of Customers—No Longer a Mystery." In *Proceedings of the Library Assessment Conference: Building Effective, Sustainable, Practical Assessment (2006)*, edited by Francine DeFalco et al., 43–52. Washington, DC: Association of Research Libraries, 2007.

Johari, Roslah and A. N. Zainab. "Identifying What Services Need to be Improved by Measuring the Library's Performance." *Malaysian Journal of Library & Information Science* 12, no. 1 (July 2007): 35–53.

Kanji, Gopal K. and Abdul Malek bin A. Tambi. "Total Quality Management in UK Higher Education Institutions." *Total Quality Management* 10, no. 1 (1999): 129–53.

Kaur, Kiran. "Quality Management Service at the University of Malaya Library." *Library Management* 27, no. 4 (2006): 249–56.

Lepik, Aira and Toomas Liivamagi. "Past Decade—Transforming Measures and Values in Estonian Library Practice." In *Proceedings of the World Library and Information Congress: 69th IFLA General Conference and Council*. The Hague, Netherlands: IFLA, 2003. www.ifla.org/IV/ifla69/papers/103e-Lepik_Liivamagi.pdf

Markless, Sharon and David Streatfield. "Supported Self-Evaluation in Assessing the Impact of HE Libraries." Paper presented at the 7th Northumbria International Conference on Performance Measurement in Libraries and Information Services, Cape Town, South Africa, August 13–16, 2007. www.informat.org/PDFs/Northumbria-7-paper.pdf

Matthews, Joseph R. *Library Assessment in Higher Education*. Westport, CT: Libraries Unlimited, 2007.

McDonald, Joseph A. and Lynda Basney Micikas. *Academic Libraries: The Dimensions of Their Effectiveness*. Westport, CT: Greenwood Press, 1994.

McGregor, Felicity. "Excellent Libraries: A Quality Assurance Perspective." In *Advances in Librarianship, Volume 28*, edited by Danuta Nitecki, 17–54. London: Academic Press, 2004.

McGregor, Felicity. "Quality Management/Change Management: Two Sides of the Same Coin?" In *Proceedings of the 25th Conference of the International Association of Technological University Libraries*. Auckland: International Association of Technological University Libraries, 2004. www.iatul.org/doclibrary/public/Conf_Proceedings/2004/Felicity20McGregor_Helen20Mandl.pdf

McNicol, Sarah and Pete Dalton. "Taking a Planned Approach to Evaluation," *SCONUL Focus* 34 (Spring 2005): 53–5.

Miller, Rush. "What Difference Do We Make?" *Journal of Academic Librarianship* 33, no. 1 (January 2007): 1–2.

Missingham, Roxanne. "Libraries and Economic Value: A Review of Recent Studies." *Performance Measurement and Metrics* 6, no. 3 (2005): 142–58.

Mistry, V. and Bob Usherwood. "Total Quality Management, British Standard Accreditation, Investors in People and Academic Libraries." *Information Research* 1, no. 3 (March 1996). Available at http://InformationR.net/ir/1-3/paper9.html

Nitecki, Danuta A. "Changing the Concept and Measure of Service Quality in Academic Libraries." *Journal of Academic Librarianship* 22, no. 3 (May 1996): 181–90.

Oakleaf, Megan. "Using Rubrics to Collect Evidence for Decision-Making: What do Librarians Need to Learn?" *Evidence Based Library and Information Practice* 2, no. 3 (2007): 27–42.

Ochoa, Paula and Leonor Gaspar Pinto. "Quality—An On-Going Practice and Reflection in a Governmental Library (1996–2006)." In *Proceedings of the World Library and Information Congress: 72nd IFLA General Conference and Council*. The Hague, Netherlands: IFLA, 2006. www.ifla.org/IV/ifla72/papers/078-Ochoa_Pinto-en.pdf

OIS (International Organization for Standardization), *Information and Documentation—Library Performance Indicators: ISO 11620*. Geneva: International Organization for Standardization, 1998.

Osman, Zaiton, Carole Ann Goon, and Wan Hajrah Wan Aris. "Quality Services: Policies and Practices in Malaysia." *Library Management* 19, no 7 (1998): 426–36.

Partridge, Helen L., Clare E. Thorpe, and Sylvia L. Edwards. "The Practitioner's Experience and Conception of Evidence Based Library and Information Practice: An Exploratory Analysis." Paper presented at the 4th International Evidence Based Library and Information Practice Conference, Chapel Hill-Durham, NC, May 6–11, 2007. Available at http://eprints.qut.edu.au/archive/ 00009946/01/9946.pdf

Pernat, Marie. "From Planning to Improvement: Monash University Library's Quality Review." *AARL: Australian Academic & Research Libraries* 35, no. 4 (December 2004).

Poll, Roswitha. "Quality and Quality Systems in Libraries." In *Proceedings of Implementation of Quality Systems and Certification of Biomedical Libraries, EAHIL Workshop*. Maarssen, The Netherlands: European Association for Health Information and Libraries, 2005. www.eahil.net/conferences/ palermo_2005/eahil_oral_docs/pdfcd/Poll-doc.pdf

— and Peter te Boekhorst. *Measuring Quality: International Guidelines for Performance Measurement in Academic Libraries*. IFLA Publication 76. Munchen: K.G. Saur, 1996.

Pritchard, Sarah. "Determining Quality in Academic Libraries." *Library Trends* 44, no. 3 (Winter 1996): 572–94.

Quinn, Brian. "Adapting Service Quality Concepts to Academic Libraries." *The Journal of Academic Librarianship* 23, no. 5 (September 1997): 359–69.

Raouf, Abdul. "Monitoring and Managing of Quality in Higher Education." In *Proceedings of the First International Conference on Assessing Quality in Higher Education*. Melbourne, Australia: Asia-Pacific Quality Network, 2006. www.apqn.org/events/past/details/103/presentations/files/13_monitoring_ and_managing_of_quality_in_higher_education.pdf

Rowley, Jennifer. "Making Sense of the Quality Maze: Perspectives for Public and Academic Libraries." *Library Management* 26, no. 8/9 (2005): 508–18.

Sacchetti, Luciana. "ISO Quality as a Driver of Continuous Improvement." *Performance Measurement and Metrics* 8, no. 2 (2007): 88–97.

Sakthivel, P. B., G. Rajendran and R. Raju. "TQM Implementation and Students' Satisfaction of Academic Performance." *The TQM Magazine* 17, no. 6 (2005): 573–89.

Simmonds, Patience L. and Syed Saad Andaleeb. "Usage of Academic Libraries: The Role of Service Quality, Resources, and User Characteristics." *Library Trends* 49, no. 4 (Spring 2001): 626–34.

Stein, Joan. "Measurement-Based Change in Libraries: Case Studies from an Academic Library." In *Statistics in Practice—Measuring & Managing 2002*. Leicestershire: Loughborough University Library and Information Statistics Unit, LISU Occasional Paper #32, 2003. www.lboro.ac.uk/departments/dlis/ lisu/downloads/statsinpractice-pdfs/stein.pdf

Tam, Lawrence W. H. "Quality Management Theory and Practice: Some Observations of Practices in Australian Academic Libraries." *Library Management* 21, no. 7 (2000): 349–56.

Town, J. Stephen. "Performance or Measurement?" *Performance Measurement and Metrics* 1, no. 1 (2000): 43–54.

——. "E-measures: A Comprehensive Waste of Time?" *VINE: The Journal of Information and Knowledge Management Systems* 34, no. 4 (2004): 190–5.

——. "Academic Library Performance, Quality and Evaluation in the UK and Europe." In *Library Assessment Conference: Thessaloniki 13–15 June 2005: Conference Papers*, edited by Mersini Moreleli-Cacouris, 29–39. Washington, DC: Association of Research Libraries, 2006. www.arl.org/bm~doc/lac-greece-2005.pdf

Trahn, Isabella et al. "Analysing the Quality Gap: Reflections on Results from an Australasian Universitas 21 Libraries Standard Survey of Service Quality." *Australian Academic & Research Libraries* 32, no. 2 (June 2001).

Troll, Denise A. "How and Why Libraries Are Changing: What We Know and What We Need to Know." *portal: Libraries and the Academy* 2, no. 1 (January 2002): 99–123.

Troll Covey, Denise. *Usage and Usability Assessment: Library Practices and Concerns*. Washington, DC: Digital Library Federation, Council on Library and Information Resources, 2002.

——. "Academic Library Assessment: New Duties and Dilemmas." *New Library World* 103, no. 4/5 (2002): 156–64.

Tuomi, Ville. "Quality of Academic Library Services: A Customers [*sic*] Point of View." Paper presented at the European Group of Public Administration Conference, Vassa, Finland, September 5–8, 2001. www.soc.kuleuven.ac.be/pol/io/egpa/qual/vaasa/paper_vaasa_tuomi.pdf

Van House, Nancy A. et al. *Output Measures for Public Libraries: A Manual of Standardized Procedures*. 2nd ed. Chicago: American Library Association, 1987.

Van House, Nancy A., Beth R. Weil, and Charles R. McClure. *Measuring Academic Library Performance: A Practical Approach*. Chicago: American Library Association, 1990.

Virkus, Sirje and Silvi Metsar. "General Introduction to the Role of the Library for University Education." *LIBER Quarterly* 14, no. 3/4 (2004): 290–305.

Walker, Clare M. "Service Excellence: A Campaign to Build Capacity to Match Service Demands in a Large South African University Library." In *Proceedings of the World Library and Information Congress: 71st IFLA General Conference and Council*. The Hague, Netherlands: IFLA, 2005. www.ifla.org/IV/ifla71/papers/142e-Walker.pdf

Wang, Hong. "From 'User' to 'Customer': TQM in Academic Libraries?" *Library Management* 27, no. 9 (2006): 606–20.

Westerheijden, Don F., Bjorn Stensaker and Maria Joao Rosa, eds. *Quality Assurance in Higher Education: Trends in Regulation, Translation and Transformation*. Dordrecht, Netherlands: Springer, 2007.

Wright, Stephanie and Lynda S. White. *Library Assessment*. SPEC Kit 303. Washington, DC: Association of Research Libraries, 2007.

2

Creating a culture of assessment

Introduction

Academic libraries have been considered unique organizations, and this has encouraged academic librarians to develop a myopic view of the library in society. The long-held view that academic libraries provided a fundamental societal "good" fostered a belief that there was no need to justify or defend them. One result of this view was the creation, over time, of a distinctive culture in academic libraries. This culture was reflected in the widely held belief that librarians were the gate keepers to knowledge and, in such an important position librarians could believe they knew what was best for their patrons. There was no need to consult with patrons or collect data because librarians could make decisions based on their experience, anecdotal reports, or their feelings. As society has changed, so has the view of the supposed "good" provided by academic libraries and librarians. Today, the assumption is that academic libraries, along with other cultural and educational institutions, should justify their support by demonstrating the value of their activities and the contributions of academe to society.

A cultural change is required before academic libraries can build the capacity to justify their support and demonstrate the value of their efforts. Before an organization's culture can be changed, there must be an understanding of what culture means. Lakos and Gray define culture as part of a social system:

> Organizational culture refers to an organization's overt and covert rules, values, and principles, and is influenced by history, custom, and practices. These are an enduring set of tenets and norms that form the basis of a social system and allow the members to attribute merit and meaning to the external and internal events they experience.[1]

Changing a library's culture is a protracted process that requires sustained leadership from the library director. Unless or until the library director is convinced that cultural change is essential, it is highly unlikely that any change effort will be successful. Leadership in this undertaking must be visible to all members of the library. The belief that permanent organizational change can occur in a year or two, and without the engagement of all library personnel, is simply wishful thinking. A decade may be required before the fundamental alterations in the library's culture become embedded.

Library and management literature are both filled with various terms related to organizational change. "Culture of continuous improvement," "culture of excellence," "culture of quality," "culture of involvement," "culture of evidence," "culture of curiosity," and "quality culture" are some of the descriptive terms devised to describe transformational changes in organizational culture. Lakos introduced the concept of a "culture of assessment" to academic libraries in 1998:

> A Culture of Assessment is an organizational environment in which decisions are based on facts, research and analysis, and where services are planned and delivered in ways that maximize positive outcomes and impacts for customers and stakeholders. A Culture of Assessment exists in organizations where staff care to know what results they produce and how those results relate to customers' expectations. Organizational mission, values, structures, and systems support behavior that is performance and learning focused.[2]

The critical statement in Lakos's definition is *decisions are based on facts, research and analysis* and *services are planned and delivered in ways that maximize positive outcomes and impacts for customers and stakeholders*. Achieving these two states represents a fundamental organizational change for many libraries. Operating a library under these two conditions means abandoning management by anecdote, management by "gut" feeling, and management by the "seat of your pants." The decision to move to a culture of assessment can be daunting, and is not to be taken lightly. Every aspect of a library's operation and all library personnel will be affected.

Matthews has suggested there are a number of reasons why a culture of assessment is not frequently fostered in any library. Among them are the following:

- the perception that one can't measure what the library does
- lack of leadership
- the library not having control over its outcomes
- the possibility of using such information against the library
- lack of skills
- the move to increased demand for electronic resources and services
- old mental models
- the status quo being preferred.[3]

Covey adds further insight to the reasons for the widespread failure of libraries to move to a culture of assessment:

> In the context of rapid change and critical need for data and accountability, libraries appear to be unwilling, unable, or unaware of the need to:
>
> - articulate beliefs, behaviors, and assumptions of a culture of assessment;
> - assess the belief, behaviors, and assumptions of the existing culture;
> - identify gaps between the current and desired frame of reference;
> - develop action plans to close the gaps.[4]

In reality, librarians are comfortable in their current cultures and don't want to change, even if those cultures are outdated and their inhabitants in danger of extinction.

The concept of a culture of assessment was revised further and updated in 2002 by Lakos and Phipps with their description of the hallmarks of an assessment culture:

> A Culture of Assessment exists when:
>
> - The organization's mission, planning, and policies are focused on supporting the customer's information and communication needs.
> - Performance measures are included in organizational planning documents such as strategic plans.
> - Administrators are committed to supporting assessment.
> - Staff and leaders recognize the value of assessment and support and participate in assessment as part of their regular assignments. Individual and organizational responsibility for assessment is addressed explicitly.

- Continuous communication with customers is maintained through needs assessment, quality outcome and satisfaction measurements. Relevant data and user feedback is routinely collected, analyzed, and used to set priorities, allocate resources and make decisions.

Support System:

- Assessment activities can be supported by a Management Information System or Decision Support System.
- All services, programs and products are evaluated for quality and impact.
- Staff continuously improve their capability to serve customers and are rewarded for this. Rewards support removing barriers to quality customer service.
- On-going staff development in the area of assessment is provided and supported. Staff appreciates feedback and support for achievement of performance and learning goals.
- Units have defined measures for their processes and services from the customer point of view.
- Units and staff have customer focused S*M*A*R*T goals which are monitored regularly.[5]

Evaluating your library's culture

Even a cursory review of the above characteristics should permit a librarian to determine whether they work in an organizational culture of assessment. It is unusual for many academic librarians to conclude from this listing that a culture of assessment exists in their libraries. Before making a decision to begin the process of changing the organizational culture, there should be a more formal evaluation or assessment to determine where the library's present culture lies along the path to becoming a culture of assessment. Lakos, Wilson, and Phipps have created a questionnaire that can be useful in making this organizational evaluation (Figure 2.1).

The results of the questionnaire can be instructive, and can reveal to library leadership how much work needs to be done toward establishing the foundation for a culture of assessment. Cullen cautions against indiscriminate use of the questionnaire, noting: "this instrument, while useful when used at the organizational or library leadership level is less appropriate to investigate the extent a culture of assessment has permeated to the lower levels of staffing, and in particular, to those managing operational units, or at the cutting edge of customer service."[6] This is an important distinction to make, as it is clear that an organization's culture exists at different levels. It is critical that the view from all ranks and levels within a library organization be known and understood, but it is not at all evident that there is a suitable instrument for distribution to the lower levels of staffing. Until all levels of the organization are polled, the result may be an organizational view of library culture that is inaccurate or wrong. This possibility affirms the fact that cultural change is a lengthy process.

Matthews proposes a quick way to evaluate the culture of assessment in a library by considering a series of questions. Does your library

- articulate a clear vision of the future that inspires employees?
- maintain consistency between words and actions?
- know what customers/users really care most about?
- know how well the library is doing to satisfy customers in terms of what the customers care most about?
- encourage the use of performance measures and analysis to assess problems and services?
- use resources efficiently? (Are we doing things right?)
- use resources effectively? (Are we doing the right things?)
- encourage employees to develop performance measurement skills?
- know how the library's policies and practices make the library "difficult" to do business with?
- demonstrate a constant pursuit of excellence?
- recruit talented people?
- learn from its mistakes?
- seize opportunities when they present themselves?
- work constantly to improve productivity and eliminate bureaucracy?
- communicate the value of your library to interested and key stakeholders?[7]

Once a library has determined where it is on the path to establishing a culture of assessment, there are a number of issues identified by Lakos that must be examined. Some of these must be explored in the context of the parent institution, i.e.,

- Where does the institution focus its efforts and resources to make the most effective transformation to a culture of assessment?

Figure 2.1 Evaluation questionnaire "Do you have a culture of assessment?"

DO YOU HAVE A "CULTURE OF ASSESSMENT?"

Background: If your organization has developed a culture of assessment it will have "built in mechanisms" that will embed and reinforce a focus on customers, continuous assessment, and the use of measurement for planning and decision-making.

Directions: Below is a list of possible mechanisms that would be evidence of an 'operating' culture of assessment. Read each item and evaluate whether your culture is weak or strong. For each item circle the number that most represents reality in your organization.

1 = NOT AT ALL OR NEVER
6 = IN ALL CASES OR ALL THE TIME

- The organization's mission, planning, and policies are focused externally—on supporting the customers' need for access to information

1	2	3	4	5	6

- How performance will be measured is included in organizational planning documents such as strategic plans

1	2	3	4	5	6

- Leadership commits to and financially supports assessment activities.

1	2	3	4	5	6

- Staff recognize the value of assessment and engage in assessment as part of their regular assignments.

1	2	3	4	5	6

- Individual and organizational responsibility for assessment is addressed explicitly—in job descriptions or is otherwise communicated formally.

1	2	3	4	5	6

- Relevant data and user feedback is routinely collected, analyzed, and used to set priorities, allocate resources and make decisions.

1	2	3	4	5	6

| Figure 2.1 | Evaluation questionnaire "Do you have a culture of assessment?" (*Cont'd*) |

SUPPORT SYSTEMS

- Assessment activities are supported by a Management Information System or Decision Support System.

| 1 | 2 | 3 | 4 | 5 | 6 |

- Services, programs and products are evaluated for quality and impact (outcome).

| 1 | 2 | 3 | 4 | 5 | 6 |

- Staff are supported to continuously improve their capability to serve customers and are rewarded for this

| 1 | 2 | 3 | 4 | 5 | 6 |

- Staff are rewarded for work that demonstrates improved service quality or better outcomes for customers.

| 1 | 2 | 3 | 4 | 5 | 6 |

- On-going staff development in how to do effective assessment and measurement of results is provided and supported

| 1 | 2 | 3 | 4 | 5 | 6 |

- Units within the Library have defined their critical processes and established measures of success from the customer point of view

| 1 | 2 | 3 | 4 | 5 | 6 |

- Individual staff have specific and measurable goals and progress toward them is reviewed periodically with others in the unit or their supervisor.

| 1 | 2 | 3 | 4 | 5 | 6 |

Adapted from Amos Lakos (University of Waterloo) and Betsy Wilson (University of Washington) – 1998
Revised and updated by Shelley Phipps (University of Arizona) – 2002

Source: Reprinted with permission of Amos Lakos from *http://lakmau.com/ CulAssessToolkit/Culture-of-Assessment-revofiq.pdf.*

- What are the characteristics of leadership that bring about the transformation toward a culture of assessment?

- How do we sustain a culture of assessment over time?

- How can we balance assessment that stresses collaboration with the one-on-one nature of student and faculty relationship? How can we balance the tension between collaboration and one-on-one approaches?

- How do we transform a traditional research culture so that it values scholarship of assessment?

- What steps are necessary to keep the focus on student learning outcomes?

- How is institutional culture formed/shaped/changed? Who sets the norms and constraints that define institutional culture? Who are the drivers/definers of culture in an institution? How do internal and external forces affect culture?

- Given increasing globalization, where can we make international comparisons of assessment approaches?[8]

What happens if, after answering these questions, a disconnect is apparent between the institutional and library cultures? How can they be brought into alignment? What can the librarians do if the various stakeholder groups have potentially conflicting cultures? As noted earlier, establishing a culture of assessment is not easy, and it will not happen quickly. Change will happen slowly, and in concert with the larger institution. Lakos again provides a series of hallmarks to guide libraries in their efforts to focus efforts toward establishing a culture of assessment:

The library needs to be externally focused. The focus has to be on delivering value to customers. In libraries, the purpose is defined by creating learning and research outcomes for the customers, listening to the voice of the customer and closing the decision-making loop in the library's processes to create outcomes that are needed and measurable.

- The library's mission, planning, and policies are focused on supporting the customer's information and communication needs.

- Performance measures are included in library planning documents such as strategic plans.

- Library administrators are committed to supporting assessment.

- Staff and leaders recognize the value of assessment and support and participate in assessment as part of their regular assignments.

Individual and organizational responsibility for assessment is addressed explicitly.

- Continuous communication with customers is maintained through needs assessment, quality outcome and satisfaction measurements. Relevant data and user feedback is routinely collected, analyzed, and used to set priorities, allocate resources and make decisions.

- A Management Information System or Decision Support System supports assessment.

- All library services, programs and products are evaluated for quality and impact.

- Service standards are identified and services and processes are measured against these standards.

- Staff continuously improve their capability to serve customers and are rewarded for this. Rewards support removing barriers to quality customer service.

- Units and staff have customer focused S*M*A*R*T goals which are monitored regularly.

- On-going staff development in the area of assessment is provided and supported.[9]

Many libraries may be meeting some of the prerequisites, or meeting them partially. Internationally, there may even be a handful of libraries that meet all of them. For most libraries, it seems futile to hope that all of the conditions can be met simultaneously. The task of deciding which elements to focus on first will depend on conditions within the library and the parent institution. There are two conditions in Lakos's above list that deserve immediate attention: performance measures, and a Management Information System.

Blixrud has listed a more concise list of essential assets for the academic library moving toward a culture of assessment. They include:

- resources (i.e., time and money)
- individual and institutional buy-in
- access to individuals to evaluate
- expertise to conduct evaluation
- project management experience
- appropriate benchmarks

- conceptual clarity
- measurement and design requirements
- instrument validity and reliability.[10]

In addition to these assets, Matthews suggests four initiatives that must be firmly established to assist the library in moving toward a culture of assessment: listening to the voices of

- the customer
- the library's staff members
- the process
- the organization.[11]

Locating the library's position along the path to a culture of assessment is a first step. It can be based on a very brief and necessarily limited analysis of what the library is doing. However, a more thorough and extensive assessment is essential before the library can begin to make significant changes to its organizational structure. Fortunately, there are a number of quality or excellence frameworks to lend structure and stability to the library's further investigations. The decision to use one of these frameworks should be carefully considered, as each requires substantial investment of time and resources, but they also will provide the clearest indication of the challenges ahead for the library. This underscores the reality that creating a culture of assessment will be slow and sometimes painful, but absolutely necessary if the library is to respond successfully to future institutional and societal expectations.

Notes

1. Lakos and Gray, "Personalized Library," 170.
2. Lakos, "Culture of Assessment as a Catalyst," 313.
3. Matthews, *Library Assessment in Higher Education*, 6–7.
4. Troll Covey, "Academic Library Assessment," 163.
5. Lakos, "Building a Culture of Assessment."
6. Cullen, "Operationalising the Focus/Values/Purpose Matrix," 87.
7. Matthews, *Strategic Planning and Management*, 105.
8. Lakos, "Culture of Assessment as a Catalyst," 313.
9. *Ibid.*, 313–16.
10. Blixrud, "Mainstreaming New Measures," 4.
11. Matthews, *Strategic Planning and Management*, 100.

Bibliography

Blixrud, Julia C. "Mainstreaming New Measures," *ARL Bimonthly Report 230/231* (October/December, 2003): 1–8.

Cullen, Rowena. "Operationalising the Focus/Values/Purpose Matrix: A Tool for Libraries to Measure their Ability to Deliver Service Quality." *Performance Measurement and Metrics* 7, no. 2 (2006): 83–99.

Dole, Wanda V., Anne Liebst, and Jitka M. Hurych. "Core Competencies for Library Leaders: Is Assessment a Core Competency?" In *Libraries, Globalisation, and Cooperation: Papers from the International Conference Held in Sofia, Bulgaria, 3–5 November 2004*, edited by Herbert Achleitner and Alexander Dimchev. Sofia: St. Kliment Ohridski University of Sofia, 2005.

Holloway, Karen. "The Significance of Organizational Development in Academic Research Libraries." *Library Trends* 53, no. 1 (Summer 2004): 5–16.

Jantti, M. H.. "Developing a Culture that Values the Need for Assessment and Continuous Improvement: The Growth of a Learning Organization." Paper presented at Peformance Measurement for Libraries and Information Services, Sydney, March 21–22, 2005. http://ro.uow.edu.au/asdpapers/21

Kaarst-Brown, Michelle L. et al. "Organizational Cultures of Libraries as a Strategic Resource." *Library Trends* 53, no.1 (Summer 2004): 33–53.

Lakos, Amos. "Library Management Information Systems in the Client Server Environment—A Proposed New Model." In *Proceedings of the 2nd Northumbria International Conference on Performance Measurement in Libraries and Information Services*, 277–86. Newcastle upon Tyne: Information North, 1997.

——. "Building a Culture of Assessment in Academic Libraries—Obstacles and Possibilities." Paper presented at Living the Future II Conference, Tucson, Arizona, April 22, 1998. http://lakmau.com/Present/Arizona98/Ariztext98.html [retrieved July 9, 2008]

——. "Culture of Assessment as a Catalyst for Organizational Culture Change in Libraries." In *Proceedings of the 4th Northumbria International Conference on Performance Measurement in Library and Information Services*, 311–19. Washington, DC: Association of Research Libraries, 2002.

——. "Evidence Based Library Management—A View to the Future." In *Proceedings of the Library Assessment Conference: Building Effective, Sustainable, Practical Assessment (2006)*, edited by Francine DeFalco, 159–70. Washington, DC: Association of Research Libraries, 2007.

——. "Evidence-Based Library Management: The Leadership Challenge." *portal: Libraries and the Academy* 7, no. 4 (October 2007): 431–50.

Lakos, Amos and Chris Gray. "Personalized Library Portals as an Organizational Culture Change Agent." *Information Technology and Libraries* 19, no. 4 (December 2000): 169–74.

Lakos, Amos and Shelley Phipps. "Creating a Culture of Assessment: A Catalyst for Organizational Change." *portal: Libraries and the Academy* 4, no. 3 (July 2004): 345–61.

McKnight, Sue. "Managing Cultural Change: The Challenge of Merging Library Services, Curriculum Development and Academic Professional Development." In *Proceedings of the World Library and Information Congress: 68th IFLA General Conference and Council*. The Hague, Netherlands: IFLA, 2002. www.ifla.org/IV/ifla68/papers/123-106e.pdf

Martin, M. Jason. "'That's the Way We Do Things Around Here': An Overview of Organizational Culture." *Electronic Journal of Academic and Special Librarianship* 7, no. 1 (Spring 2006). http://southernlibrarianship.icaap.org/content/v07n01/martin_m01.htm

Matthews, Joseph R. *Strategic Planning and Management for Library Managers*. Westport, CT: Libraries Unlimited, 2005.

——. *Library Assessment in Higher Education*. Westport, CT: Libraries Unlimited, 2007.

Oltmanns, Gail V. "Organization and Staff Renewal Using Assessment." *Library Trends* 53, no. 1 (Summer 2004): 156–71.

Phipps, Shelley. "Beyond Measuring Service Quality: Learning from the Voices of the Customers, the Staff, the Processes, and the Organization." *Library Trends* 49, no. 4 (Spring 2001): 635–61.

Pinto, Leonor Gaspar. "Building a Culture of Assessment in Lisbon Public Libraries: A Knowledge Management Approach." In *Proceedings of the World Library and Information Congress: 72nd IFLA General Conference and Council*. The Hague, Netherlands: IFLA, 2006. www.ifla.org/IV/ifla72/papers/146-Pinto-en.pdf

Shepstone, Carol and Lyn Currie. "Assessing Organizational Culture: Moving Towards Organizational Change and Renewal." In *Proceedings of the Library Assessment Conference: Building Effective, Sustainable, Practical Assessment (2006)*, edited by Francine DeFalco et al., 369–79. Washington, DC: Association of Research Libraries, 2007.

Stoffle, Carla and Shelley Phipps. "Creating a Culture of Assessment: The University of Arizona Experience." *ARL: A Bimonthly Report on Research Library Issues and Actions from ARL, CNI, and SPARC*. No. 230/231 (October/December 2003): 26–27.

Troll Covey, Denise. "Academic Library Assessment: New Duties and Dilemmas," *New Library World* 103, no. 4/5 (2002): 156–64.

3

Frameworks for quality improvement

In the early 1980s global recognition by the private sector economy of quality as a key concept resulted in the development of a number of assessment/measurement instruments to evaluate an organization's quality standing. The first of these instruments to be established was the Malcolm Baldrige National Quality Award, formally created in 1987. The next year, with the endorsement of the European Commission, 14 companies formed the European Foundation for Quality Management. During the same period, a third framework was developed, the Australian Business Excellence Framework, formerly known as the Australian Quality Council's Framework. All three frameworks are remarkably similar. Following their lead, many US states and nations have created their own quality or excellence frameworks using one of the three as a model.

These quality frameworks, as well as the many derived from them, are based on a self-assessment conducted by an organization to seek confirmation of its quality standing. Porter and Tanner define self-assessment as "a comprehensive, systematic and regular review of an organization's activities and results referenced against an appropriate business excellence model."[1] Regardless of the model chosen, the steps of the self-assessment process are universal, and they underscore a prerequisite organizational commitment:

1. Define objectives and scope of the self-assessment
2. Select the quality framework to be used
3. Select the assessment team
4. Plan the assessment
5. Collect the needed data
6. Access the data and information, including clarifications
7. Prepare the feedback
8. Review the feedback and begin action planning.

Malcolm Baldrige National Quality Award

The growing lack of competitiveness within the American economy during the 1980s prompted US President Ronald Reagan and the US Congress to commission a study of the underlying causes. The study concluded that there had been a widespread failure of quality, and acknowledged that action must be taken. One of the recommendations was to establish a prestigious award to be given to private sector organizations that exemplified extraordinary quality in their operations. The US Congress passed legislation in 1987 to create the Malcolm Baldrige National Quality Award for Performance Excellence. Initially, the award was intended for large corporations, and the first was presented in 1988 to Motorola. There was immediate interest in the process supporting the award from small businesses, health-care organizations, government agencies, and educational institutions.

Interest within the education sector was set against a background of debate about the appropriateness of the Baldrige framework for educational organizations. Winn and Cameron summarized the issues thus:

> Among the areas of controversy are the relevance of the term customer in education, the uniqueness of the production system in education, the independence (professionalism) of organization members in education organizations, and the difficulty in specifying and measuring outcomes and improvements in, especially higher education.[2]

The debate continues today, reflected by the fairly limited use of the framework by higher education institutions, which resulted in the later development of separate versions for health care, government, and education. The version for education was completed in 1992, and the first award to a university was made in 2001, to the University of Wisconsin-Stout.

An organization may choose to submit application materials for consideration for the Performance Excellence in Education Award, or it may use the self-assessment process solely for internal purposes. Many organizations choose the latter option. It is important to note that the process is scalable; the organization could be a university, a college, a community college, or a division, college, or department within a larger institution. There is no size requirement.

All versions of the Baldrige Award are based on the concept of self-assessment, which implies internal study and learning. An early step in the self-assessment process is completion of an organizational profile as outlined in the annual Educational Criteria for Performance Excellence. The profile comprises two sections. The first focuses on a description of the organization, with sub-sections concentrating on organizational environment and organizational relationships. The second section covers organizational challenges, with sub-sections concentrating on the competitive environment, strategic context, and performance improvement system. According to the *Education Criteria for Performance Excellence*, the organizational profile is of critical importance because

- it is the most approprite starting point for self-assessment and for writing an application;
- it helps you identify potential gaps in key information and focus on key performance requirements and results;
- it is used by the Examiners and Judges in application review, including the site visit, to understand your organization and what you consider important (you will be assessed using the Criteria requirements in relation to your organization's environment, relationships, influences, and challenges, as presented in your Organizational Profile); and
- it also may be used by itself for an initial self-assessment. If you identify topics for which conflicting, little or no information is available, it is possible that the Organizational Profile can serve as your complete assessment, and you can use these topics for action planning.[3]

The last bullet statement could be adopted by most educational organizations as the first step in any self-assessment, and provides a good sense of the challenge the organization may face if completing the full application. This is particularly useful for the organization trying to build its culture of assessment.

The *Education Criteria for Performance Excellence* are based on a set of interrelated core values and concepts that includes:

- visionary leadership
- learning-centered education
- organizational and personal learning
- valuing workforce members and partners

- agility
- focus on the future
- managing for innovation
- management by fact
- social responsibility
- focus on results and creating value
- systems perspective.[4]

Seven criteria make up the Baldrige Education Excellence framework. They and their relationships are illustrated in Figure 3.1.

The criteria are focused on a purposely limited set of key organizational performance areas, and leadership is evident as the critical force of the framework. Leadership drives strategic planning and ensures focus on students, stakeholders, and market. All activity in these criteria influences and informs Criterion 4: Measurement, Analysis and Knowledge Management. Criteria 1–4 control Workforce (faculty and staff) focus, as

Figure 3.1   **The seven criteria of the Baldrige Education Excellence framework**

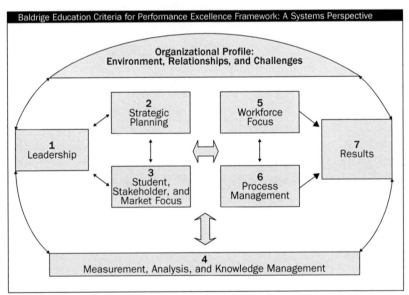

Source: Reprinted from *Education Criteria for Performance Excellence, 2008.* Baldrige National Quality Program, National Institute of Standards and Technology, U.S. Department of Commerce: Gaithersburg, MD: 2008, p. iv.

well as Criterion 6, Process Management activities. Together, these six criteria lead to Criterion 7, Results. The double-headed arrow in the middle of the chart represents feedback from results to leadership, informing the development of a continuous series of action plans and programs. The criteria are based on results-oriented requirements, but do not prescribe

- how your organization should be structured;
- that your organization should or should not have departments for quality, planning, ethics, or other functions; or
- that different units in your organization should be managed in the same way.[5]

Each criterion has sub-criteria that, in turn, have questions associated with them. The questions provide the basis for self-assessment of each criterion as follows:

Leadership

1.1   Senior Leadership

How do your senior leaders lead?

1.2   Governance and Social Responsibilities

How do you govern and address your social responsibilities?

Strategic Planning

2.1   Strategy Development

How do you develop your strategy?

2.2   Strategy Deployment

How do you deploy your strategy?

Student, Stakeholder, and Market Focus

3.1   Student, Stakeholder and Market Knowledge

How do you obtain and use student, stakeholder and market knowledge?

3.2   Student and Stakeholder Relationships and Satisfaction

How do you build relationships and grow student and stakeholder satisfaction and loyalty?

Measurement, Analysis, and Knowledge Management

4.1   Measurement, Analysis, and Improvement of Organizational Performance

How do you measure, analyze and then improve organizational performance?

4.2 Management of Information, Information Technology, and Knowledge

How do you manage your information, information technology and organizational knowledge?

Workforce Focus

5.1 Workforce Engagement

How do you engage your workforce to achieve organizational and personal success?

5.2 Workforce Environment

How do you build an effective and supportive workforce environment?

Process Management

6.1 Work Systems Design

How do you design your work systems?

6.2 Work Process Management and Improvement

How do you manage and improve your key organizational work processes?

Results

7.1 Student Learning Outcomes

What are your student learning results?

7.2 Student- and Stakeholder-Focused Outcomes

What are your student- and stakeholder-focused performance results?

7.3 Budgetary, Financial, and Market Outcomes

What are your budgetary, financial, and market performance results?

7.4 Workforce-Focused Outcomes

What are your workforce-focused performance results?

7.5 Process Effectiveness Outcomes

What are your process effectiveness results?

7.6 Leadership Outcomes

What are your leadership results?[6]

Completing a self-assessment using these criteria and answering each question in full is too daunting a task for one person. If the self-assessment is to be successful, it must involve as many people as possible from the organization, but have strong support from leadership. Without the support of top leadership, the outcomes of a quality improvement effort are likely to be unsuccessful. The Performance Excellence Process describes the leaders' role as essential, but indirect:

> With few exceptions, leaders do not have direct impact on organizational outcomes. Their influence is felt through the systems and processes they establish and manage ... The basic management tasks of leaders—gathering and utilizing information, planning strategically, effectively managing and developing organizational employees, and designing a well-oiled process for producing outcomes—create the critical outcomes related to quality in the organization.[7]

Although a limited number of higher education institutions and their subdivisions have submitted an application for consideration for the Baldrige Award, the global impact of the Baldrige Performance Excellence Process has been significant. It has served as the basis for a number of quality improvement frameworks adapted throughout the US and Europe, including by US regional accrediting bodies.

Academic Quality Improvement Project (AQIP)

The Higher Learning Commission of the North Central Association of Colleges and Schools has developed an alternative approach to the traditional decennial accreditation/reaccreditation process for universities. The alternative, an adaptation of the Baldrige criteria for self-assessment, called the Academic Quality Improvement Project, was introduced in 1999, and by 2007 there were 180 institutions participating. The Higher Learning Commission allows an institution to maintain its accreditation while participating in the AQIP. This option is available to those institutions within the region administered by the North Central Association. Institutions outside the North Central Region may choose to pursue the AQIP as the framework for quality improvement. The Higher Learning Commission makes it quite clear that units within a university/college may participate in the AQIP framework even if the parent institution is not prepared to do so. The

Commission on Colleges of the Southern Association of Colleges and Schools has also adopted a process similar to the AQIP.

AQIP has formulated a set of 10 statements, identified as *Principles of High Performance Organizations*, which are:

- A mission and vision that focus on serving students' and other stakeholders' needs.
- Leaders and **leadership** systems that support a quality culture.
- Respect for **people** and willingness to invest in them.
- **Agility**, flexibility, and responsiveness to changing needs and conditions.
- Fact-based **information**-gathering and thinking to support analysis and decision-making.
- Broad-based faculty, staff, and administrative **involvement.**
- A **learning**-centered environment.
- **Collaboration** and a shared institutional focus.
- **Planning** for innovation and improvement.
- **Integrity** and responsible institutional citizenship.[8]

Any library fully investigating the AQIP principles will recognize that choosing this as an alternative to the Baldrige Educational Criteria for Performance Excellence is going to be just as challenging. The AQIP identifies nine categories, and similar to the Baldrige process, a series of questions falls under each category. The nine categories are:

1. Helping students learn
2. Accomplishing other distinctive objectives
3. Understanding students' and other stakeholders' needs
4. Valuing people
5. Leading and communication
6. Supporting institutional operations
7. Measuring effectiveness
8. Planning continuous improvement
9. Building collaborative relationships.[9]

Each category has one overarching question augmented by four factored groups of additional questions that an institution must be prepared to answer. The factored groups are:

Context: Questions that explain how a particular system is realized in a given college or university.

Processes: Questions that ask how an institution has designed and deployed processes that help it achieve its overall goals.

Results: Questions that ask about the performance of institutional processes, whether their performance results meet requirements of stakeholders.

Improvement: Questions that ask how the institution promotes systematic improvement of its processes and performance in each category.[10]

European Foundation for Quality Management (EFQM)

Fourteen major European corporations concerned with the issue of quality and competitiveness came together in 1988 to create the European Foundation for Quality Management (EFQM). The Malcolm Baldrige Award provided a model for the EFQM. Three years after its formation, the foundation introduced the EFQM Excellence Model®. Companies wanting to confirm the quality excellence of their operations could use the excellence model framework to determine whether or not they met the performance levels. Companies across Europe quickly moved to use the framework as a method to demonstrate their commitment to improving the quality of their operations. While recognizing that it was not a perfect match for non-profit organizations, many in the European public and non-profit sectors attempted to apply the excellence model to their activities. To better meet their needs, a public and voluntary sector version of the excellence model was introduced in 1996.

The excellence model is a diagnostic tool based on the principle of self-assessment. Hides, Davis, and Jackson have identified five self-assessment methods from which an organization can choose: questionnaire, matrix chart, workshop, pro forma, and award simulation. The excellence model is a questionnaire model, as are the models discussed earlier. Hides et al. further identified eight stages of self-assessment: creating management commitment, communicating self-assessment plans, planning self-assessment, establishing teams and training, conducting self-assessment, establishing action plans, implementing action plans, and review.[11] It is possible that some of these stages can be conducted simultaneously.

The excellence model is based on eight concepts:

1. Leadership and constancy of purpose

2. Continuous learning, innovation and improvement

3. People development and involvement

4. Partnership development

5. Customer focus

6. Management by processes and facts

7. Corporate social responsibility

8. Results orientation.

The EFQM Excellence Model® consists of nine criteria, five of which are considered enablers, and four that are identified as results. The enabler criteria are leadership, people management, policy and strategy, resources, and processes. The results criteria are people satisfaction, customer satisfaction, impact on society, and business results. The nine main criteria are supported by 32 sub-criteria.

In 2000, the Higher Education Funding Council for England (HEFCE) sponsored a project to evaluate the benefits of applying the EFQM Excellence Model® in higher education, and devised an adaptation for use in higher education institutions. The project, directed by the Centre for Integral Excellence, Sheffield Hallam University for the Consortium for Excellence in Higher Education, concluded in 2003 with the publication of *EFQM Excellence Model Higher Education Version 2003*. The six consortium members included Sheffield Hallam University, University of Durham, Cranfield University, Salford University, Ulster University and Dearne Valley FE College. The institutions tested four of the five self-assessment methods reported by Hides et al., and adapted the EFQM Excellence Model® for higher education. The concept model is illustrated in Figure 3.2.

Regarding the HE version of the EFQM Excellence Model®, Mattison and Kuldvee note that it is built upon an integrated vertical alignment at every level of the institution:

> The adapted higher education model has five developmental stages of quality management: Activity-oriented, process-oriented, system-oriented, chain-oriented, and total quality management-oriented. The lowest level—activity-oriented level—is the fundamental level

Figure 3.2 The EFQM Excellence Model®

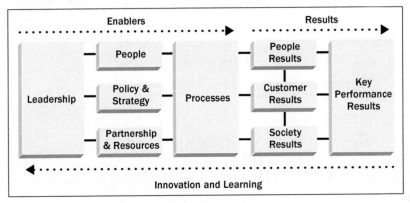

Source: © EFQM 1999–2003. Reprinted with permission.

of quality management, based on the individual responsibility for quality. Total quality management can't be achieved by the higher education institution without individuals, and especially academics, taking responsibility for it.[12]

An early step in creating the HE version of the model was to benchmark against the Baldrige Award criteria. The benchmark exercise indicated that the Baldrige Award had two additional values when compared to the HE version of the EFQM Excellence Model®, which were agility and future focus. These were included in EFQM HE version. Table 3.1 compares the EFQM Excellence Model® definitions with summarized interpretations for further and higher education.

The EFQM Excellence Model® Higher Education Version uses the same nine criteria and 32 sub-criteria as the original excellence model. The descriptions of the criteria and the details of the sub-criteria in the higher education version were modified from their original statements to reflect the special needs of higher education institutions along each of nine criteria, described briefly below.

Leadership

Outlines the responsibilities of leadership as developing the mission, vision, values and ethics of the organization; ensuring the function of management systems; engaging directly with the community and society; promoting a positive organizational climate within the university, and championing change.

Table 3.1   The EFQM Excellence Model® definitions and their interpretations for further and higher education

EFQM Excellence Model® definitions (2003)	Interpretation for further and higher education
Results orientation	
Excellence is achieving results that delight all the organization's stakeholders	Focusing clearly on and understanding students and other customers, their needs, expectations, and values.
Customer focus	
Excellence is creating sustainable customer value	Anticipating, balancing, and meeting the current and future needs of students, staff, and others.
Leadership and constancy of purpose	
Excellence is visionary and inspirational leadership, coupled with constancy of purpose.	Clearly demonstrating visionary and inspirational leadership, which is transparent and open, [and] ... which is shared by everyone in the institution.
Management by processes and facts	
Excellence is managing the organization through a set of interdependent and interrelated systems, processes and facts.	Understanding and systematically managing all activities through a set of interdependent and interrelated systems and processes.
People development and involvement	
Excellence is maximizing the contribution of employees through their development and involvement.	Developing, involving, and engaging staff, maximizing their contribution in a positive and encouraged way.
Partnership development	
Excellence is developing and maintaining value-adding partnerships.	Developing meaningful and mutually beneficial relationships, both internally and externally.
Corporate social responsibility	
Excellence is exceeding the minimum regulatory framework in which the organization operates and to strive to understand and respond to the expectations of their stakeholders in society.	Understanding, appreciating, and considering positively the way in which the institution interacts with and impacts on the local and wider society.

Table 3.1	The EFQM Excellence Model® definitions and their interpretations for further and higher education (*Cont'd*)

Continuous learning, innovation and improvement	
Excellence is challenging the status quo and effecting change by using learning to create innovation and improvement opportunities.	Stimulating, encouraging, managing, sharing, and acting on learning and experiences, making changes using innovation and creativity, and enabling continuous improvement.
Agility	
	The ability to react quickly to the changing demands of students and stakeholders in terms of speed of response and flexibility to deliver.
Future focus	
	Understanding the short- and longer-term factors that affect the organization and the education market and planning to take account of these.

Source: Consortium for Excellence in Higher Education. *EFQM Excellence Model Higher Education Version 2003*, 5.

Policy and strategy

Outlines the basis of policy and strategy to meet the present and future needs of stakeholder groups, with decision-making based on evidence from performance measurement, research, and learning; continuous review, and deployed through a framework of key processes.

People

Outlines the needs for workforce planning, management and improvement; for identifying, developing and sustaining competencies; enabling an involved and empowered workforce that is listened to, recognized, and rewarded.

Partnerships and resources

Outlines the necessity of developing and managing internal and external partnerships, finances, physical assets, technology and information and knowledge.

Processes

Processes are systematically designed, managed and improved to generate value for students, staff and other stakeholders and are innovative in their approach. Academic programs are designed and developed based on stakeholder needs and expectations.

Customer results

Measures of perception, as well as internal performance indicators are used to monitor, understand, predict and improve university performance.

People results

Measures of perception, as well as internal performance indicators are used to monitor, understand, predict and improve staff performance.

Society results

Measures of perception, as well as internal performance indicators are used to monitor, understand, predict and improve performance for the local community.

Key performance results

Key performance indicators are used to monitor, understand, predict and improve key performance outcomes.[13]

The same self-assessment options mentioned earlier for the original excellence model are applicable to the HE version. The simplest and easiest option is the questionnaire method. It is the most direct way to begin, and the questionnaire can be distributed to an entire library staff, allowing for the best sense of the organization status vis-à-vis the culture of assessment. If the library staff is ready for a more extensive self-assessment effort, using workshops to prepare them for a more rigorous organizational self-analysis is an appropriate step. The EFQM HE version suggests that the workshop approach comprises five distinct phases:

1. Training

2. Data collection

3. A scoring workshop

4. Prioritization of improvement actions

5. A review of progress.[14]

Finally, simulating the process of applying for an EFQM Excellence Model® Award will be the most challenging, but has the highest potential for reward. There is no obligation to actually submit the analysis for award consideration, but following the process may yield enormous benefits for the organization.

The original excellence model provides a structure, called a pro forma, for each of the 32 sub-criteria. Completing these forms can be an exhausting task for any organization, but again, the information gained would be invaluable for organizational quality improvement. Although the HE version of the EFQM Excellence Model® is widely available, it has not been adopted widely by higher education institutions. This is not surprising, given the natural conservatism of academe, mixed with an antipathy toward any measurement/analysis tool from the private sector. In spite of the approach taken in many European countries of mandating some type of quality improvement effort, the professoriate has demonstrated great tenacity in preserving the status quo.

The long-term successful application of the EFQM Excellence Model® Higher Education Version, or any national adaptation, will depend upon leadership decisions at the very top of the institution and its governing authorities. Such leadership would have to be extraordinarily stable and politically astute in order to persevere in establishing a culture of quality excellence—a process that may take, at a minimum, a decade.

Australian Business Excellence Framework (ABEF)

The Australian Business Excellence Framework was developed in 1987, the result of a joint effort by the Australian government and industry. The ABEF is similar to the previous two frameworks in structure, providing eight principles, seven categories, and 17 items. There are three types of category: drivers, enablers, and results, defined as follows:

> An organisation's strategies are usually Drivers. Enablers are the processes, tools and approaches that support an organisation's pursuit of its goals and objectives. "Results" are the organization's measures of success; they provide comparison against past performance and organizational objectives.[15]

The eight principles are:

Leadership: Lead by example, provide clear direction, build organizational alignment and focus on sustainable achievement of goals

Customers: Understand what markets and customers value, now and into the future, and use this to drive organizational design, strategy, products and services

Systems thinking: Continuously improve the system

People: Develop and value people's capability and release their skills, resourcefulness and creativity to change and improve the organization

Continuous improvement: Develop agility, adaptability and responsiveness based on a culture of continual improvement, innovation and learning

Information and knowledge: Improve performance through the use of data, information and knowledge to understand variability and to improve strategic and operational decision-making

Corporate/social responsibility: Behave in an ethically, socially and environmentally responsible manner

Sustainable results: Focus on sustainable results, value and outcomes.[16]

The seven categories of the ABEF and the supporting items are distributed as shown in Table 3.2.

The ABEF provides an assessment matrix, enabling an organization to evaluate its position in relationship to the business excellence principles. This is accomplished using a feature called the "learning cycle" that consists of four factors: approach, deployment, results, and improvement. Each factor has a series of questions that is used to determine the organization's position in terms of performance and business excellence (Table 3.3).

The University of Wollongong Library won the Australian Business Excellence Award in 2001: the culmination of many years of leadership within the library, the commitment of library staff, and the establishment of a strong culture of assessment.

The three quality frameworks discussed in this chapter are so similar that it is not evident there are advantages to adopting one over another. The important action is to make a choice, and prepare the library for the

Table 3.2   Australian Business Excellence Framework categories and supporting items

Category	Supporting item
Leadership	Leadership throughout the organization
	Leading the organizational culture
	Society, community and environmental responsibility
Strategy and planning	Strategic direction
	The planning process
Information and knowledge	Generating, collecting and analyzing the right data to inform decision-making
	Creating value through applying knowledge
People	A great place to work
	Building organizational capability through people
Customer and market focus	Gaining and using knowledge of customers and markets
	Effective management of customer relationships
	Customer perception of value
Process management, improvement, and innovation	Identification and management of processes
	Process improvement and innovation
	Process outputs
Success and sustainability	Measuring and communicating organizational performance
	Achieving sustainability

Source: SAI Global, *The Business Excellence Framework*, 16–29.

process of self-assessment. Self-assessment using an excellence/quality framework will result in a thorough examination of the library's strengths and weaknesses. It will be a demanding exercise if done with thoughtfulness, an understanding of why the self-assessment is necessary, and the involvement and participation of all library staff. However, the

Table 3.3 The Australian Business Excellence Framework learning cycle

Factor	Questions
Approach—Thinking and planning	What are you trying to achieve for the item—what is your intent?
	What goals have been established?
	What strategies, structures and processes have been developed to achieve your intent, and why did you choose them?
	What quantitative and qualitative performance indicators have been designed to track progress?
	How does your approach align with the Business Excellence Principles?
Deployment—Implementing and doing	How have those strategies, structures and processes been put into practice?
	What is the depth and breadth of their implementation throughout the organisation?
	To what extent have they been accepted and integrated as part of normal operation?
Results—Monitoring and evaluating	What are the trends in the performance indicators for this item?
	How do these results compare with best-known performance?
Improvement—Learning and adapting	What is the process to review the appropriateness and effectiveness of the Approach and its Deployment for the Item?
	How do you use the Results from the Item to do this?
	What have you learned, how have you captured this learning, and how have you used the learning to improve the Approach and its Deployment?

Source: SAI Global, *The Business Excellence Framework*, 33.

potential benefits are exciting to consider, as is suggested by Porter and Tanner:

> Organizations using self-assessment quickly realize a wide range of benefits. Studies of leading European companies carried out at the

European Centre for Total Quality Management have found the companies:

- Experience a greater focus on continuous improvement
- Are able to measure the progress of the organization more effectively
- Experience improved senior management commitment to continuous improvement
- Have increased the awareness level of TQ throughout the organization
- Have more focused and strategic action planning
- Have improved employee commitment to or involvement in continuous improvement
- Have improved operational performance
- Have improved customer satisfaction
- Have improved financial performance.[17]

The results of the self-assessment will provide a strong foundation on which to build the library's strategic plan, will permit the identification of performance targets and indicators, and will ultimately facilitate the library's demonstration of its contributions to the outcomes of the parent institution.

Notes

1. Porter and Tanner, *Assessing Business Excellence*, 2.
2. Winn and Cameron, "Organizational Quality," 509.
3. Baldrige National Quality Program, *Education Criteria for Performance Excellence, 2008*, 4.
4. *Ibid.*, 48.
5. *Ibid.*, 54.
6. *Ibid.*, 33–47.
7. *Ibid.*, 508.
8. Academic Quality Improvement Program, *Introduction to AQIP*, 2.
9. Dew and Nearing, *Continuous Quality Improvement in Higher Education*, 70–1.
10. *Ibid.*, 2
11. Hides et al., "Implementation of EFQM Excellence Model," 196–7.
12. Mattisen and Kuldvee, "Quality Management vs Quality Control," 1–2
13. *Ibid.*, 18, 20, 22, 24, 26, 28, 30, 32, 34, 36.
14. *Ibid.*, 198.
15. SAI Global, *The Business Excellence Framework*, 14.
16. *Ibid.*, 10–11.
17. Porter and Tanner, *Assessing Business Excellence*, 161–3.

Bibliography

Academic Quality Improvement Program. *Principles and Categories for Improving Academic Quality*. Chicago: Academic Quality Improvement Program, The Higher Learning Commission, 2005. www.aqip.org [retrieved February 14, 2008]

——. *AQIP's Expectations on Assessing Student Learning*. Chicago: Academic Quality Improvement Program, The Higher Learning Commission, 2006. www.aqip.org

——. *Introduction to AQIP*. Chicago: Academic Quality Improvement Program, The Higher Learning Commission, 2007. www.aqip.org

Akyuz, Asuman. "Application of EFQM Excellence Model to the Sabanci University IC," 2005. http://eprints.rclis.org/archive/00005450/01/3012800000002.pdf

Anyamele, Stephen Chukwu. "Applying Leadership Criterion of the European Excellence Model for Achieving Quality Management in Higher Education Institutions." *Academic Leadership: The Online Journal 5*, no.2 (July 31, 2007). www.academicleadership.org.

Baker, Ronald L. "Evaluating Quality and Effectiveness: Regional Accreditation Principles and Practices." *Journal of Academic Librarianship* 28, no. 2 (January/March 2002): 3–7.

Baldrige National Quality Program. *Education Criteria for Performance Excellence, 2008*. Gaithersburg, MD: Baldrige National Quality Program, National Institute of Standards and Technology, U.S. Department of Commerce, 2008.

Bokhari, Syed Ali Hassan. "Use of EFQM, BNQA, ISO 9001 in Higher Education: A Practitioner's Approach." In *Proceedings of the First International Conference on Assessing Quality in Higher Education*. Melbourne, Australia: Asia-Pacific Quality Network, 2006. www.apqn.org/events/past/details/103/presentations/files/15_use_of_efqm_in_he.pdf

Booz, Allen Hamilton. *Assessment of Leadership Attitudes about the Baldrige National Quality Program: Final Report*. Gaithersburg, MD: Baldrige National Quality Program, National Institute of Standards and Technology, U.S. Department of Commerce, 2003. www.quality.nist.gov/PDF_files/Assessment_Leadership.pdf

Calvo-Mora, Arturo, Antonio Leal, and Jose L. Roldan. "Relationships Between the EFQM Model Criteria: A Study in Spanish Universities." *Total Quality Management* 16, no. 6 (August 2005): 741–70.

Center for Institutional Effectiveness. "Self-Help for Higher Education: Baldrige Performance Criteria Improve Academia and Bring Positive Institutional Change." An interview with Kendall Rice in *The Higher Education Digest* 16, January 2005. www.internetviz-newsletters.com/datatel/e_article000347721.cfm?x=b11,0

Consortium for Excellence in Higher Education. *Applying Self-Assessment Against the EFQM Excellence Model in Further and Higher Education*. Sheffield, UK: Centre for Integral Excellence, Sheffield Hallam University, 2003.

——. *EFQM Excellence Model Higher Education Version 2003*. Sheffield, UK: Centre for Integral Excellence, Sheffield Hallam University, 2003

——. *Embracing Excellence in Education.* Sheffield, UK: Centre for Integral Excellence, Sheffield Hallam University, 2003.

——. *Linking the EFQM Excellence Model to Other Management Models and Tools.* Sheffield, UK: Centre for Integral Excellence, Sheffield Hallam University, 2003.

——. *Organizational Learning and the Future of Higher Education.* Sheffield, UK: Centre for Integral Excellence, Sheffield Hallam University, 2003

Davies, John. "Integration Issues in the Implementation of the EFQM Excellence Model in UK Universities." In *Proceedings of Integrating for Excellence, 1st International Conference.* Sheffield, UK: Centre for Integral Excellence, Sheffield Hallam University, 2005. www.shu.ac.uk/research/integral excellence/downloads/ConferenceProceedings2005.pdf

Dew, John Robert and Molly McGowan Nearing. *Continuous Quality Improvement in Higher Education.* American Council on Education Series on Higher Education. Westport, CT: Praeger, 2004

Ensby, Michael, and Farzad Mahmoodi. "Using the Baldrige Award Criteria in College Classrooms." *Quality Progress* 30, no. 4 (April 1997): 85–91.

European Foundation for Quality Management. *The Fundamental Concepts of Excellence.* Brussels: European Foundation for Quality Management, 1999–2003.

——. *Introducing Excellence.* Brussels: European Foundation for Quality Management, 1999–2003.

Fenske, Robert H. "Higher Performing Colleges: The Malcolm Baldridge National Quality Award as a Framework for Improving Higher Education." *Journal of College Student Development* (July/August 1997). http://findarticles.com/p/articles/mi_qa3752/is_199707?tag=artBody;col1

Furst-Bowe, Julie A. and Roy A. Bauer. "Application of the Baldrige Model for Innovation in Higher Education." In *Managing for Innovation: New Directions for Higher Education #137*, edited by Theodore S. Glickman and Susan C. White, 5–14. Jossey Bass, 2007.

Hakes, Chris. *The EFQM Excellence Model for Assessing Organizational Performance: A Management Guide.* Zaltbommel: Van Haren Publishing, 2007.

Harer, John B. and Bryan R. Cole. "The Importance of the Stakeholder in Performance Measurement: Critical Processes and Performance Measures for Assessing and Improving Academic Library Services and Programs." *College and Research Libraries* 66, no. 2 (March 2005): 149–70.

Hides, Michael Trevor, John Davies, and Sue Jackson. "Implementation of EFQM Excellence Model Self-Assessment in the UK Higher Education Sector—Lessons Learned from Other Sectors." *The TQM Magazine* 16, no. 3 (2004): 194–201.

Izadi, Mahyar, Ali E. Kashef, and Ronald W. Stadt. "Quality in Higher Education: Lessons Learned from the Baldrige Award, Deming Prize, and ISO 9000 Registration." *Journal of Industrial Teacher Education* 33, no. 2 (Winter 1996).

Jantti, Margie H. "Minding Your Own Business: Can a Business Excellence Framework Translate to the Education Sector?" In *Proceedings of the 2002 Annual International Conference of the Higher Education Research and*

Development Society of Australasia (HERDSA), edited by Alan Goody, Jan Herrington, and Maria Northcote. Jamison Centre, Australia: HERDSA, 2002. www.ecu.edu.au/conferences/herdsa/main/papers/nonref/pdf/MargieJantti .pdf

Jones, Kathryn, Margaret Kinnell, and Bob Usherwood. "The Development of Self-Assessment Tool-Kits for the Library and Information Sector." *The Journal of Documentation* 56, no. 2 (March 2000): 119–35.

McAdam, Rodney and William Welsh. "A Critical Review of the Business Excellence Quality Model Applied to Further Education Colleges." *Quality Assurance in Education* 8, no. 3 (2000): 120–31.

Mattisen, Heli and Birgit Kuldvee. "Quality Management vs. Quality Control: Latest Developments in Estonian Higher Education." Paper presented at the 2006 *European Quality Assurance Forum: Embedding Quality Culture in Higher Education*, Munich, 2006. www.eua.be/fileadmin/user_upload/ files/QAForum_2006/GS_I_3_Mattisen.pdf [retrieved February 14, 2008]

Nicholson, Scott. "A Conceptual Framework for the Holistic Measurement and Cumulative Evaluation of Library Services." *Journal of Documentation* 60, no. 2 (2004): 164–82.

Ololube, Nwachukwu Prince. "An Approach to Quality Improvement of Education in Nigeria through EFQM Excellence Model." *The African Symposium: An On Line Journal of the African Educational Research Network* 6, no. 1/2 (June 2006): 7–22. www.ncsu.edu/aern/TAS6.1.2/TAS6 .1.2_rev.pdf

Osseo-Asare, A. Ernest, and David Longbottom. "The Need for Education and Training in the Use of the EFQM Model for Quality Management in UK Higher Education Institutions." *Quality Assurance in Education* 10, no. 1 (2002): 26–36.

Osseo-Asare, Augustus E., David Longbottom, and William D. Murphy. "Leadership Best Practices for Sustaining Quality in UK Higher Education from the Perspective of the EFQM Excellence Model." *Quality Assurance in Education* 13, no. 2 (2005): 148–70.

Penniman, W. David. "Quality Reward and Awards: Quality Has its own Reward, But an Award Helps Speed the Process." In *Integrating Total Quality Management in a Library Setting*, edited by Susan Jurow and Susan B. Barnard. New York: The Haworth Press, 1993.

Porter, Leslie J. and S. J. Tanner. *Assessing Business Excellence: A Guide to Self-Assessment*. Oxford: Butterworth, Heinemann, 1996.

Pupius, Mike. "Achieving Excellence in Education and Training." Paper presented at the European Quality Congress, Volume 44, Volume S (2000): 28–35. http://excellence.shu.ac.uk/publications/eoq_budapest.doc

Rice, G. Kendell, and Donna C. Taylor. "Continuous-Improvement Strategies in Higher Education: A Progress Report." *Research Bulletin, Educause Center for Applied Research*, Volume 2003, Issue 20, September 30, 2003.

Rosa, Maria Joao and Alberto Amaral. "A Self-Assessment of Higher Education Institutions from the Perspective of the EFQM Excellence Model." In *Quality Assurance in Higher Education*, edited by Don F. Westerheijden, Bjorn Stensaker, and Maria Joao Rosa, 181–207. Dordrecht, Netherlands: Springer, 2007.

Rosa, Maria Joao, Pedro M. Saraiva, and Henrique Diz. "The Development of an Excellence Model for Portuguese Higher Education Institutions." *Total Quality Management* 12, no. 7&8 (2001): 1010–17.

SAI Global. *The Business Excellence Framework*. Sydney: SAI Global, March 2007.

Sorensen, Charles W. and Meridith Wentz. "From Crisis to Quality: Using the Malcolm Baldrige National Quality Award Criteria to Redefine Leadership Systems." *Higher Education Digest*, Issue 14, October 2004. www.internetviz-newsletters.com/datatel/e_article000309321.cfm? x=b3MtDqh,b1kH7SfV

Sorensen, Charles W., Julie A. Furst-Bowe and Diane M. Moen, editors. *Quality and Performance Excellence in Higher Education: Baldrige on Campus*. Bolton, MA: Anker Publishing, 2005.

Steed, Carol and Mike Pupius. *EFQM Excellence Model® Higher Education Version 2003*. Sheffield: Sheffield Hallam University, 2003.

Steed, Carol, Dmitry Maslow, and Anna Mazaletskaya. "The EFQM Excellence Model for Deploying Quality Management: A British–Russian Journey." *Higher Education in Europe* 30, no. 3–4 (October–December 2005): 307–19.

Stella, Antony. *Understanding Quality Assurance Frameworks in the Asia-Pacific Region: Indicators of Quality*. Project Group Report. Melbourne: Asia Pacific Quality Network, May 2007. www.apqn.org/project_groups/reports/?referrer=vl

Tari, Juan Jose. "An EFQM Model of Self-Assessment Exercise at a Spanish University." *Journal of Educational Administration* 44, no. 2 (2006): 170–88.

Temple, Paul. "The EFQM Excellence Model: Higher Education's Latest Management Fad?" *Higher Education Quarterly* 59, no. 4 (October 2005): 261–74.

Truccolo, Ivana et al. "EFQM (European Foundation for Quality Management) and Libraries: An Organisational Challenge for Improving the Provided Services." In *Proceedings of Implementation of Quality Systems and Certification of Biomedical Libraries, EAHIL Workshop*. Maarssen, The Netherlands: European Association for Health Information and Libraries, 2005. www.cro.sanita.fvg.it/reposCRO/Biblioteca/eahil_2005_Truccolo-doc.pdf

White, Tatiana. "Knowledge Management in an Academic Library Based on the Case Study 'KM within OULS'." In *Proceedings of the World Library and Information Congress: 70th IFLA General Conference and Council*. The Hague, Netherlands: IFLA, 2004. www.ifla.org/IV/ifla70/papers/089e-White.pdf

Winn, Bradley A., and Kim S. Cameron. "Organizational Quality: An Examination of the Malcolm Baldrige National Quality Framework." *Research in Higher Education* 39, no. 5 (1998): 491–512.

Zink, Klaus J., and Wolfgang Voss. "The New EFQM Excellence Model and Its Impact on Higher Education Institutions." In *Conference Proceedings from TQM for Higher Education Institutions, Higher Education Institutions and the Issue of Total Quality* (1999): 241–55.

4

Strategic planning, the Balanced Scorecard and benchmarking

Strategic planning

Strategic planning has been an integral part of the business world since the mid twentieth century. Its adoption by the academic community came somewhat later, during the 1970s, although the acceptance of strategic planning throughout academe has been less than thorough. Presidents, chancellors, rectors, vice presidents, vice chancellors, and vice rectors embraced the process, but its reception at lower levels of the academic administration was less than enthusiastic. Deans, directors, and department chairs were reluctant to adopt this intrusion from the business world, arguing that their activities were different, and not amenable to the constraints of planning.

Eventually, strategic planning was accepted by the deans, directors, and department chairs for their units. Faculty and staff went through the motions, and the resulting documents were often exercises in fiction that ended up in an administrator's bottom desk drawer. The demand for greater accountability focused attention on strategic planning, and its potential for requiring organizational units to commit action to funding was attractive to administrators. Linking strategic planning to budget preparation and funding requests had a remarkable influence on the willingness of middle management to engage in the planning process.

When creating a strategic plan, the academic library should be aware that its plan will be a subset of the parent institution's strategic plan. Linkages between the institutional plan and the library plan must be evident. The process of establishing any strategic plan must be clearly defined, and must be an integral part of the institutional management system. There are three questions the university strategic planning group should ask the library:

- How can information resources and technologies best support institutional priorities?
- How can we best organize our information resources and technologies to make the strongest contribution to the identified priorities?
- How can we best deploy our limited human and fiscal information technology resources so that all graduates are information literate?[1]

By the time a library has determined its developmental position as a culture of assessment and has used a strong framework for initial self-assessment, it should have a wealth of information to share with the strategic planning group. The planning group should use this information as it moves through the well-known steps of strategic planning: mission, vision, values, SWOT (strengths, weaknesses, opportunities, and threats), goals and objectives.

The best goals and objectives are SMART, an acronym for specific, measurable, achievable, realistic, and timely. There is no specific sequence to be followed in creating SMART objectives, but each descriptor must be met. The SMART acronym has been frequently discussed in popular business media, but its origin is uncertain. Briefly, SMART goals and objectives are:

Specific: Goal and objective statements are concrete, detailed, well-defined, and actionable. They describe action to be taken, explain why the action is important, identify who will be responsible, and describe the condition or status that will exist when they are reached.

Measurable: The outcome of a goal or objective must be measurable. If an outcome can be observed or recorded, then it is measurable, and a measure and accompanying metric should be identified. The best measures have the capacity to track progress toward a goal or objective, and help motivate those involved in the action. *If you can measure it, you can manage it.*

Achievable: Goals and objectives must be practical and achievable. If the outcome(s) are set too far into the future, involve factors not under the library's control, or present insurmountable limitations or constraints on action, then they will be impossible to achieve. They should stretch the library organization, but not break it.

Realistic: Goals and objectives that are achievable may not always be realistic. They do not have to be easy, but the library should have the resources and the means to achieve them—funds, staff with the required knowledge and skills, a reasonable timeline, and leadership support. The library should be able to achieve them without radically reordering its priorities.

Time-bound: Also referred to as "timely" in some SMART descriptions, means setting a deadline for the achievement of the goal or objective. Deadlines need to be both achievable and realistic. If no timeline is projected, it undermines any sense of urgency, reduces motivation, and permits other priorities to intervene. Too short a deadline creates resistance; too long a deadline creates apathy.

Goals and objectives that aren't SMART are fundamentally useless. There is no possibility of achievement, and certainly no possibility that anyone will be held accountable.

When the planning process is at the goal-setting stage and goals have been set, people often consider the exercise complete. If that is the view, strategic planning will never accomplish what it is capable of achieving. There are three additional steps: the formation of targets or action plans, the establishment of milestones, and the identification of desired outcomes. Follow-through after goal setting is essential if the strategic plan is to be fully implemented. These three critical elements are most commonly missing from library strategic plans. One reason is lack of commitment; another is fear. If there are targets/action plans, milestones, and outcomes, the library becomes immediately more accountable. In these instances, any positive results of strategic planning are sheer luck. Dew and Nearing summarize the process of action planning as:

> The objective of creating action plans is to define what specific steps will occur to implement a key strategic action, to define who will be responsible for each step, and to define a time frame for the completion of each step. A major action plan may include numerous steps with completion dates (sometimes called milestones) defined for each step. In some cases, it is beneficial to define points in time when progress on the implementation of a plan will be formally reviewed. It may also be beneficial to clarify or define the end point of an action plan.[2]

Markless and Streatfield add three important points regarding the use of milestones, or targets, which can be easily overlooked in planning.

1. A mixture of process and impact targets should be used.

Process targets are intended to make changes in what people do ... It is usual to see development plans bristling with process items. Process targets are important, but processes can be changed radically without leading to real differences in the impact of services.

Impact targets are aimed at improving the quality of the service; they are focused on real achievements ... Impact targets can be concerned with the whole community or parts of it. Impact targets lend themselves to more precise quantification than process targets but it would be a mistake to see them all in terms of numbers ...

2. Failure will result if too many impact targets are adopted at the same time, because this will lead to confusion rather than concentrated effort. Each impact target will necessarily drag a raft of process targets along in its wake.

3. When setting targets it may be helpful to consider target zones ...

- the historic zone. Targets in this zone are those which are behind current performance, which is hidden to the extent that others are not aware of its quality. By this means, standstill can be represented as improvement—it is a means of "domesticating" any threats that targets may offer.

- the comfort zone. Targets in this zone seek to keep improvement very much within reach. They often reflect a belief that there is really no need to improve.

- the smart zone. Targets in this zone are sufficiently ahead of the present state of play to make a difference.

- the unlikely zone. Targets in this zone seek large improvements through determination and high aspirations, or recklessness. They can be a recipe for high risk and high stress.[3]

If librarians are honest with themselves, how many would acknowledge that most of their targets/action plans (if they have even created them) fall into the "historic" or "comfort" zones? These misconceptions allow librarians to claim engagement in strategic planning when, in reality, they are just going through the motions. The challenge is to select targets/action plans that make a difference and that people really care about, but are not within the "unlikely" zone. There can be enough stress in an organization without setting its members up to fail at fulfilling their targets/action plans.

At the conclusion of the strategic planning process, every individual staff member should be able to identify the strategies the library will pursue to set itself apart from its competitors and move it toward its vision of the future. Matthews identifies "three types of broad or generic strategies that can be considered should any library wish to be more responsive to those it serves: Operational excellence; innovative services; and customer intimacy."[4] He notes that, regardless of the strategy chosen, "there is only one fundamental question: How? Organizational strategies concern how to grow the organization, how to satisfy customers, how to overcome the pressures of competitors, how to respond to changing market conditions, and how to manage the organization and develop organizational capabilities."[5]

Measurement systems and the Balanced Scorecard

Libraries have had the most difficulty with the "measurable" component of the SMART acronym, and this bedevils the process throughout—in setting targets, creating actions, identifying milestones, and describing outcomes. Once identified and defined, measures are most useful as part of an integrated comprehensive measurement system within the library. Without relevant associated measures, milestones and outcomes are nothing more than wishful thinking. Jacobson and Sparks provide the following advice to consider when identifying measures and creating measurement systems.

1. Measure objectives or outcomes for each strategic objective ... Identify at least one measure. The measures can be qualitative and quantitative and often you may choose to assign more than one indicator to each objective. What is important is that the measures be outcomes or "effect" indicators ...

2. Measure selective inputs or drivers—selectively measure the inputs or drivers to the strategic plan ...

3. Define target points and include manager's comments for each measure that you define, [and] try to identify a target value ...

4. Keep it simple—one of the traps that measurement systems fall into is that they quickly become too burdensome and complex ...

5. Communicate the system with an effective plan describing the purposes and mechanics of the measurement system ...

6. Revise the measurement system—strategy does not exist in a vacuum but in a real work setting that is constantly changing or shifting ...[6]

If strategic planning is to be successful, it must reflect the library-wide involvement of all professional and non-professional staff. Leadership must be exercised from the very top for a sustained and sustainable process. Even when these conditions are met, there are barriers that affect the success of strategic planning. The Balanced Scorecard Collaborative has identified four barriers to the successful implementation of a strategic plan:

1. Vision barrier: No one in the organization understands the strategies of the organization.
2. People barrier: Most people have objectives that are not linked to the strategy of the organization.
3. Resource barrier: Time, energy and money are not allocated to those things that are critical to the organization. For example, budgets are not linked to strategy, resulting in wasted resources.
4. Management barrier: Management spends too little time on strategy and too much time on short-term tactical decision-making.[7]

These barriers continue beyond the strategic planning phase and, with slight variation, can threaten all organizational activity. At one time or another any library engaged in strategic planning has been affected by one or more of these barriers. The challenge is to recognize that action must be taken to protect the strategic plan from failure. Leadership must recognize the challenges these barriers present, and take responsibility for overcoming them.

The Balanced Scorecard framework (Figure 4.1), introduced in 1992 by Robert S. Kaplan and David P. Norton, was the result of two years' work with a selected group of businesses.[8] The motivation for creating the Balanced Scorecard was to provide a more holistic system for the development and deployment of strategic plans, one taking into account more than financial performance. The framework focuses on achieving a balance between short- and long-term objectives, financial and non-financial measures, lagging and leading indicators, and external and internal performance perspectives. The Scorecard comprises four perspectives—financial, customer, internal business process, and learning and growth/innovation. Each of these perspectives poses a question to help focus goal setting:

- Financial: how do we look to shareholders?
- Customer: how do customers see us?
- Internal business process: what must we excel at?
- Learning and growth/innovation: can we continue to improve and create value?

Each of the perspectives should have a very limited number of goals—no more than four. Similarly, there should be only one measure for each goal. It can be argued that if a goal has more than one measure, then there really is more than one goal. The emphasis of the Balanced Scorecard is to focus on goals that are most critical to the success of the company. In their work, Kaplan and Norton found that, about 20 percent of the time, goals were established for which no data could be collected. Kaplan and Norton make the importance of measurement very clear:

> Measurement matters: "If you can't measure it, you can't manage it." An organization's measurement system strongly reflects the behavior of people both inside and outside the organization. If companies are to survive and prosper in information age competition, they must use measurement and management systems derived from their strategies and capabilities. Unfortunately, many

Figure 4.1   Kaplan and Norton's Balanced Scorecard

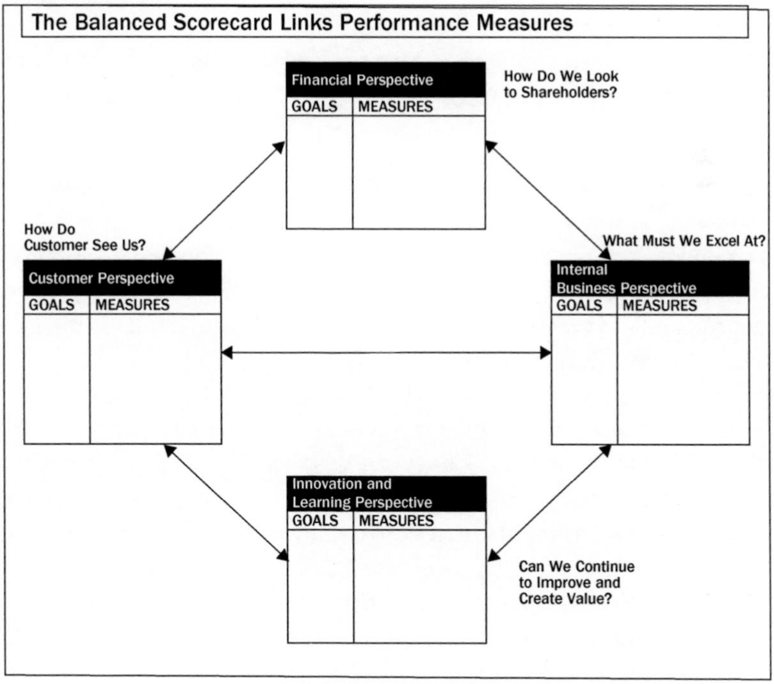

Source: Reprinted with permission of Harvard Business School Publishing from Robert S. Kaplan and David P. Norton. "The Balanced Scorecard—Measures that Drive Performance," *Harvard Business Review* 70, no. 1 (January/February 1992): 72.

organizations espouse strategies about customer relationships, core competencies, and organizational capabilities while motivating and measuring performance only with financial measures.[9]

An essential requirement of the Balanced Scorecard is a cause-and-effect relationship between each of the four perspectives. For example, goals for the learning and growth/innovation perspective must have clear, causal relationships with the effects found in either the internal business process or customer perspectives. Further, goals in these two perspectives must have a causal relationship with the effects in the financial perspective.

Since the Balanced Scorecard was developed in the for-profit sector, there may be a tendency to focus on the financial perspective as the most important of the four. However, Kaplan and Norton make it clear that three types of intangible assets in the learning and growth/innovation perspective are essential for implementing business strategy:

- Human capital: The skills, talents, and knowledge that a company's employees possess.

- Information capital: The company's databases, information systems, networks, and technology infrastructure.

- Organization capital: The company's culture, its leadership, how aligned its people are with its strategic goals and employees' ability to share knowledge.[10]

These intangible assets are just as essential, and perhaps more essential, in the public and non-profit sector as the for-profit sector.

The Balanced Scorecard drew immediate interest from public and non-profit sectors, and Kaplan and Norton recognized these types of organizations had certain difficulties and limitations in implementing the Scorecard, which Kaplan noted directly:

> In my experience, nonprofits have considerable difficulty in clearly defining their strategy. I have seen "strategy" documents that run upwards of fifty pages. And most of the documents, once the mission and vision are articulated, consist of lists of programs and initiatives rather than outcomes the organization is trying to achieve. Such organizations, when implementing a performance measurement system, typically measure progress in achieving milestones on their initiatives. This is backwards. Initiatives should exist to help the organization achieve its strategic objectives. They are means, not ends. Strategy and performance measurement should

focus on what output and outcomes the organization intends to achieve, not what programs and initiatives are being implemented.[11]

Kaplan's statement unwittingly, but accurately, describes the reality of strategic planning and measurement for many academic libraries.

During the 1990s, significant steps towards instituting well-defined quality programs were taken in many countries in Europe, the US, Japan, Singapore, Australia, and New Zealand. As implementation efforts moved forward, the Balanced Scorecard was considered a useful tool, but with one significant shortcoming for public and non-profit organizations: that it put too little emphasis on the customer perspective and too much emphasis on the financial perspective. Government organizations and non-profit groups, such as higher education and libraries, are not committed to building shareholder equity, so financials were not the ultimate goal. Instead, high-quality customer service was the goal.

To develop an integrated quality library management system for academic libraries, three German academic/state libraries (the University and Regional Library, Münster, the Bavarian State Library, Munich, and the State and University Library, Bremen) decided to adapt the Balanced Scorecard for academic libraries. Speaking about the process, Poll noted that adaptation

"translates" the planning perspective of an institution (mission, strategic vision and goals) into a system of performance indicators that covers all important perspectives of performance: finances, users, internal processes and improvement activities.

The system thus integrates

- Financial and non-financial data
- Input and output data
- External perspective (funding institution, users) and the internal perspective (processes, staff)
- Goals and measures taken
- Causes and results.[12]

Representatives of the three libraries decided to reorient the Balanced Scorecard (Figure 4.2). The result, illustrated below, places the customer (users) perspective at the top, and the financial (finances) perspective to the left, to reflect its fundamental importance, but only in service to the customer (users).[13]

Figure 4.2 The Balanced Scorecard reoriented for library use

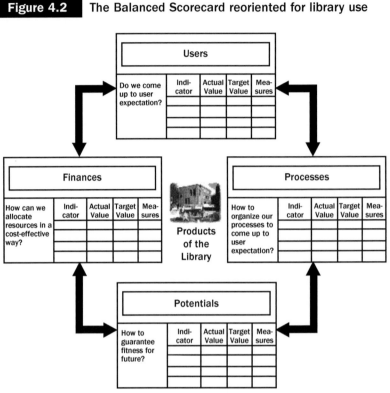

The illustration of the Balanced Scorecard framework for libraries shows the relationship between the measure or metric, the target value, the actual value achieved, and an indicator. Poll noted: "One great advantage of the Balanced Scorecard is that it can visualize relationships of cause and effect among target values, evaluation data, and actions taken."[14] The general methodology of the Balanced Scorecard was retained, and limitation of goals and development of appropriate measurements were considered critical to the success of the method in academic libraries.

Another example of the adaptability of the Balanced Scorecard to higher education comes from the University of Southern California, Rossier School of Education. A faculty committee revised the scorecard for use in the school and:

made some minor modifications in the wording of the four perspectives and of the questions that define them. "Financial perspective" was replaced with "academic management perspective," and instead of asking "How do we look to shareholders?" we asked, "How do we look to our university leadership?" (In public institutions, this question might be expanded to include "statewide coordinating boards" or "system wide administrators.") For the original "customer perspective" we substituted "stakeholder perspective" and identified students and employers as our most significant stakeholders. (For public institutions, this stakeholder set could be expanded to include elected officials and other stakeholders who have influence over budget appropriations for higher education.) We kept the original names of the two remaining perspectives.[15]

The University of Virginia (UVA) Library, which has a long history of data gathering and statistical reporting among US academic libraries, decided to implement the Balanced Scorecard in the late 1990s. James Self noted the rationale for adoption as:

> In essence the Balanced Scorecard enables us to gain better control of our statistical operations. By limiting the number of scorecard metrics, it forces us to decide what is important, and to identify those numbers that truly make a difference. It also introduces some balance into our statistical work. Like many libraries, we have collected many data regarding resources and user services, but other areas have not received the same attention. The BSC compels us to take a focused look at finances, internal processes, and the future. Another important aspect of the BSC is the assigning of targets for goals. We not only decide what measures are important; we also state what constitutes success for each measurement.[16]

The UVA Library assigns two targets to each goal. One is a stretch target, which challenges library staff to achieve significant change. The other target is less challenging, but represents meaningful progress toward the goal. In discussing UVA Library's implementation of the scorecard, Self noted a general staff opinion that choosing the appropriate metrics may be the most critical step in implementation, for the choice of metrics reflects the values of the library. Adopting the scorecard requires a library to confront decisions that historically have been avoided. While choosing the metric or measurement is critical, technique is an equally important aspect of choice:

The nature of the measurement is equally important. Do we count the number of times we perform a task? Do we measure the cost of performing a task? Do we calculate the time it typically takes to do the task? Or do we survey our customers and ask them how well we perform the task? Any of these techniques might be appropriate, but our choice of techniques is reflective of the library's priorities.[17]

The UVA Library is one of the few US academic libraries to have fully adopted the Balanced Scorecard, and its Management Information Services unit maintains a well-developed website to present complete scorecard metrics, targets, and results along the four perspectives.[18] Several Australian university libraries have implemented the scorecard, notably Monash University, which also publishes its scorecard results.[19]

Organizations considering the Balanced Scorecard approach to total quality management have been advised by Niven to first address the following tasks:

- Developing your rationale for using the Balanced Scorecard.
- Determining resource requirements and availability.
- Deciding where to build your first scorecard.
- Gaining senior leadership support and sponsorship.
- Forming your Balanced Scorecard team.
- Providing training to your team and other key stakeholders.
- Developing a communications plan for your Balanced Scorecard implementation.[20]

Niven also provides a number of key steps in establishing a Balanced Scorecard system for government and non-profit agencies. These steps represent a substantial departure from traditional library management thinking:

1. Develop or confirm your mission, values, vision, and strategy.
2. Confirm the role of the Balanced Scorecard in your Performance Management framework.
3. Select your Scorecard perspectives.
4. Review relevant background materials.
5. Conduct executive interviews.
6. Create your strategy maps.
7. Gather feedback.

8. Develop performance measures.

9. Develop targets and initiatives.

10. Develop the ongoing implementation plan.[21]

The decision to employ the Balanced Scorecard should not be taken without extensive and thorough consideration of its impacts on the library. As with any quality improvement system, the decision commits already scarce staff resources and time to successful implementation.

Benchmarking

The notion of benchmarking comes from the business world and it has been widely used in industry for a number of years. Benchmarking simply means measuring something against a standard, and may have its earliest meaning as a notch or mark made on the surface of a workbench for use as a measurement template. In writing about libraries, Shaughnessy notes that benchmarking can benefit an organization in several ways.

- It permits the best practices from any industry to be incorporated into an organization's processes or operations;
- It can help break down ingrained operational and behavioral responses and create a more receptive climate for change;
- It can facilitate innovation through the substitution of technologies or other systems designed to improve performance.[22]

The practice of benchmarking in higher education, and specifically in academic libraries, has been sporadic. Although librarians have prided themselves in their willingness to share information and knowledge, they have been reluctant to embark on sustained benchmarking. One reason for this may be that, properly done, benchmarking requires a significant investment of time and careful preparation. It typically takes much longer to accomplish than is planned. Finding partners who are willing to make the investment of time and resources also can be an obstacle. There have been many informal benchmarking exercises, but formal, continuous benchmarking has been a rare practice. Formal or informal, very little has been written about benchmarking activities among academic libraries, with the exception of Australian libraries. They have pursued benchmarking in a more formal manner and have written about their experiences.

There are many definitions of benchmarking, all of which are remarkably similar. White presented this definition:

> Benchmarking is an ongoing, systematic process for measuring and comparing the work processes of one organization to those of others that exhibit functional "best practices." The goal is to provide an external standard for measuring the quality and cost of internal processes, and to help identify where there may be opportunities for improvement.[23]

A fundamental problem in this definition is the identification of "best practices." Although statements of good practice have been released by library associations, there is no comprehensive clearinghouse to identify and collect information on best practices. There are no standards to describe best practices exactly, or review panels to determine what libraries follow them.

The Consortium for Excellence in Higher Education (UK) provides some clarification of the general term "best practice" in its description of the essential characteristics of benchmarking.

> **Continuous:** Benchmarking should not be treated as a "one-off" exercise; it should be incorporated into the regular planning cycle of the organization and the management of key processes.
>
> **Systematic:** It is important to ensure that a consistent methodology is adopted by the organization and that it is followed. It is equally important that processes are in place to ensure that good practice is shared across the organization.
>
> **Implementation:** Benchmarking helps to identify gaps that exist between current performance and "Best Practice", and also how "Best Practice" performance has been achieved but in order for improvement to occur, a set of actions must be implemented.
>
> **Best practice:** It is not necessary to identify the absolute "Best Practice" in the world in order for benchmarking to be successful. "Good or Superior" practice is probably a more accurate phrase.[24]

Some authors have identified four categories of benchmarking, while others have listed five, but the Centre for Integral Excellence defines no fewer than seven different types of benchmarking.

> **Performance or competitive benchmarking:** A process whereby organizations use performance measures to compare themselves against

similar organizations. This is common practice in higher education where universities compare themselves with others in terms of market share, retention rates, research performance and costs. Benchmarking using this approach can also be undertaken within an organization by comparing the performance of individual business units.

Functional or generic benchmarking: Functional or generic benchmarking involves partnerships of organizations drawn from different sectors that wish to improve some specific activity or process.

External benchmarking: This type of benchmarking can enable the comparison of the organization's functions and key processes against good practice organizations. The key driver can be the search for improvement or breakthrough opportunities in business processes.

Internal good practice benchmarking: This is achieved by the establishing of good practice organization-wide through the comparison of internal activities or operations. The key driver is the sharing of good practice in cross-cutting activities, for example, by carrying out process improvement.

International benchmarking: ... benchmarking can be undertaken internationally as well as nationally.

Process benchmarking: This approach focuses on specific processes or operations. In higher education examples might be enquiry management, enrolment or timetabling.

Product benchmarking: Of relevance in the private sector and increasingly in the HE sector is product benchmarking, a practice that would seek to identify opportunities for improvement from comparisons of product in terms of cost, quality and features. In the HE case this would be equivalent to comparing courses or programmes of teaching.[25]

While any of these approaches to benchmarking could be applied by an academic library, *functional* benchmarking is probably the most familiar and widely applied type. Librarians usually want to compare what is being done in functional departments, e.g., cataloging, interlibrary loan, stacks maintenance, etc. There should be plenty of opportunity for internal benchmarking, but little appears to have been written about libraries conducting this type of investigation. Benchmarking in libraries has focused on data collection for comparison of inputs and outputs. As the interest in performance measurement has grown, one might expect the focus to shift toward benchmarking outcomes, but this does not seem to be happening.

Assuming there is some interest in benchmarking, exactly how would the library proceed? First, it would be important to know your own library as an organization, understand its goals and objectives, and know its internal and external customers. Peischl suggests the following steps for benchmarking in academic libraries:

Pre-benchmarking: Deciding what is to be measured; how to measure; and what partners or criterion will be used in the process.

Benchmarking: During this stage the process of gathering data, measuring outputs and estimating targets is formulated. This lengthy process involves many staff and much organization time.

Post-benchmarking: The results are in; the process of analysis is started and the future goals are formulated. An action plan, a strategy, is created and set in motion.

Review/renew: During this phase review of the strategy, resetting goals and continuous planning for improvement lead back to the first step of pre-benchmarking.[26]

Determining what to benchmark and how it will be measured is important, but even more critical may be finding a partner(s) for the project. All parties to benchmarking should expect that collecting data will be more time consuming than anticipated. If processes are being benchmarked, there may be very little documentation to describe them. If there is documentation, it may have little relevance to the way in which the process is actually performed. It is also possible that staff may not be terribly enthusiastic about sharing how they do their work. Before embarking on a benchmarking project, a number of considerations need to be addressed by library administration:

- Commitment is essential from both participants in the project and management.
- Process thinking: All staff have to stop thinking in terms of distinct functional areas and start thinking in terms of processes. Establishing cross-functional benchmarking teams encourages this change.
- Benchmarking methodology: Benchmarking works best when it is guided by a structural approach, which outlines the main steps and provides guidance for the team.
- Involvement in all aspects of the project by the participants.
- Planning is essential.

- Training to equip benchmarkers with the skills to: Analyse processes; collect and analyse data; develop performance indicators and measures; manage projects; liaise with other organizations and communicate, and where appropriate implement findings. Apply continuous improvement and benchmarking tools such as: flowcharting, cause and effect diagrams, brainstorming, performance gap analysis, work mapping, Imagineering, multivoting, and surveys, questionnaires and focus groups.

- Continuous improvement culture: Successful organizations operate in an environment where improvement strategies are integrated into the way things are done.

- Benchmarking is a gradual process that takes time and happens in small steps.

- The project chosen must be meaningful to the library and fit in with its strategic plan.[27]

It is easy to understand why so many librarians abandon benchmarking before they begin. Even when willing and ready to engage in benchmarking, there are opportunities for error, which Henczel enumerates, and which are restated below:

Collaboration versus competition: Benchmarking is often difficult when potential external partners are also competitors, as "commercial sensitivity" often prevents them from revealing details of their processes.

Non-standard data collection methods: Methods for collecting data are not consistent or standardized, so comparisons may not be valid.

Changing environment: Continuous measurement and comparison does not easily reflect change in environmental variables.

Reliance: There is a danger of becoming reliant on benchmarking rather than seeking inventive or innovative process improvements, and it can stifle creativity.

Resources: Benchmarking requires a significant commitment of resources with no real guarantee of tangible benefit.

Identifying partners: Identifying potential benchmarking partners can be difficult.

The people factor: Often the adaptation of a process is not successful, as its success was dependent on the skills and expertise of those using it in the initiating environment. It can be difficult to distinguish human talent as a factor separate from internal processes.

Inappropriate adaptation: It may be tempting to benchmark processes that are not strategically important just because you think that someone else may be doing them better than you.

Innovative and efficient processes: Benchmarking is less useful to organizations in the lead, especially in unique environments. It can, however, be very useful to followers who are looking for better ways of doing things.

Best practice: Best practice is not always appropriate. Best practice can be unique to an environment or situation and will not necessarily adapt successfully to a different environment.[28]

Unless leadership is committed to benchmarking, the process won't succeed. One of the most difficult and challenging activities is determining what to benchmark—that is, to develop performance indicators. Librarians in Europe, Asia, and Australia are acquainted with the importance of performance measures, but librarians in the US have not developed a similar level of familiarity. Garrod and Kinnell note that "Performance indicators provide hard quantitative data on the relationship between different variables and thus enable comparisons to be made, e.g. between different time periods and different operational methods."[29] Performance indicators must be established before a benchmarking project begins, and must be agreed to by all partners in the project. This creates a competitive hurdle if one library believes a particular performance indicator gives another of the partners an unfair advantage. In a perfect world, Poll suggests that performance indicators would:

- Mirror the full extent of library services,
- Consider electronic as well as traditional services,
- Help to demonstrate the importance and impact of libraries,
- Further comparison between the participating libraries,
- Avoid unfair treatment of individual libraries,
- Allow for special conditions in the libraries (every library seems to be unique!)
- Yield results that are easily understandable, even for politicians
- And, in spite of all that, consist of only a few measures that should preferably be collected from the normal library statistics.[30]

Whether or not a library chooses benchmarking as a quality improvement practice, performance indicators have to be addressed, for they provide the basis of measurement and the development of meaningful library metrics. Benchmarks are embedded into the Balanced Scorecard method, which uses them to set targets and report results. Chapter 5 reviews established performance indicators adopted by various library organizations, as well as the role of indicators in determining impacts and outcomes.

Notes

1. Birdsall, "Strategic Planning in Academic Libraries."
2. Dew and Nearing, *Continuous Quality Improvement in Higher Education*, 85–6.
3. Markless and Streatfield, "Developing Performance and Impact Indicators and Targets," 175.
4. Matthews, *Strategic Planning and Management*, 43.
5. *Ibid.*, 5.
6. Jacobson and Sparks, "Creating Value," 20.
7. Financial Management Training Center, "Excellence in Financial Management Course 11: The Balanced Scorecard," prepared by Matt H. Evans. [Retrieved July 10, 2008 from www.exinfm.com/training/index.html]
8. Kaplan and Norton, "The Balanced Scorecard," 72.
9. Kaplan and Norton, *The Balanced Scorecard*, 21.
10. Kaplan and Norton, "Measuring the Strategic Readiness of Intangible Assets," 55.
11. Kaplan, "Strategic Performance Measurements and Management," 358.
12. Poll, "Managing Service Quality," 2.
13. *Ibid.*, 6.
14. Poll, "Performance, Processes, and Costs," 715.
15. Harold F. O'Neil, Jr. et al., "Designing and Implementing an Academic Scorecard," 36.
16. Self, "Using Data to Make Choices," 28.
17. *Ibid.*
18. The University of Virginia Library's Balanced Scorecard pages are located at www.lib.virginia.edu/bsc/metrics/all0304.html.
19. Monash University's 2006 Balanced Scorecard report is located at www.lib.monash.edu.au/reports/annual/2006/appendix.html.
20. Niven, *Balanced Scorecard Step-by-Step*, 68.
21. *Ibid.*, 70.
22. Shaughnessy, "Benchmarking," 9.
23. White, "The University of Virginia's Experiment with Benchmarking," 14.
24. Consortium for Excellence in Higher Education, *Benchmarking Methods and Experiences*, 4–5.

25. *Ibid.*, 6.
26. Peischl, "Benchmarking: A Process for Improvement," 120–1.
27. Wilson and Pitman, *Best Practice Handbook*, 7–8.
28. Henczel, "Benchmarking, Measuring and Comparing," 3.
29. Garrod and Kinnell, "Benchmarking Development Needs," 112.
30. Poll, "Quality Measures on a National Scale," 2–3.

Bibliography

Anderson, Henrik V., Gavin Lawrie, and Michael Shulver. "The Balanced Scorecard vs. the EFQM Business Excellence Model—Which is the Better Strategic Management Tool?" 2CG Working Paper. Berkshire, UK: 2CG Limited, 2000. www.mpowerasia.com/BSC%20vs%20BEM.pdf

Baker, Bill. "Scorecards." *DM Review* 17, no. 2 (February 2007): 50–2.

Birdsall, Douglas G. "Strategic Planning in Academic Libraries: A Political Perspective." Chicago: ALA-Association of College & Research Libraries, 1997. www.ala.org/ala/acrlbucket/pil49restructuri/birdsall.htm [retrieved July 9, 2008]

Brodie, Maxine and Meredith Martinelli. "Creating a New Library for Macquarie University: Are We There Yet?" *Library Management* 28, no. 8/9 (2007): 557–68.

Chen, Shun-Hsing, Ching Chow Yang, and Jiun-Yan Shiau. "The Application of Balanced Scorecard in the Performance Evaluation of Higher Education." *The TQM Magazine* 18, no. 2 (2006): 190–205.

Claggett, Laura. "Create, Organize and Expedite a Strategic Plan: How to Use the Balanced Scorecard and the Stage-Gate Funnel." *Information Outlook* (March 2005). http://findarticles.com/p/articles/mi_m0FWE/is_3_9?tag=untagged

Consortium for Excellence in Higher Education. *Benchmarking Methods and Experiences*. Sheffield, UK: Centre for Integral Excellence, Sheffield Hallam University, 2003.

Cribb, Gulcin. "Human Resource Development: Impacting on All Four Perspectives of the Balanced Scorecard." In *Proceedings of the World Library and Information Congress: 71st IFLA General Conference and Council*. The Hague, Netherlands: IFLA, 2005. www.ifla.org/IV/ifla71/papers/075e-Cribb.pdf

—— and Chris Hogan. "Balanced Scorecard: Linking Strategic Planning to Measurement and Communication." Paper presented at the 24th Annual IATUL Conference, June 2–5, 2003, Ankara,Turkey. http://epublications.bond.edu.au/cgi/viewcontent.cgi?article=1006&context=library_pubs

Cullen, Rowena. "Benchmarking Overview and Context." In *Proceedings of the World Library and Information Congress: 69th IFLA General Conference and Council*. The Hague, Netherlands: IFLA, 2003. www.ifla.org/IV/ifla69/papers/015e-Cullen.pdf

Dew, John Robert and Molly McGowan Nearing. *Continuous Quality Improvement in Higher Education*. American Council on Education Series on Higher Education. Westport, CT: Praeger, 2004

Dougherty, Richard M. "Planning for New Library Futures." *Library Journal* 126, no 9 (May 15, 2002): 38–41

Dugan, Robert E. "Managing Technology in an Assessment Environment." *Journal of Academic Librarianship* 28, No. 1 (January/March 2001): 56–8.

European Benchmarking Initiative (EBI) in Higher Education. "Background, Definitions and Approaches of Benchmarking." Brussels: EBI, 2007. www.esmu.be/fileadmin/documents/DEAN_members/documents/Background _paper_EBI_Symposium.pdf

Ford, Geoffrey. "Strategic Uses of Evaluation and Performance Measurement." In *Proceedings of the 4th Northumbria International Conference on Performance Measurement in Library and Information Services*, 19–30. Washington, DC: Association of Research Libraries, 2002. www.libqual .org/documents/admin/ford.pdf

Fulweiler, Rebecca D. "The Role of Management Information Systems." *Journal of Academic Librarianship* 27, no. 5 (September 2001): 386–90.

Garrod, Penny and Margaret Kinnell. "Benchmarking Development Needs in the LIS Sector." *Journal of Information Science* 23, no. 2 (1997): 111–18.

Gorman, G. E. "Collecting Data Sensibly in Information Settings." *IFLA Journal* 26, no. 2 (2000): 115–19.

Hart, Liz. "Benchmarking for Improvement." In *Statistics in Practice— Measuring & Managing 2002*. Leicestershire: Loughborough University Library and Information Statistics Unit, LISU Occasional Paper #32, 2003. www.lboro.ac.uk/departments/dils/lisu/pages/publications/ifla-ab-pr.html

Henczel, Sue. "Benchmarking, Measuring and Comparing." *Information Outlook* 6, no. 7 (July 2002). http://findarticles.com/p/articles/mi_m0FWE/ is_7_6/ai_89397531] [retrieved July 11, 2008]

——. "Measuring and Evaluating the Library's Contribution to Organizational Success: Developing a Strategic Measurement Model." *Performance Measurement and Metrics* 7, no. 1 (2006): 7–16.

Hernon, Peter and Philip J. Calvert. "Methods for Measuring Service Quality in University Libraries in New Zealand." *Journal of Academic Librarianship* 22, no. 5 (January 1996): 387–8.

—— and Robert E. Dugan. *An Action Plan for Outcomes Assessment in Your Library*. Chicago: American Library Association, 2002.

Jackson Feinman, Valerie. "Five Steps Toward Planning Today for Tomorrow's Needs." *Computers in Libraries* 19, no. 1 (January 1999): 19–21.

Jacobson, Alvin L. and JoAnne L. Sparks. "Creating Value: Building the Strategy-Focused Library." *Information Outlook* 5, no. 9 (September 2001): 15–20.

Kaplan, Robert S. "Strategic Performance Measurement and Management in Nonprofit Organizations." *Nonprofit Management and Leadership* 11, no. 3 (Spring 2001): 353–70.

Kaplan, Robert S. and David P. Norton. "The Balanced Scorecard—Measures that Drive Performance." *Harvard Business Review* (January–February 1992): 71–9.

—— and ——. "Putting the Balanced Scorecard to Work." *Harvard Business Review* (September–October 1993): 134–47.

—— and ——. *The Balanced Scorecard, Translating Strategy into Action*. Boston: Harvard Business School Press, 1996.

—— and ——. "Using the Balanced Scorecard as a Strategic Management System." *Harvard Business Review* (January–February 1996): 75–85.

—— and ——. "Linking the Balanced Scorecard to Strategy." *California Management Review* 39, no. 1 (September 1996): 53–79.

—— and ——. "Having Trouble with Your Strategy? Then Map It." *Harvard Business Review* (September–October 2000): 167–76.

—— and ——. "Measuring the Strategic Readiness of Intangible Assets." *Harvard Business Review* (February 2004): 52–63.

—— and ——. *Strategy Maps, Converting Intangible Assets into Tangible Outcomes*. Boston: Harvard Business School Press, 2004.

—— and ——. "The Office of Strategy Management." *Harvard Business Review* (October 2005): 72–80.

Karathanos, Demetrius and Patricia Karathanos. "Applying the Balanced Scorecard to Education." *Journal of Education for Business* 80, no. 4 (March/April 2005): 222–30.

Kettunen, Juha. "The Strategic Evaluation of Academic Libraries." *Library Hi Tech* 25, no. 3 (2007): 409–21.

Kinnell, Margret and Penny Garrod. "Benchmarking and Its Relevance to the Library and Information Sector. Interim Findings." In *Proceedings of the 1st Northumbria International Conference on Performance Measurement in Libraries and Information Services*. Newcastle upon Tyne: Information North, 1995.

Laeven, Hubert and Anja Smit. "A Project to Benchmark University Libraries in the Netherlands." *Library Management* 24, no. 6/7 (2003): 291–304.

Levinge, Leanne and Karen Tang. "The Impact of Leadership on Library Quality: Outcomes of a Benchmarking Project Between ATN Libraries." In *Proceedings ALIA 2006 Biennial Conference: CLICK '06*. Deakin, Australia: Australian Library and Information Association, 2006 http://conferences.alia.org.au/alia2006/presentations/Levinge.pdf

Lloyd, Stratton. "Building Library Success Using the Balanced Scorecard." *Library Quarterly* 76, no. 3 (2006): 352–61.

Lorenzen, Michael. "Strategic Planning for Academic Library Instructional Programming: An Overview." www.libraryinstruction.com/strategic-planning.html

McGregor, Felicity. "Performance Measures, Benchmarking and Value." In *Proceedings of the Australian Library and Information Association (ALIA) 2000 Conference*. Deakin, Australia: Australian Library and Information Association, 2000. http://conferences.alia.org.au/alia2000/proceedings/felicity.mcgregor.html

——. "Benchmarking with the Best." Paper presented at the 5th Northumbria Conference on Performance Measurement in Libraries and Information Services, Durham, England. July 28–31, 2003.

McNicol, Sarah. "The Challenges of Strategic Planning in Academic Libraries." *New Library World* 106, no. 11/12 (2005): 495–509.

MacStravic, Scott. "A Really Balanced Scorecard." *Health Forum Journal* 42 (May/June 1999): 64–7.

Markless, Sharon and David Streatfield. "Developing Performance and Impact Indicators and Targets in Public and Education Libraries," *International Journal of Information Management* 21, no. 2 (April 2001): 167–79.

Markless, Sharon and David Streatfield. "Gathering and Applying Evidence of the Impact of UK University Libraries on Student Learning and Research: A Facilitated Action Research Approach." *International Journal of Information Management* 26, no. 1 (February 2006): 3–15.

Matthews, Joseph R. *Strategic Planning and Management for Library Managers*. Westport, CT: Libraries Unlimited, 2005.

Melo, Luiza Baptista, Cestalina Pires, and Ana Tavelra. "Recognizing Best Practice in Portuguese Higher Education Libraries." *IFLA Journal* 34, no. 1 (2008): 34–54.

Mullany, Fiona. "Bridging the Evidence Gap—the eVALUEd Toolkit Project." *SCONUL Focus* 34 (Spring 2005): 49–51.

Mundt, Sebastian. "Benchmarking User Satisfaction in Academic Libraries—A Case Study." *Library and Information Research* 27, no. 87 (Winter 2003): 29–37.

Nawe, Julita. "Planning and Policy Issues in Academic Libraries in Tanzania." *Library Management* 24, no. 8/9 (2003): 417–22.

Nicholson, Scott. "The Bibliomining Process: Data Warehousing and Data Mining for Library Decision Making." *ITAL: Information Technology and Libraries* 22, no. 4 (2003): 146–51.

——. "Approaching Librarianship from the Data: Using Bibliomining for Evidence-Based Librarianship." *Library Hi Tech* 24, no. 3 (2006): 369–75.

Niven, Paul R. *Balanced Scorecard Step-by-Step for Government and Nonprofit Agencies*. Hoboken, NJ: Wiley & Sons, Inc., 2003.

O'Neil, Jr., Harold F. et al. "Designing and Implementing an Academic Scorecard." *Change* 31, no. 6 (November/December 1999): 32–40.

Oppenheim, Charles, Joan Stenson, and Richard M. S. Wilson. "The Attributes of Information as an Asset, Its Measurement and Role in Enhancing Organizational Effectiveness." In *Proceedings of the 4th Northumbria International Conference on Performance Measurement in Library and Information Services*, 197–202. Washington, DC: Association of Research Libraries, 2002. www.libqual.org/documents/admin/4np_secure.pdf

Pacios, Ana R. "Strategic Plans and Long-Range Plans: Is There a Difference?" *Library Management* 25, no. 6/7 (2004): 259–69.

Papadimitriou, Antigoni et al. "Examination of the Best Practices in Administrative and Organizational Functions of the Greek Universities." In *Proceedings of Integrating for Excellence, 1st International Conference*, 136–42. Sheffield, UK: Centre for Integral Excellence, Sheffield Hallam University, 2005. www.shu.ac.uk/research/integralexcellence/downloads/ConferenceProceedings2005.pdf

Peischl, Thomas M. "Benchmarking: A Process for Improvement." In *Total Quality Management in Academic Libraries: Initial Implementation Efforts, Proceedings from the International Conference on TQM and Academic Libraries*, edited by Laura Rounds and Michael Matthews, 119–22. Washington, DC: Association of Research Libraries, 1995. http://eric.ed.gov/ERICDocs/data/ericdocs2sql/content_storage_01/0000019b/ 80/14/5c/56.pdf

Pienaar, Heila and Cecilia Penzhorn. "Using the Balanced Scorecard to Facilitate Strategic Management at an Academic Information Service." *Libri* 50, no. 3 (September 2000): 202–9. www.librijournal.org/pdf/2000-3pp202-209.pdf

Pitman, Leeanne, Isabella Trahn, and Anne Wilson. "Working Towards Best Practice in Australian University Libraries: Reflections on a National Project." *Australian Academic & Research Libraries* 32, no. 1 (May 2001). http://alia.org.au/publishing/aarl/32.1/full.text/ptw.html

Poll, Roswitha. "Performance, Processes and Costs: Managing Service Quality with the Balanced Scorecard." *Library Trends* 49, no. 4 (Spring 2001): 709–17.

——. "Managing Service Quality with the Balanced Scorecard." In *Proceedings of the World Library and Information Congress: 67th IFLA General Conference and Council*. The Hague, Netherlands: IFLA, 2001. www.ifla.org/IV/ifla67/papers/042-135e.pdf [retrieved July 10, 2008]

——. "Quality Measures on a National Scale—Comparison of Projects." In *Proceedings of the World Library and Information Congress: 72nd IFLA General Conference and Council*. The Hague, Netherlands: IFLA, 2006. www.ifla.org/IV/ifla72/papers/105-Poll-en.pdf

——. "Benchmarking with Quality Indicators: National Projects." *Performance Measurement and Metrics* 8, no. 1 (2007): 41–53.

Porter, Michael E. "What is Strategy?" *Harvard Business Review* 74, no. 6 (November/December 1996): 61–78.

Raven's Brain blog. "10 Tips for Setting SMART Goals/Objectives." http://ravenyoung.spaces.live.com/?_c11_BlogPart_BlogPart=blogview&_c=BlogPart&partqs=amonth%3d12%26ayear%3d2006

Reichmann, Gerhard and Margit Sommersguter-Reichmann. "University Library Benchmarking: An International Comparison Using DEA." *International Journal of Production Economics* 100, no. 1 (March 2006): 131–47.

Robertson, Margaret and Isabella Trahn. "Benchmarking Academic Libraries: An Australian Case Study." *Australian Academic & Research Libraries* 28, no. 2 (1997): 126–44. Author version at: http://eprints.qut.edu.au/archive/00000048/

Rompho, N. "Building the Balanced Scorecard for the University Case Study: The University in Thailand." In *Proceedings of the Fourth International Conference, Performance Measurement and Management: Public and Private*. Cranfield, UK: Centre for Business Performance, Cranfield School of Management, 2004. Author version at: http://qa.tu.ac.th/acrd/Knowledge/Building_the_BSC_for_the_University.pdf.

Rosa, Maria Joao, Pedro M. Saraiva, and Henrique Diz. "Defining Strategic and Excellence Bases for the Development of Portuguese Higher Education." *European Journal of Education* 40, no. 2 (2005): 205–21.

Schulz, Lisa. "Strategic Planning in a University Library." *Marketing Library Services* 12, no. 5 (July/August 1998). www.infotoday.com/mls/jul98/story.htm

Self, James. "From Values to Metrics: Implementation of the Balanced Scorecard at a University Library." *Performance Measurement and Metrics* 4, no. 2 (2003): 57–63.

——. "Using Data to Make Choices: The Balanced Scorecard at the University of Virginia Library." *ARL: A Bimonthly Report on Research Library Issues and Actions from ARL, CNI, and SPARC*, No. 230/231 (October/December 2003): 28–9. www.arl.org/newsltr/230/balscorecard.html [retrieved July 10, 2008]

——. "Metrics and Management: Applying the Results of the Balanced Scorecard." *Performance Measurement and Metrics* 5, no. 3 (2004): 101–5.

Shaughnessy, Thomas W. "Benchmarking, Total Quality Management, and Libraries." *Library Administration and Management* 7, no. 1 (Winter 1993): 7–12.

Shim, Wonsik. "Applying DEA Techniques to Library Evaluation in Academic Research Libraries." *Library Trends* 51, no. 3 (Winter 2003): 312–32.

Shorb, Stephen R. and Lori Driscoll. "LibQUAL+ Meets Strategic Planning at the University of Florida." *The Journal of Library Administration* 40, no. 3/4 (2004): 173–80.

Snead, John T. et al. "Developing Best-Fit Evaluation Strategies." In *Proceedings of the Library Assessment Conference: Building Effective, Sustainable, Practical Assessment (2006)*, edited by Francine DeFalco et al., 225–32. Washington, DC: Association of Research Libraries, 2007.

Speckbacher, Gerhard. "The Economics of Performance Management in Nonprofit Organizations." *Nonprofit Management & Leadership* 13, no. 3 (Spring 2003): 267–81.

Thebridge, Stella. "Evaluating Electronic Information Services: A Toolkit for Practitioners." *Library and Information Research* 27, no. 87 (Winter 2003): 38–46.

Town, J. Stephen. "Benchmarking and Performance Measurement." In *Proceedings of the 1st Northumbria International Conference on Performance Measurement in Libraries and Information Services.* Newcastle upon Tyne: Information North, 1995. http://eric.ed.gov/ERICDocs/data/ericdocs2sql/content_storage_01/0000019b/80/16/6a/05.pdf

Townley, Charles T. "Knowledge Management and Academic Libraries." *College & Research Libraries* 62, no. 1 (January 2001): 44–57.

Valiris, George, Panagiotis Chytas, and Michael Glykas. "Making Decisions Using the Balanced Scorecard and the Simple Multi-Attribute Rating Technique." *Performance Measurement and Metrics* 6, no. 3 (2005): 159–71.

White, Lynda S. "The University of Virginia Library's Experiment with Benchmarking." *Virginia Libraries* 48, no. 4 (Winter 2002). http://scholar.lib.vt.edu/ejournals/VALib/v48_n4?white.html [retrieved July 10, 2008]

Wilson, Anne and Leeanne Pitman. *Best Practice Handbook for Australian University Libraries.* Commonwealth of Australia: Department of Education, Training and Youth Affairs, Higher Education Division, 2000.

Wilson, Frankie and J. Stephen Town. "Benchmarking and Library Quality Maturity." *Performance Measurement and Metrics* 7, no. 2 (2006): 75–82.

Winkworth, Ian. "Innovative United Kingdom Approaches to Measuring Service Quality." *Library Trends* 49, no. 4 (Spring 2001): 718–31.

Wongrassamee, P., P. D. Gardiner, and J. E. L. Simmons. "Performance Measurement Tools: The Balanced Scorecard and the EFQM Excellence Model." *Measuring Business Excellence* 7, no. 1 (2003): 14–29.

Zucca, Joe. "Traces in the Clickstream: Early Work on a Management Information Repository at the University of Pennsylvania." *Information Technology and Libraries* 22, no. 4 (December 2003): 175–9.

5

Performance indicators

Introduction

In pursuit of establishing a culture of assessment, librarians have conducted self-assessments using a variety of quality frameworks, created strategic plans to set goals, considered benchmarking internally or externally, and linked their strategic plans to a Balanced Scorecard structure that focuses on a handful of performance measures to document whether the library is moving forward according to plan. The key action at this stage becomes performance measurement.

> Performance measurement means collection of statistical and other data describing the performance of the library and the analysis of these data in order to evaluate the performance. Or, in other words: Comparing what a library is doing (performance) with what it is meant to do (mission) and wants to achieve (goals).[1]

Librarians have been collecting statistical data about their libraries for decades, but nearly all of these have been about inputs to the library (financial resources, staff, equipment, etc.) or outputs (books circulated, volumes added, reference questions answered, interlibrary lending and borrowing, etc.). Data have been compiled and reported vigorously, but whether or not they were analyzed within the contexts of library mission or goals has been quite another matter. Authors writing about library performance have used the terms "performance indicators," "performance measures," and "performance criteria" interchangeably. For our purposes, we will use the term "performance indicators."

During the late 1980s, a growing international interest in conducting more focused forms of performance measurement arose. An IFLA

Working Group was established to develop guidelines for performance measurement and, early in the process, agreed upon its intentions:

- To concentrate on academic libraries (according to the section).

- To include only measures that would be applicable in all countries (developing as well as developed) and to all kinds of academic libraries (small or big, computerized or not, with free access or closed stacks).

- To measure effectiveness, not efficiency (cost-effectiveness). Because of the immense differences between budgetary and financial conditions for libraries in different countries, we could not hope to develop indicators suitable for all ...

- To include "overall" indicators (for example user satisfaction with the whole library) as well as indicators for separate activities.

- To concentrate on user-oriented indicators (that excludes, for example, indicators for collection preservation).[2]

The group's efforts resulted in the 1996 publication of the IFLA *Guidelines for Performance Measurement*. A revision of the *Guidelines* is currently in process (2008) and, unfortunately, not available as of this writing. The focus of the 1996 *Guidelines* was the description of a series of performance indicators. Performance indicators were defined as "a qualified statement used to evaluate and compare performance of a library in achieving its objectives." They can be categorized generally as input, process, output, and outcome. The *Guidelines* qualify performance indicators in a series of statements:

- A performance indicator should be appropriate (valid) for what it is supposed to measure ... A performance indicator is applied in order to answer a particular question, and the results should provide the answer.

- It should be reliable (accurate). This means it should be devoid of ambiguity. This is an ideal demand which will not always be fulfilled, e.g. where performance indicators try to analyze an attitude or opinion, the results of which cannot be numeric.

- It should be reproducible; the same things should always be counted or measured in the same way. To achieve this, the separate steps of the indicator should be exactly described, and the activities, persons or things measured precisely defined.

Given these qualifiers, it seems immediately obvious that identifying and establishing good performance indicators can be a slippery business. It is critical that the library has complete control of the collections, services, and programs it seeks to measure. Otherwise the library will be measuring performance, but with limited potential for action to improve that performance.

Establishing library performance indicators

Matthews enumerates seven attributes of a sound performance measurement system, including clarity of purpose, focus on service objectives, alignment with library goals and objectives, balance across overall library performance, the regularity with which performance indicators are reviewed, and the vigor of the performance indicators selected. He emphasizes the importance of selecting a balanced array of performance indicators that describe and represent all aspects of library operation. For example, he advises a mix of absolute and relative indicators, or those which "stand on their own" and those useful for comparison to other libraries; those which examine processes such as cataloging; and those which examine broader services. He advises considering both leading and lagging indicators, especially those with potential diagnostic value, and including both qualitative and quantitative measures in the mix. Vigorous performance indicators are clearly defined and relevant, and do not lend themselves to manipulation.[3]

One message in Matthews's discussion is a reminder that the proof of a good performance measurement system is in its application. If a library is going to commit to developing a set of indicators, then it should commit equally to making use of the data and of the results generated from them.

The *Guidelines* document provides a foundational list of performance indicators that reflect agreement on an international scale, and that include 17 indicators covering general library use and facilities, collection quality, catalog quality, availability of documents in the collection, reference service, remote use, and user satisfaction. There are no indicators for electronic resources and services in the 1996 *Guidelines*, reflecting its age and no doubt providing added impetus for the revision now (2008) in process. Information on each of the 17 indicators includes a definition of the indicator, a description of what it is intended to measure, a description of how data might be collected and results calculated, a review of how the results might appear, and a bibliography of additional readings. Although it was agreed not to include performance indicators on cost, there is a relatively lengthy section on cost-effectiveness, as the Working Group recognized there would be questions about costs and cost-effectiveness and wanted to equip librarians to provide answers.

Poll, who has been a force in developing international guidelines for performance measurement, and in library quality improvement in general, provides an advance look at the forthcoming revision of the *Guidelines*, which:

> offers seven indicators especially intended for electronic services; a great part of the other indicators combine the quality assessment of both traditional and electronic services ... six indicators dealing with costs of expenditures and seven indicators for measuring the efficiency of processes ... three indicators for the library's information and teaching services ... The topic "library as a physical place" is represented by six indicators ...[4]

She explains the purpose of the new indicators:

- to cover the full range of resources and services generally offered in academic and public libraries;
- to consider traditional services as well as new electronic services and, if possible, to combine them in "merged" indicators;
- to select indicators that have been tested and documented, at least in a similar form to what is described in the handbook; and
- to cover the different aspects of service quality as shown in the Balanced Scorecard, including indicators for the aspect of development and potentials.[5]

The new edition of the *Guidelines* will clearly reflect the significant changes of the past decade in academic library environments, and by incorporating public libraries in its coverage reflect the many similarities of purpose in performance measurement and improvement between academic and public libraries. Poll also notes that six of the original indicators have been deleted from the new edition, as their actual use proved to be too difficult. She makes it very clear that the indicators in the new edition do not include measures for outcomes, but they are still under development. The total number of indicators will be 40. It was decided "to develop and test two new indicators, as some crucial aspects seemed to be missing, one for the quality of the library website, another for the overall cost of usage, including traditional forms of use (loans, in-house use) as well as downloads."[6]

The International Organization for Standardization (OIS) published a list of performance indicators for libraries in 1998, and an amendment in 2003. OIS is also working on an updated list of library performance indicators. The 1998 OIS list does not include any performance indicators involving electronic/networked technologies, services, or collections, which will undoubtedly be corrected in the forthcoming edition. Each OIS performance indicator contains an objective, a definition, methods for gathering data and calculating the indicator, an interpretation, factors affecting the indicators, sources, and related indicators.

While there are similarities between the OIS and IFLA lists, there are also significant differences. Te Boekhorst describes them as primarily differences in purpose:

Most of them [the differences] are directly related to the fact that the ISO document is to provide a standard which is especially useful in regard to terminology whereas the IFLA Guidelines are a selection of user-oriented indicators:

- The ISO standard is "concerned with the evaluation of libraries of all types" which makes it more difficult for librarians to decide whether an indicator is useful for their type of library. The IFLA Guidelines restrict themselves to academic libraries.

- In contrast to the IFLA Guidelines the ISO standards include cost indicators, e.g., cost per title catalogued or cost per loan.

- The description of the ISO indicators is less detailed than that of the IFLA indicators which might negatively influence their practical application.

- In the interest of a precise definition the ISO performance indicators have been thinned out or isolated, while the IFLA indicators are more like clusters that are analyzed together in the interest of practical application.[7]

A review of the literature on performance measurement projects reveals that libraries have drawn performance indicators from both the IFLA and OIS lists, and often supplemented them with unique local indicators. No clear consensus was apparent, and the number of indicators selected varied greatly. Nuut reported on a project in Estonia in which 20 performance indicators were chosen for analysis.[8] Derfert-Wolf wrote about a project in Poland involving library statistics and performance indicators and listed 13 that had been used.[9] A Swiss benchmarking project involving a set of 87 primary data elements resulted in 41 performance indicators, as reported by Niederer.[10] The development of a quality assurance system in South African higher education was documented by de Jager, in which the more modest number of 10 performance indicators were selected for use in the system.[11] A benchmarking project in Portugal, described by Melo, Pires, and Tavelra, used 20 performance indicators.[12] In all of these cases, the performance indicators represented an amalgam of both the IFLA and OIS lists. Librarians appear to be selecting what makes best sense for their individual libraries, given the local environment and politics, and this makes good sense, for one size does not fit all. Niederer presented a most interesting set of performance indicators involving the use of staff time, perhaps to reveal something about the nature of the library's work climate:

- hours of absence (sick leave, etc.) per total staff hours;
- hours of further education per total staff hours; and
- hours of meetings per total staff hours.[13]

These are fascinating indicators, revealing both positive and negative aspects of the library climate. Excessive hours of absence, especially unplanned absence such as sick leave, may indicate morale problems; that staff feel stressed or pressured to work harder. High per-staff hours of further education may indicate that skill deficiencies are being addressed by remedial training, or that the library values staff knowledge as a strong asset. It is also possible that hours of further education could be a "leading" indicator of change if preparations are underway to receive new equipment, or launch new initiatives. Unusually high numbers of hours spent in meetings may reveal an enormous waste of staff resources, or simply high staff involvement in decision making and a highly participative management style within the library. Performance indicators are indeed useful, but measurement alone is not an evaluation. Interpreting data in its most meaningful context remains as the ultimate challenge.

In their article on Portuguese academic libraries, Melo, Pires, and Tavelra discuss staff performance indicators for gauging "impact on society," which in their setting meant:

1. Collaborator satisfaction

2. Amount of academic publication

3. Amount of academic publications and papers by library staff

4. Amount of training sessions for library users

5. The adoption of sustained development principles.[14]

Item three, "academic publications and papers by library staff," is unique in the literature, or at least is an indicator not found otherwise in this review. It raises questions related to the tenure model, and to financial support and encouragement for library faculty and staff to research, write, and present. "Sustained development principles," as used in their article, refers to conservation or "green" principles. This indicator was not found elsewhere, but it was evidently meaningful and important to the library or libraries under consideration.

Seissl reported on an unsuccessful benchmarking project in Austria that used 11 performance indicators.[15] At the conclusion of the project, the libraries decided to associate with an effort in Germany known as BIX— The Library Index. The BIX project began in 1999, first involving public libraries in Germany, and expanding in 2002 to include academic libraries. The BIX Index for academic libraries groups 17 ratio or percentage data indicators into four broad categories: resources/infrastructure, usage, efficiency, and development. BIX is now operated and managed by the German Library Association, standing as an example of successful collaboration in benchmarking.[16]

About the time BIX was created, the University and Regional Library, Münster, the Bavarian State Library, and the State and University of Bremen Library began a collaborative project to develop performance indicators to support strategic objectives and actions. Their aim was a set of 20 performance indicators that could be used within the balanced scorecard framework, which was adapted by moving the financial perspective to the bottom of the hierarchy and replacing it with users/customers perspective. The rationale was that although academic libraries don't have to make a profit, they do have to fulfill the expectations of their users. As analyzed by Ceynowa, the selected performance indicators and their equivalent balanced scorecard perspectives are enumerated in Table 5.1.

In essence, this is the list of IFLA performance indicators updated to fill the gap in performance data for electronic/networked technologies, resources, and services. It is unclear whether the list of performance indicators in the revised IFLA and OIS publications will include additional items, or will remain the same in number. If the numbers remain the same, some of the more traditional indicators may be dropped. The comparison in Table 5.2, prepared by the authors on the basis of present IFLA and ISO indicators, indicates their closest relationships.[17]

Table 5.1 Performance indicator by adapted Balanced Scorecard perspective

Perspective	Performance indicator
User	Percentage of target group attained (proportion of registered users in the primary user group)
	User satisfaction quota
	Ratio of opening hours to demand
	Incidence of use per member of the primary user group
	Availability quota (proportion of immediate loans to total loans)
	Proportion of the primary user group using the library's electronic services
	Proportion of logins to electronic services from outside the library (campus and external) to the total number of logins
Finance	Per capita library costs for the primary user group
	Library costs for each case of use
	Relation of media budget to staff budget
	Proportion of staff costs per library service to total staff costs
	Proportion of expenditure on electronic resources to total media budget
Business	Staff productivity: processes handled per person, per year
	Average media throughput times (from receipt of delivery to availability)
	The number of stages involved in providing a product unit (for every library service)
	The relation of staff costs for electronic services to processing and the provision of electronic media
	The relation of staff costs for conventional services to process and provision of printed media
Future	Share of the library budget in the overall budget of the university or provider institution
	Share of the expenditure for information and communication technology
	Number of in-service training measures per person (by service area)
	Number of short periods of illness per person

Source: Klaus Ceynowa, "Managing Academic Information Provision with the Balanced Scorecard," 159–62.

Table 5.2 Comparison of IFLA and OIS performance indicators

IFLA performance indicators		OIS performance indicators	
User satisfaction	Two levels of user satisfaction to be measured: general user satisfaction with services of the library as a whole and user satisfaction with individual services or components thereof.	User satisfaction	To assess the degree to which users are satisfied with the library services as a whole or with different services of the library.
Market penetration	The proportion of the library's potential users who actually use the library.	Percentage of target population reached	To assess the success of the library in reaching a target population.
No matching indicator		Cost per user	To assess the cost of the service of the library related to the number of users.
Opening hours compared to demand	Relates the actual number and distribution of opening hours to the number and distribution of opening hours as desired by the users.	No matching indicator	
No matching indicator		Library visits per capita	To assess the library's success in attracting users of the services.

Table 5.2	Comparison of IFLA and OIS performance indicators (*Cont'd*)

IFLA performance indicators		OIS performance indicators	
Expert checklists	The percentage of titles enumerated in an expert list or in a bibliography which are in possession of the library.	No matching indicator	
No matching indicator		Titles availability	To assess to what extent titles owned by the library are actually available to the users if required.
Availability	The proportion of the material requested by the user that can be used in the library (including copying) or taken home immediately.	Required titles availability	To assess to what extent titles owned by the library and in demand by the users are actually available when required.
No matching indicator		Percentage of required titles in the collection	To assess to what extent titles in demand by the users are owned by the library.
Document delivery time	The average time between the moment a user starts with the necessary procedures to borrow a document and the moment the item is checked out or available at the issue desk.	Required titles extended availability	To assess to what extent titles in demand by the users are immediately available or can be made available within a specified period of time.
No matching indicator		In-library use per capita	To assess the amount of usage of materials within the library.

Table 5.2   Comparison of IFLA and OIS performance
indicators (*Cont'd*)

IFLA performance indicators		OIS performance indicators	
Collection use	The ratio between the number of document uses within a certain period of time and the total number of documents in the collection.	Document use rate	To assess the overall use of the collection by estimating the proportion of documents in use at any one time.
Documents not used	The percentage of documents in the lending collection not used within a certain period of time.	Proportion of stock not used	To assess the amount of stock not used during a specified period.
No matching indicator		Shelving accuracy	To assess to what extent documents that are recorded in the library's catalog are in their correct place on the shelves.
No matching indicator		Median time of document retrieval from closed stacks	To assess whether the retrieval system is effective.
No matching indicator		Median time of document retrieval from open access areas	To assess whether self-explanatory signposting and correct shelving all prompt access to documents.
No matching indicator		Collection turnover	To assess the overall rate of use of a loan collection

Table 5.2 Comparison of IFLA and OIS performance indicators (*Cont'd*)

IFLA performance indicators		OIS performance indicators	
No matching indicator		Loans per capita	To assess the rate of use of library collections by the population to be served. May also be used to assess the quality of the collections and the library's ability to promote the use of the collections.
No matching indicator		Documents on loan per capita	To assess the overall rate of use of the collection by the population to be served.
No matching indicator		Cost per loan	To assess the cost of the services of the library in relation to the number of loans.
No matching indicator		Loans per employee	To assess the staff resources of the library in relation to the number of loans.
No matching indicator		Proportion of stock on loan	To assess the overall rate of use of the loan collection at a specified point in time.
Interlibrary loan speed	The proportion of documents requested through local and international interlibrary loans that are supplied within a certain period of time, say 7, 14, 21 and 21+ days (i.e., availability).	Speed of interlibrary lending	To assess whether the library is providing an efficient interlibrary lending service to its users.

Table 5.2   Comparison of IFLA and OIS performance
indicators (*Cont'd*)

IFLA performance indicators		OIS performance indicators	
Correct answer fill rate	The proportion of test questions which are correctly answered by the reference service.	**Correct answer fill rate**	To assess to what extent the staff are able to fulfill the primary requirements for a good reference service, namely to provide correct answers to enquiries.
Known-item search	The proportion of titles sought by the user and registered in the catalog that the user manages to find.	**Title catalog search success rate**	To assess the library's success in informing the users where and how to find a title through catalogs.
Subject search	The proportion of titles in the subject or classified catalog matching the user's subject that are found by the user.	**Subject catalog search success rate**	To assess the library's success in matching the user's subject search in the catalog and in informing the user where and how to find literature on a subject.
No matching indicator		**Facilities availability**	To assess to what extent specified facilities provided by the library are actually available to the users.
No matching indicator		**Facilities use rate**	To assess the rate of use of specified facilities provided by the library.

Table 5.2 Comparison of IFLA and OIS performance indicators (*Cont'd*)

IFLA performance indicators		OIS performance indicators	
No matching indicator		Seat occupancy rate	To assess the overall rate of use of seats provided for reading or studying in the library, by estimating the proportion of seats in use at any given time.
No matching indicator		Automated systems availability	To assess to what extent the automated system of the library is actually available to the users.
Acquisition speed	The time period between the day a title is published and the day it arrives at the library. Two aspects: ordering speed and delivery speed.	Median time of document acquisition	To assess the degree to which suppliers of library materials are effective, in terms of speed.
Book processing speed	The time period between the day a document arrives at the library and the day it is available on the shelf and/or in the catalog.	Median time of document processing	To assess whether the different forms of processing procedures are effective as to speed.
No matching indicator		Cost per title cataloged	To assess the cost of a specific policy for producing bibliographic records.
No matching indicator		User services staff per capita	To identify the number of employees directly serving users per member of the population to be served.

Table 5.2   Comparison of IFLA and OIS performance indicators (*Cont'd*)

IFLA performance indicators		OIS performance indicators	
No matching indicator		User services staff as a percentage of total staff	To determine the library's effort devoted to public services in relation to the background services.
Remote uses per capita	The number of remote uses from access points outside the library or its branches by members of the primary user group during a year in relation to the primary user group.	No matching indicator	
User satisfaction with services offered for remote use	Users' rating of their satisfaction with the library's services offered for remote use from access points outside the library or its branch libraries.	No matching indicator	

After cost-related indicators are removed from the OIS list, some interesting differences emerge. Are some of the remaining OIS indicators omitted from the IFLA list because they were considered too public library oriented? That could be argued for "library visits per capita," "loans per capita," "documents on loan per capita," "proportion of stock on loan," and "facilities use rate." Whatever the rationale, it remains that many academic libraries select indicators from both lists.

Recognizing that many knowledgeable librarians are working to develop reliable metrics in the electronic and networked environment, Hsieh presents an interesting list of possible performance indicators for the virtual library. His work identified 20 different indicators with 44 data elements.[18] Again, librarians prove that they are nothing if not thorough.

Impacts and outcomes

Once a library has chosen it performance indicators, it is still to be proven that they will help in determining the library's contributions to its institution's outcomes. If a library cannot identify its contributions toward the outcomes established within the institution's strategic plan, it runs the risk of being marginalized in the life of the institution.

The first hurdle facing the library is to determine whether its parent institution has created a culture or environment that facilitates the identification and selection of outcomes to fulfill institutional strategic plans, goals, and objectives. There is an understandable assumption that, institutionally, the structure of the strategic plan and its goals and objectives is such that outcomes are evident and unequivocal. This is not necessarily the case. Fraser, McClure, and Leahy created a series of questions to examine its institutional environment for outcomes. The essential questions, which examine the library's relationship to the larger institution, are summarized below.

- Is there a culture of assessment at your university? At your library?
- How does your university articulate its core values?
- Does your university measure itself—its outcomes—in terms of core values?
- Has the culture of assessment remained constant at your university (and at your library), or has it changed relatively recently?
- What does your university expect from the library in terms of contributing to university outcomes?
- What does your university expect from the library in terms of reporting data?
- How receptive do you believe your university administration is or would be to library reporting based on outcomes assessment?
- Does your library currently focus on campus-wide, university-based outcomes?
- Does your library collect data on its outcomes (impacts, effects)—and/or on university outcomes—that occur outside the library's domain?
- How do you see the way you assess your library's performance changing in the next few years?
- Assuming your library does not already do so, if it were to measure and report its data in terms of university outcomes, would that affect the way the library is viewed and funded by your university's administration?

- What are the key activities that your library does to support the research, education, and service goals of your university?[19]

Several of Fraser et al.'s questions challenge most libraries. "What does your university expect from the library in terms of contributing to university outcomes?" How many universities have explicitly and publicly stated the outcomes they want to achieve? Not many. When a university has made known the outcomes it seeks to achieve, how often has there been a specific, focused discussion outlining its expectations for the library? This type of discussion rarely takes place between the academic leader and the library director. "Does your library collect data on its outcomes (impacts, effects)—and/or university outcomes—that occur outside the library's domain?" Some libraries may collect data on their own outcomes (if they have identified them), but it is unlikely that any libraries collect data on other units' outcomes. There may reasons why this is not practical, feasible, or politically advisable. If so, then not having outcome data for academic computing, for example, could prevent the development of effective and rewarding collaborations.

Answers to the entire list of questions could provide a baseline from which the library could move forward in pursuit of outcomes, impacts, values, and benefits. Here it may be useful to look at the definitions and relationships various authors have provided for four terms: outcomes, impacts, values, and benefits. "Outcome" and "impact" have been used interchangeably and synonymously, which only adds to the confusion.

Outcomes

Troll Covey states that "outcomes are measures of the impact or effect that using library collections and services has on users. Good outcome measures are tied to specific library objectives and indicate whether these objectives have been achieved."[20] Cram differentiates further:

> Distinguishing between intermediate outcomes and longer-term outcomes draws attention to cause–effect linkages and identifies lower-level outcomes that are within the control of the library. The library may not be solely responsible for long-term outcomes, but I suggest that though you may be judged on immediate outcomes, those immediate outcomes cannot be established without reference to the long-term outcomes which are a reminder of the moral imperative that underlies all public service.[21]

Fraser, McClure, and Leahy provide their research definition of outcomes:

> An outcome is a clearly identified result or end product that occurs as a consequence of individual or combined activities from units at the institution. It is a preferred or desired state and ideally clarifies specific expectations of what should be products from the institution. An institutional outcome can be defined and measured in such a way that evidence is available to determine the amount or degree to which the outcome does, in fact, occur.[22]

They go on to identify three types: outcomes of interest, desired outcomes, and actual outcomes. Outcomes of interest:

> are those outcomes—relatively few in number—on which a particular university chooses to focus its attention at a given time, taking into account the complex, ever-changing array of relevant, local values ... desired outcomes are the aspirational levels of achievement or production an institution should set in advance to determine whether it has attained success at a future time on some important dimension of its operation. In other words, they are specific goals or quality standards for outcomes of interest. Actual outcomes are the real achievement or production levels for an outcome of interest as measured at a given time.[23]

Gratch-Lindauer observes that "the word 'outcomes' is reserved for the realized goals valued by various campus constituents."[24] Bertot and McClure write that outcomes:

- Include the notion of an impact, benefit, difference or change in a user, group, or institution based on the use of or involvement with a library service or resource;
- Are predetermined based on a service/resource/planning process in which the library engages to produce desired service/resource outcomes through the setting of service/resource goals and objectives; and
- Involve measuring and demonstrating the extent to which library services/resources meet the anticipated outcomes determined by the library or imposed by the community the library serves (e.g., academic institution, county, city).[25]

They go on to describe three types of outcomes:

Anticipated: These are the outcomes for which the library plans and by which the library intends to measure its success/failure in goals and objectives attainment. The library expects to achieve certain outcomes through its services/resources and then seeks to ascertain the extent to which its services/resources achieved the anticipated outcomes ...

Emergent: These are outcomes that emerge through the service/resource planning and implementation process. Such outcomes are not the immediate focus of the service/resource goals and objective—either library or externally imposed ...

Unanticipated: Once a service/resource is in operation, these are those outcomes that derive from actual service/resource use or interaction and can be ones that neither the library nor others predicted—nor planned to assess.[26]

Poll writes that "definitions of library outcomes generally highlight the effect on individual users or on users collectively."[27] She lists four characteristics of outcomes, based on research. They "are not always predictable, are generally rather an addition to previous experience than a radical change in attitudes, will be higher if a gain in skills and competences or a change in behaviour seems promising to the user, often become visible only in long-term development."[28] Thebridge and Dalton define outcomes as "the ways in which users are changed as a result of coming into contact with the library's collections and services."[29] They further note that outcomes are directly linked to institutional goals. The Association of College and Research Libraries (ACRL) Outcomes Assessment Task Force declared that outcomes "are the ways in which library users are changed as a result of their contact with the library's resources and programs. Satisfaction on the part of the user is an outcome."[30]

Impacts

According to Brophy, an impact

can be defined in different ways, but in the context of library services it may be most helpful to think of it as any effect of a service, product or other "event" on an individual or group. It

- may be positive or negative
- may be what was intended or something entirely different
- may result in changed

- attitudes
- behaviors
- outputs (ie what an individual or group produces during or after interaction with the service)
  - may be short or long term
  - may be critical or trivial.[31]

Cram defines impacts as user driven: "the impact of a library is the impact of the choices an individual makes of which items and services he or she uses and the sequence in which he or she will use them."[32] Gratch-Lindauer ties impacts to institutional effectiveness: "the word impact(s) is used for those direct effects the library has on institutional outcomes, or more indirect, the enabling effects that contribute to these outcomes."[33] Poll views impacts as the connections between outcomes and library goals and objectives, and with institutional goals and objectives. She defines an impact simply as "the effect or influence of one person, thing, or action on another."[34] Thebridge and Dalton take an unreasonably comprehensive approach to impacts as being "any effects, intentional or not, of a user's contact with a service …"[35]

Value

Cram observes that "value is a psychological construct. It may be intrinsic or extrinsic, but it is always subjective."[36] Poll defines value as "the importance or preciousness of something, the perception of actual or potential benefits."[37] It is surprising that librarians have not had more to say about value. Perhaps user satisfaction is sometimes confused with value? Is it possible for outcomes to be without value? If an outcome is linked to the strategic plan goals and objectives, does it automatically have value? If so, then how can value be described, then quantified? Is it possible for an outcome to be valued by stakeholders within the institution and not valued by stakeholders outside the institution or library? Value might be better examined as the value of a benefit.

Benefit

Poll defines benefit as "the helpful or useful effect that something has."[38] She links value to benefit, which necessitates some consideration of individuals' perceptions. Perhaps this is another instance when "user satisfaction" has been used as a surrogate for "benefit"? Can an outcome have both value and benefit? Is one short term and the other long term?

These are difficult questions to wrestle with, particularly when most librarians are just beginning to address the matter of performance indicators, not to mention outcomes and impacts. As librarians begin to consider assessing outcomes they should keep in mind four areas of assessment:

- Economic value. Assessing the market value or proxy price of the library's services or a single service.

- Social impact. Assessing the imputed value of the library, e.g. by social audits.

- Information literacy/information retrieval. Assessing the impact of library services on users' information skills and the library's role in information retrieval.

- Academic professional success. Assessing the relation of academic/ professional success to the use of library services.[39]

There do not seem to be any recognized, established measures for assessing academic library outcomes, and this has challenged our profession. Poll describes them best:

Trying to show an impact of libraries on individuals and society is obviously a much more difficult venture than counting outputs. The following problems have appeared in most studies:

- A service can have different value and outcome for different user groups. A training session in special databases will have less effect on freshmen than on postgraduates who need these resources directly for their work.

- Data that could be relevant for demonstrating impact are not available because of data protection rules (e.g. individual data about grades in exams).

- The data or correlations found in projects until now are in most cases not comparable, as differing methods were used. Standardization of methods will be necessary to allow for benchmarking of results.

- Long-term effects can often not be assessed if the users are no more available for tests or surveys.

- All methods that have been tested until now are time-consuming.[40]

It is tempting to ask "Why bother?" There are so many challenges organizationally and statistically, and resolving them puts an enormous stress on administrative leadership. Yet, this fact remains: if the library can't describe its contributions to the institution's success in measurable ways, its future is uncertain.

Poll suggests "the most urgent issue is to promote the library's role, to show what one library, what all libraries can do for their users and society."[41] Library researchers have identified a number of impact indicators very similar in construction to many of the performance indicators mentioned earlier. Powell notes that a number of performance indicators are good potential impact indicators, and has drawn up a list to include:

1. Test scores
2. Employer satisfaction
3. Number and amount of research grants received
4. Publications
5. Course evaluations
6. Course grades
7. Time saved
8. Quality of papers
9. Ideas
10. Understanding
11. Plans
12. Skills
13. Progress.[42]

He recognized that many of the indicators in his list have been identified elsewhere as performance or effectiveness indicators, but he believed these might serve beyond being measures of outputs or performance. Each library must decide the value of this, on the basis of institutional reality. Can these indicators provide accurate and realistic assessments of student learning or faculty success? The ACRL Task Force has provided a set of questions that outcome assessment should attempt to answer:

- Is the academic performance of students improved through their contact with the library?
- By using the library, do students improve their chances of having a successful career?

- Are undergraduates who used the library more likely to succeed in graduate school?

- Does the library's bibliographic instruction program result in a high level of "information literacy" among students?

- As a result of collaboration with the library staff, are faculty members more likely to view use of the library as an integral part of their courses?

- Are students who use the library more likely to lead fuller and more satisfying lives?[43]

ACRL's focus is centered entirely on undergraduate students, and this might be reasonable if the sole mission of most institutions were to educate undergraduate students. While most of the performance indicators listed by Powell and ACRL's questions would be applicable to both undergraduate and graduate students, are there others that would be more appropriate for graduate students? Similarly, what about outcomes for faculty? What role does the library play in successful faculty teaching and research, and in the success of undergraduate and postgraduate education?

Notes

1. Poll and te Boekhorst, *Measuring Quality*, 16.
2. te Boekhorst, "Measuring Quality," 278.
3. Matthews, *Strategic Planning and Management*, 115–16.
4. Poll, "Ten Years After," 27.
5. *Ibid.*, 31.
6. *Ibid.*, 32.
7. te Boekhorst, "Measuring Quality," 281.
8. Nuut et al., "Developing Performance Measurement and Quality Evaluation," 164.
9. Derfert-Wolf et al., "Management Based on Reliable Comparative Data," 12.
10. Niederer, "'L'appetit Vient en Comparant'," 157.
11. de Jager, "Towards Establishing an Integrated System," 111.
12. Melo et al., "Recognizing Best Practice," 37.
13. Niederer, "L'appetit Vient en Comparant," 157.
14. Melo et al., "Recognizing Best Practice," 37.
15. Seissl, "Benchmarking Efforts in Austrian University Libraries," 2.
16. Wimmer, "BIX—the Library Index."
17. Comparison table developed from indicators provided in OIS, *Information and Documentation* and IFLA performance indicators from Roswitha Poll and Peter te Boekhorst, *Measuring Quality*.

18. Hsieh et al., "The Performance Indicators of University E-library in Taiwan," 329.
19. Fraser et al., "Toward a Framework," 524–5.
20. Troll Covey, *Usage and Usability Assessment*, 89.
21. Cram, "'Six Impossible Things'."
22. Fraser et al., "Toward a Framework," 506.
23. *Ibid.*, 506–7.
24. Gratch-Lindauer, "Defining and Measuring the Library's Impact," 550.
25. Bertot and McClure, "Outcomes Assessment in the Networked Environment," 594.
26. *Ibid.*, 601.
27. Poll and Payne, "Impact Measures for Libraries," 548.
28. *Ibid.*, 549.
29. Thebridge and Dalton, "Working Towards Outcomes Assessment," 94.
30. Association of College and Research Libraries, *Task Force on Academic Library Outcomes Assessment Report*, 2.
31. Brophy, "The Development of a Model," 43.
32. Cram, "'Six Impossible Things'," 2.
33. Gratch-Lindauer, "Defining and Measuring the Library's Impact," 550.
34. Poll, "Measuring Impact and Outcome," 5.
35. Thebridge, "Working Towards Outcomes Assessment," 94.
36. Cram, "'Six Impossible Things'," 2.
37. Poll, "Measuring Impact and Outcome," 5.
38. *Ibid.*, 5.
39. *Ibid.*, 7.
40. Poll and Payne, "Impact Measures for Libraries," 550.
41. *Ibid.*, 555.
42. Powell, "Impact Assessment of University Libraries," 251–2.
43. Association of College and Research Libraries, *Task Force on Academic Library Outcomes Assessment Report*, 2–3.

Bibliography

Ambrozic, Melita. "A Few Countries Measure Impact and Outcomes—Most Would Like to Measure at Least Something." *Performance Measurement and Metrics* 4, no. 2 (2003): 64–78.

Association of College and Research Libraries. *Task Force on Academic Library Outcomes Assessment Report*. Chicago: ALA-Association of College and Research Libraries, June 27, 1998. www.ala.org/ala/acrl/acrlpubs/whitepapers/taskforceacademic.cfm [retrieved July 12, 2008]

——. "Information Literacy Competency Standards for Higher Education." Chicago: ALA-Association of College and Research Libraries, 2000. www.ala.org/ala/acrl/acrlstandards/standards.pdf

——. "Standards for Libraries in Higher Education." Chicago: ALA-Association of College and Research Libraries, June 2004. www.ala.org/ala/acrl/acrl standards/standardslibraries.cfm

Atkinson, Jeremy. "Quality Assurance in Higher Education: Mission (im)possible." *SCONUL Focus* 38 (Summer/Autumn 2006): 139–41.

Bauer, Kent. "Key Performance Indicators: The Multiple Dimensions, The Power of Metrics." *DM Review,* October 2004. www.dmreview.com/issues/20041001/1011028-1.html

Bertot, John Carlos and Charles R. McClure. "Outcomes Assessment in the Networked Environment: Research Questions, Issues, Considerations, and Moving Forward," *Library Trends* 51, no. 4 (Spring 2003): 590–613.

Blixrud, Julia C. "The Association of Research Libraries Statistics and Measurement Program: From Descriptive Data to Performance Measures." In *Proceedings of the World Library and Information Congress: 67th IFLA General Conference and Council.* The Hague, Netherlands: IFLA, 2001. www.ifla.org/IV/ifla67/papers/034-135e.pdf

——. "Assessing Library Performance: New Measures, Methods, and Models." In *Proceedings of the 24th Conference of the International Association of Technological University Libraries Conference.* Auckland: International Association of Technological University Libraries, 2003. http://iatul.org/doclibrary/public/Conf_Proceedings/2003/Blixrud_fulltext.pdf

——. "Mainstreaming New Measures." *ARL Bimonthly Report 230/231.* (October/December 2003).

——. "Measures for Electronic Use: The ARL E-Metrics Project." In *Statistics in Practice—Measuring & Managing 2002,* 73–84. Leicestershire: Loughborough University Library and Information Statistics Unit, LISU Occasional Paper #32, 2003. www.lboro.ac.uk/departments/ls/lisu/downloads/statsinpractice-pdfs/blixrud.pdf

Bommer, Michael R., Ronald W. Chorba, and Walter Grattidge. "Performance Assessment Model for Academic Libraries." *Journal of the American Society for Information Science* 30, no. 2 (March 1979): 93–9.

Booth, Andrew. "Counting What Counts: Performance Measurement and Evidence-Based Practice." *Performance Measurement and Metrics* 7, no. 2 (2006): 63–74.

Brinkley, Monica. "Performance Measurement and Quality Management for the Hybrid Library: An Update on the EQUINOX Project. *Exploit Interactive,* Issue 7 (October 2000). www.exploit-lib.org/issue7/equinox

Brophy, Peter. "The Development of a Model for Assessing the Level of Impact of Information and Library Services." *Library and Information Research* 29, no. 93 (Winter 2005): 43–9.

——. *Measuring Library Performance: Principles and Techniques.* London: Facet Publishing, 2006.

—— et al. "EQUINOX, Library Performance Measurement and Quality Management System, Performance Indicators for Electronic Library Services." November 2000. http://equinox.dcu.ie/reports/pilist.html

Ceynowa, Klaus. "Managing Academic Information Provision with the Balanced Scorecard: A Project of the German Research Association." *Performance Measurement and Metrics* 1, no. 3 (2000): 157–64.

Conyers, Angela, and Philip Payne. "Making an Impact: The SCONUL/LIRG Measuring Impact Initiative." *SCONUL Focus* 31 (Spring 2004): 24–5.

Cotter, Rosemary. "Performance Indicators for Reference and Information Services—Round 1." In *Proceedings of the 17th Conference of the*

International Association of Technological University Libraries. Auckland: International Association of Technological University Libraries, 1996 http://iatul.org/conferences/pastconferences/1996proceedings.asp

Cram, Jennifer. "'Six Impossible Things Before Breakfast': A Multidimensional Approach to Measuring the Value of Libraries." Paper presented at the 3rd Northumbria International Conference on Performance Measurement in Libraries and Information Services, August 27–31, 1999. Author version at: www.alia.org.au/~jcram/six_things.html [retrieved July 12, 2008]

de Jager, Karin. "Impacts and Outcomes: Searching for the Most Elusive Indicators of Academic Library Performance." In *Proceedings of the 4th Northumbria International Conference on Performance Measurement in Library and Information Services*, 291–7. Washington, DC: Association of Research Libraries, 2002. www.libqual.org/documents/admin/dejager.pdf

——. "Successful Students: Does the Library Make a Difference?" *Performance Measurement and Metrics* 3, no. 3 (2002): 140–4.

——. "Towards Establishing an Integrated System of Quality Assurance in South African Higher Education Libraries." *IFLA Journal* 33, no. 2 (2007): 109–16.

Derfert-Wolf, Lidia, Marek M. Gorski, and Marzena Marcinek. "Management Based on Reliable Comparative Data. Library Statistics and Performance indicators. A Common Project of Polish Research Libraries." In *Proceedings of the 25th Conference of the International Association of Technological University Libraries*. Auckland: International Association of Technological University Libraries, 2004. www.iatul.org/conferences/pastconferences/] www.iatul.org/doclibrary/public/Conf_Proceedings/2004/Lidia20Derfert-Wolf_Marek20M.Gorski_Marzena20Marcinek.pdf [retrieved July 12, 2008]

Dixon, Pat, Alison Pickard, and Heather Robson. "Developing a Criteria-Based Quality Framework for Measuring Value." *Performance Measurement and Metrics* 3, no. 1 (2002): 5–9.

Dole, Wanda V., Anne Liebst, and Jitka M. Hurych. "Using Performance Measurement for Decision Making in Mid-Sized Academic Libraries." *Performance Measurement and Metrics* 7, no. 3 (2006): 173–84.

Dugan, Robert E., and Peter Hernon. "Outcomes Assessment: Not Synonymous with Inputs and Outputs." *Journal of Academic Librarianship* 28, no. 6 (November 2002): 376–80.

Everest, Katherine, and Philip Payne. "The Impact of Libraries on Learning, Teaching and Research." *SCONUL Newsletter* 24 (Winter 2001): 60–3.

Fraser, Bruce T., Charles R. McClure, and Emily H. Leahy. "Toward a Framework for Assessing Library and Institutional Outcomes." *portal: Libraries and the Academy*, 2, no. 4 (October 2002): 505–28.

Gedye, Richard J. and Peter T. Shepherd. "COUNTER and the Development of Meaningful Measures." In *Proceedings of the World Library and Information Congress: 71st IFLA General Conference and Council*. The Hague, Netherlands: IFLA, 2005. www.ifla.org/IV/ifla71/papers/090e-Gedye_Shepherd.pdf

German Library Association, "BIX—the Library Index: Basic information in English—Working Paper" (Berlin: German Library Association, April 24, 2007) www.bix-bibliotheksindex.de/index.php?id=115 [retrieved July 11, 2008]

Goodall, Deborah L. "Performance Measurement: A Historical Perspective." *Journal of Librarianship and Information Science* 20, no. 2 (April 1988): 128–44.

Grasenick, Karin and Jonathan Low. "Shaken, Not Stirred: Defining and Connecting Indicators for the Measurement and Valuation of Intangibles." *Journal of Intellectual Capital 5*, no. 2 (2004): 268–81.

Gratch-Lindauer, Bonnie. "Defining and Measuring the Library's Impact on Campuswide Outcomes." *College & Research Libraries 59*, no. 6 (November 1998): 546–63.

Hernon, Peter. "Editorial: The Practice of Outcomes Assessment." *Journal of Academic Librarianship 28*, no. 1 (January/March 2002): 1–2.

——. "Quality: New Directions in the Research." *Journal of Academic Librarianship 28*, no. 4 (July 2002): 224–31.

Hiller, Steve. "'But What Does It Mean?' Using Statistical Data for Decision Making in Academic Libraries." In *Statistics in Practice—Measuring & Managing 2002*, 10–23. Leicestershire: Loughborough University Library and Information Statistics Unit, LISU Occasional Paper #32, 2003. www.lboro.ac.uk/departments/dils/lisu/downloads/statsinpractice-pdfs/hiller.pdf

Hiller, Steve and Cathie Jilovsky. "Measuring Value: A Comparison of Performance Quality Measures and Outcomes Identified by Australian and North American Libraries." In *Proceedings of the 3rd International Evidence Based Librarianship Conference*. Kingston, Australia: Australian Library and Information Association, 2005. http://conferences.alia.org.au/ebl2005/Hiller.pdf

Hooper-Greenhill, Eilean. "Measuring Learning Outcomes in Museums, Archives and Libraries: The Learning Impact Research Project (LIRP)." *International Journal of Heritage Studies 10*, no. 2 (May 2004): 151–74.

Hsieh, Ling-Feng, Jiung-Bin Chin and Mu-Chen Wu. "The Performance Indicators of University E-Library in Taiwan." *The Electronic Library 22*, no. 4 (2004): 325–30.

——, ——, and ——. "Performance Evaluation for University Electronic Libraries in Taiwan." *The Electronic Library 24*, no. 2 (2006): 212–4.

International Organization for Standardization (IOS). *Information and Documentation—Library Performance Indicators: ISO 11620*. Geneva: International Organization for Standardization, 1998.

——. *Information and Documentation—Library Performance Indicators: AMENDMENT 1: Additional Performance Indicators for Libraries: ISO 11620 Amendment 1*. Geneva: International Organization for Standardization, 2003.

Julien, Heidi and Stuart Boon. "Assessing Instructional Outcomes in Canadian Academic Libraries." *Library & Information Science Research 26*, no. 2 (Spring 2004): 121–39.

Kyrillidou, Martha. "An Overview of Performance Measures in Higher Education." *Journal of Library Administration 55*, no. 4 (2001): 7–18.

——. "From Input and Output Measures to Quality and Outcome Measures, or from the User in the Life of the Library to the Library in the Life of the User." *Journal of Academic Librarianship 28*, no. 1 (January–March 2002): 42–6.

Lane, Gina. "Developing Outcome-Based Indicators: Resource's Learning and Access Standard." In *Proceedings of the 4th Northumbria International Conference on Performance Measurement in Library and Information Services*, 137–43. Washington, DC: Association of Research Libraries, 2002. www.libqual.org/documents/admin/lane1.pdf

Markless, Sharon and David Streatfield. "Developing Performance and Impact Indicators and Targets in Public and Education Libraries." *International Journal of Information Management* 21, no. 2 (April 2001): 167–79.

Matthews, Joseph R. *Strategic Planning and Management for Library Managers.* Westport, CT: Libraries Unlimited, 2005.

McNeeney, Anthony. "Selecting the Right Key Performance Indicators." *Maintenance Technology* (April 2005). http://mt-online.com/articles/0405 meridium.cfm?pf=1

Melo, Luiza Baptista and Maria Imaculada Cardoso Sampaio. "Quality Measures for Academic Libraries and Information Services: Two Implementation Initiatives—Mixed Model CAF-BSC-AHP and PAQ-SIBI-USP." In *Proceedings of the 27th Conference of the International Association of Technological University Libraries.* Auckland: International Association of Technological University Libraries, 2006. www.iatul.org/doclibrary/public/ Conf_Proceedings/2006/MeloSampaiopaper.pdf

Melo, Luiza Baptista, Cestalina Pires, and Ana Tavelra. "Recognizing Best Practice in Portuguese Higher Education Libraries," *IFLA Journal* 34, no. 1 (2008): 34–54.

Micheli, Pietro and Mike Kennerley. "Performance Measurement Frameworks in Public and Non-Profit Sectors." *Production Planning & Control* 16, no. 2 (March 2005): 125–34.

Niederer, Ulrich. "'L'appetit Vient en Comparant': The Swiss Benchmarking Project." In *Proceedings of the 4th Northumbria International Conference on Performance Measurement in Library and Information Services,* 155–8. Washington, DC: Association of Research Libraries, 2002. www.libqual.org/ documents/admin/niederer.pdf

Nitecki, Danuta A. and Brinley Franklin. "New Measures for Research Libraries." *Journal of Academic Librarianship* 25, no. 6 (November 1999): 484–7.

Nuut, Anu, Aira Lepik, and Toomas Viivamagi. "Developing Performance Measurement and Quality Evaluation in Estonian Research Libraries: Survey of Current Situation." In *Proceedings of the 4th Northumbria International Conference on Performance Measurement in Library and Information Services,* 159–69. Washington, DC: Association of Research Libraries, 2002. www.libqual.org/documents/admin/nuut.pdf

Payne, Philip, and Angela Conyers. "Measuring the Impact of Higher Education Libraries: The LIRG/SCONUL Impact Implementation Initiative." *Library and Information Research* 29, no. 91 (Spring 2005).

Payne, Philip, John Crawford, and Wendy Fiander. "Counting on Making a Difference: Assessing Our Impact." *VINE: The Journal of Information and Knowledge Management Systems* 34, no. 4 (2004): 176–83.

Poll, Roswitha. "Impact/Outcome Measures for Libraries." *Liber Quarterly* 13, no. 3/4 (2003): 329–42.

——. "Measuring Impact and Outcome of Libraries." *Performance Measurement and Metrics* 4, no. 1 (2003): 5–12.

——. "Library Management with Cost Data." In *Proceedings of the World Library and Information Congress: 71st IFLA General Conference and Council.* The Hague, Netherlands: IFLA, 2005. www.ifla.org/IV/ifla70/ papers/099e-Poll.pdf

——. "Measuring the Impact of New Library Services." In *Proceedings of the World Library and Information Congress: 71st IFLA General Conference and Council*. The Hague, Netherlands: IFLA, 2005. www.ifla.org/IV/ifla71/papers/081e-Poll.pdf

——. "Standardized Measures in the Changing Information Environment." *Performance Measurement and Metrics* 7, no. 3 (2006): 127–41.

——. "Ten Years After: Measuring Quality Revised." *Performance Measurement and Metrics* 9, no. 1 (2008): 26–37.

—— and Peter te Boekhorst. *Measuring Quality: International Guidelines for Performance Measurement in Academic Libraries*. IFLA Publication 76. Munchen: K. G. Saur, 1996.

—— and Christina Jonsson-Adrial. "Performance Indicators for National Libraries: A List of Possible Indicators, Taken from the New Draft of the Standard ISO 11620 and from Practical Examples Rested by National or Regional Libraries." The Hague, Netherlands: IFLA, August 30, 2006. www.ifla.org/VII/s1/pub/s1-PerformanceIndicators2006.pdf

—— and Philip Payne. "Impact Measures for Libraries and Information Services." *Library Hi Tech* 24, no. 4 (2006): 547–62.

Powell, Ronald R. "Impact Assessment of University Libraries: A Consideration of Issues and Research Methodologies." *Library and Information Science Research* 14, no. 3 (September 1992): 245–57.

Rabine, Julie and Catherine Cardwell. "Start Making Sense: Practical Approaches to Outcomes Assessment for Libraries." *Research Strategies* 17, no. 4 (2000): 319–35.

Reh, F. John. "Key Performance Indicators (KPI): How an Organization Defines and Measures Progress Toward its Goals." About.com: Management. http://management.about.com/cs/generalmanagement/a/keyperfindic.htm?P=1

Rose, Steve and Valerie Stevenson. "The Measure of All Things: Assessing the Impact of Academic Libraries: SCONUL Autumn Conference, 28 November 2006." *SCONUL Focus* 39 (Winter 2005): 55–9.

Seissl, Maria. "Benchmarking Efforts in Austrian University Libraries." In *Proceedings of the World Library and Information Congress: 72nd IFLA General Conference and Council*. The Hague, Netherlands: IFLA, 2006. www.ifla.org/IV/ifla72/papers/105-Seissl-en.pdf [retrieved July 12, 2008]

Smith, K. R. "New Roles and Responsibilities for the University Library: Advancing Student Learning through Outcomes Assessment." *ARL: Bimonthly Report on Research Library Issues and Actions from ARL, CNI, and SPARC*. No. 213 (2000): 2–5.

Tammaro, Anna Maria. "Performance Indicators in Library and Information Science (LIS) Education: Towards Crossborder Quality Assurance in Europe." In Proceedings of the 38th Congres Annue, Corporation des Bibliothecaires Professionels du Quebec, 2007. www.cbpq.qc.ca/congres/congres2007/Actes/Tammaro.pdf

te Boekhorst, Peter. "Measuring Quality: The IFLA Guidelines for Performance Measurement in Academic Libraries." *IFLA Journal* 21, no. 4 (1995): 278–81.

Thebridge, Stella, and Pete Dalton. "Working Towards Outcomes Assessment in UK Academic Libraries." *Journal of Librarianship and Information Science* 35, no. 2 (June 2003): 93–104.

Thornton, Steve. "Two Years of Impact Assessments." *Performance Measurement and Metrics* 1, no. 3 (2000): 147–56.

Town, J. Stephen. "Welfare or Wisdom? Performance Measurement of Information Skills Education." In *Proceedings of the 4th Northumbria International Conference on Performance Measurement in Library and Information Services*, 203–8. Washington, DC: Association of Research Libraries, 2002. www.libqual.org/documents/admin/town.pdf

——. "The SCONUL Value and Impact Measurement Programme (VAMP): A Progress Report." *SCONUL Focus* 38 (Summer/Autumn 2006): 114–6.

——. "VAMP gets WIKI'd." *SCONUL Focus* 40 (Spring 2007): 101–4.

Troll Covey, Denise. *Usage and Usability Assessment: Library Practices and Concerns*. Washington, DC: Digital Library Federation, Council on Library and Information Resources, 2002.

Usherwood, Bob. "Value and Impact Studies." In *Proceedings of the World Library and Information Congress: 65th IFLA General Conference and Council*. The Hague, Netherlands: IFLA, 1999. www.ifla.org/IV/ifla65/papers/110-84e.htm

——. "Demonstrating Impact through Qualitative Research." *Performance Measurement and Metrics* 3, no. 3 (2002): 117–22.

Vergueiro, Waldomiro, and Telma de Carvalho. "Quality in Brazilian Academic Libraries: Proposal of Indicators from the Customers' Point of View." In *Proceedings of the 28th Annual Conference of the Canadian Association for Information Science*, 2000. www.cais-acsi.ca/proceedings/2000/vergueiro_2000.pdf

Weiner, Sharon A. "Library Quality and Impact: Is There a Relationship between New Measures and Traditional Measures?" *Journal of Academic Librarianship* 31, no. 5 (September 2005): 432–7.

Willemse, John. "Performance Assessment in IFLA and United Kingdom Academic Libraries." *South African Journal of Library & Information Science* 66, no. 4 (1998):. 161–6.

Wimmer, Ulla. "BIX—the Library Index: Basic Information in English—Working Paper." January 24, 2007. www.bix-bibliotheksindex.de

6

The library's role in successful faculty research and teaching

Libraries exist because they add value to teaching, learning, and the production and dissemination of knowledge. In general, we intuitively believe that the better the university, the better its libraries. In the past, "better" has often meant "bigger," particularly in terms of collections and financial resources. The availability of electronic access to information having eroded the prominence of print collection size as a measure of library quality, libraries have looked to other means of measuring and demonstrating their value.

This forces libraries to a single, central assumption—that value is determined by the receiver of the benefit, not by the provider of the benefit. This leaves behind most traditional performance measures and indicators, e.g., size of print collections, processing volume or work throughput, and most measures of size and efficiency. Although these are useful in describing the quality of internal operations, and some of them have been correlated to user outcomes, they do not describe or measure the value received by library users. The direct beneficiaries of the library are the university's faculty, its postgraduate and professional students, and its undergraduate or baccalaureate students. What difference does the library make to these groups? How does the library contribute to their success?

A framework for faculty success

If libraries do not assess and report their contributions toward faculty success, and instead direct their findings toward improvements in collections and services, they run the risk of being viewed as general utilities within their institutions—perhaps no more than a convenience or amenity in the minds of administrators, faculty, and librarians themselves. Library contributions to faculty success are *indirect* and can be difficult to identify and measure qualitatively. Because of this, it is easy to accept a passive role altogether, or to follow whatever best practices have been established by prestigious libraries, or to simply experiment until something seems to work. However, the library's contributions as an *enabler* of faculty success certainly can be established and considered within the larger framework of a university's mission and goals.

Faculty and the current academic environment

Faculty are a primary, perhaps the most important, user group of academic libraries. Although the institution does not exist to serve faculty per se, it can not advance knowledge or educate students without an effective faculty. Faculty are the most expensive instructional resource within institutions. Faculty salaries compose 85 to 90 percent of the direct cost of instruction.[1] If for no other reason than economics, the institution has an overwhelming interest in seeing that faculty members are effective and productive in their research, teaching, and service roles. The institution's investment in its faculty as an economic asset requires hiring the best scholar-teachers, retaining them through tenure and beyond, and ensuring their continued productivity. Although the mechanisms for this vary greatly, depending upon the history, mission, and degree offerings of the institution, libraries most certainly contribute to these important objectives in measurable ways.

Faculties are not universal, homogenous bodies of scholar-teachers. They are loose groups of individuals who may, from time to time, share characteristics that affect their library needs and use. They can be segmented by rank, employment status, and discipline, as well as by their relative degrees of productivity. They are subject to numerous time pressures and are often are faced with conflicting demands, e.g., teaching vs. research, increasing program enrollments vs. improving the quality of students admitted, and aligning program goals with sometimes disparate institutional goals. Teaching is far more than direct classroom or online instruction, and subsumes other roles—as curriculum builder, course developer, advisor, mentor, and department or program advocate within the division, college or school.

Authoring publications is only the end result, and most visible part, of research. Publication may follow months or years of examining a research pathway, identifying fruitful areas of concentration, reviewing the literature, designing studies, collecting and analyzing data or other information, and writing. Given the increasing emphasis on sponsored research within universities, we can add the process of finding and securing funding to these research tasks and processes. In some cases, securing patents or other means of establishing intellectual property rights may be as important as, or more important than, research publications. Consequently, the most productive faculty members are often those who have the least time to engage with the library, and the least predictable schedules.

Depending upon the institution, a faculty can vary greatly in composition, from part-time instructors who teach an occasional course or two, to full professors deeply engaged in sponsored or personal research. Faculty information and service needs are centered on two activities: instruction at the undergraduate and graduate levels; and research, which may or may not involve graduate students whose thesis or dissertation research they supervise. If you agree that teaching and research are the main intersections between faculty and the library, it only makes sense to study these intersections, to propose measures of the library's contribution to both teaching and research, to evaluate the findings, and to use them to drive quality improvement planning.

Critical factors in faculty research success

Time

Time may be the most critical factor in faculty productivity and success in performing research. It is a myth that faculty spend all their time outside the classroom doing research; in fact, they must struggle to find adequate time for research and "work it" into their schedules. According to the National Center for Education Statistics, US full-time faculty spent less time on research than on teaching and administrative duties, except for those in doctoral institutions, where faculty spent about 50 percent of their time teaching, 28 percent doing research, and about 22 percent on administrative activities. When all program areas in four-year or higher institutions were averaged, faculty spent 58 percent of their time on teaching, and an equal split of 21 percent on research and 21 percent on administrative activities.[2]

Despite the pressure to produce, and the amount of time available for research, the American faculty member, on average, writes about two articles over a 24-month period, as well as a book review, perhaps a book chapter, and a monograph; he or she may make four presentations at professional meetings.[3]

Full-time faculty members are chronically pressed for time and tend to work in binges, when research time is identified within their schedules. Can we demonstrate that the library saves time for faculty in performing research, and translate this into return on investment (ROI) of faculty salaries for the university, which we also know to be the highest direct cost of instruction?

Collections and access

First and foremost in the minds of faculty researchers are the library's collections. It seems obvious that access to the results of others' research is the most basic requirement to examine the research path, formulate a research agenda, identify gaps in the research, design specific studies, and select possible publishing venues. In three separate studies, John Budd has tracked faculty research productivity in institutions that were members of the Association of Research Libraries (ARL) between 1991 and 2004. In the first two studies (covering 1991–93 and 1995–97), two variables were associated with overall faculty research productivity: the number of PhDs awarded by the institution, and the total number of volumes in the institution's library. To complement the total volumes measure, in the third study (2002–4) he added total library materials expenditure as a variable and found a slightly higher correlation between overall research productivity and collection funding. Across all three studies, he found three variables to be associated with institutional productivity. In order, they were: total number of PhDs awarded, total materials expenditure by the library, and total volumes in the library. As noted earlier, faculty in doctoral institutions spend about one-third more time doing research than do other faculty, so perhaps time spent on research and materials available for research are two important factors in overall faculty research productivity. At a minimum, Budd's research certainly supports a relationship between strong collections and faculty productivity in research universities.[4]

Budd also tracked overall research productivity at ARL universities and confirmed what other studies have indicated, both in the US and internationally:[5] that research productivity among faculty has increased over time. Budd found that per capita production of journal articles increased from 3.56 per faculty member in 1991 to 4.24 in 2004. So, despite the competing demands on faculty time, on average, faculty members have become more productive researchers than in the past.

Can this be attributed in part to explosive growth in collections, particularly electronic resources? Faculty access to digital resources—their availability, ease and speed of retrieval, and ubiquity of delivery—has very likely contributed to increased faculty productivity over time. A number of studies support a relationship between the availability of electronic resources and increased research productivity.[6] Vakkari summarizes them in the introduction to his study of faculty and doctoral students at 22 Finnish universities. Study results from 767 researchers representing all the broad disciplines indicated that "use of digital libraries has led to a considerable decrease in browsing physical library collections, saving their [faculty] working time" and that "the more scholars perceive improvement in the access to literature in electronic form, the more they publish internationally."[7]

Why do academic libraries rarely point out that they have played a major role in supporting such large savings in costly faculty research time within their institutions? As expensive as online databases, full-text journal subscriptions, and e-books can be, they cost a mere fraction of the total investment the institution makes in annual faculty salaries.

In a 2008 study at the University of Illinois at Champaign-Urbana, researchers collected data from 328 faculty members about their library use in grant-writing activities and found:

> Compared with the print environment, the median time for faculty to find and access needed books and articles in electronic form dropped from 7 to 2 hours per week, although the median time spent reading did not change from 10 hours per week. Comments repeatedly emphasized how much more efficiently they operate with electronic resources to maintain current awareness, select relevant articles, read more broadly, and identify related works.[8]

If an estimate of faculty time saved could be made by other libraries, then those libraries could calculate an estimated number of faculty salary dollars saved by their electronic resource collections, and faculty time released to spend on higher-purpose activities.

In this same, very useful study, researchers provided a formula to calculate the ratio value of US$1.00 spent on the library to total grant funds awarded, and found that the ratio was 1:4.38 at the University of

Illinois at Champaign-Urbana. That is, for every library dollar spent, the university received 4.38 dollars in grant funding. Again, this is not a causal relationship, and library funding may not have a direct effect, but it is an indicator of value added to faculty salaries and of successful ROI in the library.

Communications

Competition for faculty time and attention, coupled with the growth of collections and the attendant online access/delivery mechanisms, makes communicating with faculty the third critical factor in supporting faculty research productivity. E-mail alone will not ensure effective communications, nor will offering periodic library instructional opportunities for faculty. Finding out what faculty members want to know, when they want to know it, and how they want to discover information about the library to assist them in research are crucial elements that unite faculty with research materials.

Recent studies of how faculty members use the library for research reveal a set of recurring themes. Although certainly not true for every faculty member or for researchers in every discipline, a general profile can be summarized as:

> Faculty rely heavily on electronic means to identify, retrieve and acquire materials needed for research. Faculty rely less on the library as a physical facility, visiting mainly to retrieve print items. They are the most likely users of interlibrary loan and document delivery, and most likely to extend searches beyond their "home" library. They rely on personal contacts and networks of fellow researchers, as well as on personal subscriptions gained through society or professional memberships. They tend to overestimate their knowledge of library services and resources. They prefer to have their needs anticipated, rather than asking a librarian for assistance.[9]

Of course, this profile is highly generalized and there are numerous studies examining differences in research behavior and needs in various disciplines,[10] but it underscores the need for libraries to communicate information on holdings, accessibility, and specific search tools in ways that satisfy faculty preferences for communicating with the library and that work within their individual schedules. They may be less able to schedule meetings in the library, want assistance only at the point of need, and may prefer to have assistance "waiting" for them online, rather than having to initiate a request for assistance. Determining faculty preferences for the delivery of information is the library's responsibility. Faculty resistance to formal communication and instruction has been summarized by one faculty member in the observation: "with many ICT [information and communication technology] things it takes a lot of time up front to save an uncertain amount of time in the future."[11]

Jankowska concludes a study of faculty use of ICT at the University of Idaho with the following suggestions for communicating with faculty:

> Use ICTs to enhance the marketing of the e-resources and services that are available.
>
> Create flexible training and instructions that accommodate faculty learning styles, preferences, and their busy time schedule.
>
> Provide self-service instructions and training on how to access and retrieve the e-collection and services.
>
> Create Web-based tours, remote instructional presentations, and virtual help.[12]

Critical factors in faculty teaching success

It's hard to tease out successful teaching factors from student success measures, since teaching success has been measured by student success, and has been studied primarily by engineering backwards from the latter to the former. Begun in 2000, the National Survey of Student Engagement (NSSE) has collected survey data from undergraduate students in US and Canadian four-year colleges and universities about their participation in programs and activities that institutions provide for their learning and personal development. The results provide an estimate of how undergraduates spend their time and what they gain from attending college. Survey items on the NSSE represent empirically confirmed "good practices" in undergraduate education. That is, they reflect behaviors by students and institutions that are associated with desired outcomes of college attendance. NSSE results indicate the following actions by faculty members, beyond delivering course content, that have a positive influence on student success:

1. Embrace undergraduates and their learning.
2. Set and maintain high expectations for student performance.

3. Clarify what students need to do to succeed.

4. Use engaging pedagogical approaches appropriate for course objectives and students' abilities and learning styles.

5. Build on students' knowledge, abilities and talents.

6. Provide meaningful feedback to students.

7. Weave diversity into the curriculum including out-of-class assignments.

8. Make time for students.

9. Hold students accountable for taking their share of the responsibility for their learning.

The third NSSE finding, "Clarify what students need to do to succeed," is briefly explained as:

> Do not leave students—especially newcomers—to discover on their own what it takes to be successful. Become familiar with and promote the available academic and social support resources such as writing centers and tutoring support programs.[13]

Although not mentioned explicitly, this finding may have the greatest implication for libraries. Libraries tend to be recognized for what they have to offer "good" students, e.g., strong collections, assistance finding and evaluating resources for assignments, and comfortable spaces to study and work. "Good" students are not those who trouble the faculty member, leaving him or her to wonder what more he or she could do to help the student. Library programs and services provided specifically to assist struggling students, especially newcomers, may have an impact on student persistence and retention, and are discussed at length in Chapter 8. The availability of such programs and services, and faculty awareness of them, would be significant in terms of the assistance academic libraries could offer to struggling students.

Part-time versus full-time faculty

In the US and Canada almost 50 percent of academic faculty are part-time instructors who are also referred to variously as "contingent," "non-regular," "adjunct" or "sessional." At a minimum, US part-time instructors teach 25 percent of all courses, and may teach as many as 65 percent of all courses.[14] Although not as extreme in Great Britain and India, the practice of employing part-time faculty is on an upward trend, especially in Latin American and Asian countries. More than 80 percent of faculty members in Argentina and Mexico have part-time appointments. According to the Center for International Higher Education, a study of the professoriate in 14 countries found: "A growing portion of the profession is part-time, and many full-time academics are employed in positions that do not lead to long-term appointment. The traditional full-time permanent academic professor, the 'gold standard' of academe, is increasingly rare."[15]

Assuming these part-time instructors do less research than teaching, they have an equivalent or greater need than the full-time professoriate for library information and services to support instruction. Although employed in nearly every department, the numbers of US part-timers are highest in the fine arts, business, and English and literature. They are hard to contact, have no office or campus telephone, their roster changes every semester, and often they feel no sense of affiliation with the larger campus. They may know less about collections and services offered or how to develop library assignments for the classes they teach. If these faculty members are not identified and solicited for inclusion in service activities, as well as evaluation activities that address library support for instruction, then by extension, 25 percent to 65 percent of the student instruction is not being taken into account.[16] This population can be "silent," is easily overlooked, and difficult to identify, but may have a disproportionate effect on the quality of instruction.

Communications

Communication methods developed by the library without faculty consultation may on occasion be successful, but experimentation uninformed by faculty preference wastes everyone's time, and may eventually erode the library's credibility. Faculty may not be uninterested, but they may not have time to listen when the library is ready to talk. Messages from the library may be unclear about how the faculty member will benefit from library services and collections or where to begin and what to do next; may contain incorrect assumptions about their needs; or may be delivered to the wrong audience entirely. In separate studies, Stevens (US) and McGuiness (Ireland) present information literacy as the classic example of libraries' failure to connect with faculty about what is considered an important student outcome. Stevens concludes that the library's information literacy culture was developed without the input of teaching faculty, was disaggregated from the curriculum, and paid little attention to exactly how faculty were expected to be involved in implementation.[17] From in-depth interviews with key faculty informants, McGuiness provides a snapshot of faculty thinking on the development of information-literate students as:

> [I]nformation literacy develops gradually and intuitively, through participation in a number of different scenarios. The concept of "learning by doing" featured strongly in faculty's comments, although the need for structured intervention and guidance was not a key theme. Paradoxically, students' personal motivation emerged as both a positive and a negative influence on faculty's approach to pedagogy … [faculty suggesting] that the road to ILD [information literacy development] is essentially a solitary journey, driven by the student's own personal interest.[18]

Few faculty members enter the professoriate with extensive backgrounds in learning theory or instructional design, and much of the skill they gain as teachers is learned through experience and self-initiated professional development. The information literacy "message" is huge, complex, of varying importance among disciplines, not directly involved in delivering course content, and takes a long time for faculty to teach and students to learn. To deliver the information literacy message, have it understood, and persuade faculty from many disciplines to adopt it as another priority for teaching requires transformational change at the university level. No wonder progress has been difficult so far. Librarians have suggested a number of approaches, each illustrating a different level of the instructional hierarchy as an initial focus for the task—toward faculty who develop and teach individual courses, and teach them in multiple modes, i.e., face-to-face and online; toward departments that make programmatic and curriculum decisions; and toward college and university structures such as the freshman experience or general education core. The larger and more complex the "message" to be communicated, the larger and more complex will be the audience. Information literacy may be the classic example of a large and complex message that needs to be broken down by audience level within the hierarchy, and into smaller and simpler sequential message "bites" that are presented as a benefit to the audience, rather than as another chore to be taken on by the faculty. It puts the onus on the library to be a good communicator on many levels within the organization, and not on the faculty to be good listeners. The topic of information literacy is broached here simply as an example, and will be discussed in more detail in Chapter 8.

Desirable faculty outcomes of library engagement

Depending on the local history, culture, and environment within an institution, and on whose perspective of quality is considered (administrators, faculty members, librarians, students, etc.), there could be many desirable faculty outcomes. If, however, we take only the perspective of faculty members and choose only those factors identified directly by faculty in previous research, then there are three recurring themes: time saved, increased publications and funded grants, and support for instruction.

Any estimate of time saved by faculty that arises from library offerings or services, that is not punishing to collect, and that can be replicated and tracked over time would be useful. A measure that can be replicated and tracked over time and that is meaningful in context is called a metric. The most plausible way to develop a metric of time saved may be to ask faculty members directly—by surveying a representative sample and, if the findings warrant it, analyzing further by discipline, rank, or other demographic. Such data, when averaged, could be multiplied by an average cost of one hour of faculty time to produce a metric that has meaning—a financial estimate of savings promoted by the library.

Faculty productivity in terms of publications and grants is typically counted and tracked by universities and, although it is hotly contested and much criticized, universities have been ranked according to data on faculty productivity. Since library collection expenditures are thought to be associated with improved productivity, an interesting metric might be to divide each year's expenditures for library materials by the number of publications for the year, to produce a library materials cost-per-publication figure. Similarly, each year's expenditures for library materials could be divided by the number of grants awarded, and/or expressed as a percentage of total grant funding awarded.

Support for instruction metrics might include figures such as the number of hours of instruction and service desk assistance provided to students divided by the number of hours students spent in class, to determine the percentage of total instruction and academic support provided by library staff. Students are often given an opportunity by their universities to evaluate instruction at the end of a course. Is there presently, or could there be, a question(s) about the student's evaluation of the instructor's use or non-use of library assignments or reserve readings in the course? This might produce some data on the level and value of instructor-mandated library use.

Creating customized metrics to express the value added by the library to faculty success is difficult, and depends on the environmental and cultural realities at individual institutions. The above are only meant to serve as examples of metrics that advance libraries beyond the more traditional performance measures. Performance measures have meaning to librarians, but need to be placed in a larger context in order for them to become meaningful metrics for quality improvement.

Faculty are an important user group and, as a general user category, are typically pressed for time, prefer to acquire library awareness and training through self-selected and self-controlled methods, and include a growing proportion of part-time teaching associates. In order to be successful, faculty 1) should have adequate collections and access, 2) should have an awareness of library collections and access, and 3) should use them, and expect their students to use them. Any metrics that describe current levels of these three variables in the context of faculty success can be used to establish baselines, track improvements, and identify and repair possible disconnections between the three. For example, if a library believes its collections and collection development activities to be at an adequate or optimal level, but that use is lower than expected, then perhaps faculty awareness is not what it should be, and communication would be a priority for improvement. If use is judged to be higher than expected or optimal, then additional investments in collections may be warranted.

Notes

1. Middaugh, "Measuring Higher Education Costs," 89.
2. Forrest, *2004 National Study of Post-Secondary Faculty*. Percentages taken from Table 19 E.D. TAB 2006-176.
3. Middaugh, *Understanding Faculty Productivity*, 22.
4. Budd, "Faculty Publishing Productivity," 230–9.
5. Cornet and Vollard note a number of studies in *Tackling the Journal Crisis: When Authors Pay with Money instead of Copyright* (The Hague, Netherlands: Centraal Planbureau, 2000) to illustrate the increase in numbers of journals and articles published, and summarize by saying "Until the 1960s, the number of articles published by each author was relatively small, and many members of academic societies did not publish at all. Since then, article output per author has increased. For instance, over the period 1983/84 to 1995/96 the article output of Dutch academics increased almost 70 per cent, whereas research expenditures stayed constant or declined and the number of academics started to decrease in 1994."
6. Notably and most recently, Franz Barjak's survey of scientists in seven European countries, "Research Productivity in the Internet Era," 343–60.

7. Vakkari, "Perceived Influence of the Use of Electronic Information Resources," 610.
8. Luther, "University Investment in the Library," 10.
9. This profile was compiled from numerous articles based on faculty surveys addressing their perceived needs and preferences for library resources, and how they are used in research. Significant sources included: Weber and Flatley, "What Do Faculty Want?" 1–8; Jirojwong and Wallin, "Use of Formal and Informal Methods to Gain Information," 68–73; and Leckie, "Desperately Seeking Citations," 201–8.
10. Discipline-based studies of faculty library needs, preferences and user behaviors generally support the profile, but take into account variations in scholarly communications and online availability of resources. Examples of recent studies include: Wallis, "Information-Seeking Behavior of Faculty," 441–6; Boyce et al., "Not All Users Are Alike," 237–43; Belefant-Miller and King, "How, What, and Why Science Faculty Read," 91–112.
11. Jankowska, "Identifying University Professors' Information Needs," 58.
12. *Ibid.*, 62.
13. Kinzie, *Promoting Student Success.*
14. Comments by Steve Street, reporting on the Tri-national Conference on Contingent Academic Labor held in Vancouver, British Columbia on August 10–13, 2006, included an estimate that 45–50 percent of teaching is done by part-time faculty in Canada, and two-thirds of the teaching is done by part-time faculty in the United States. [Retrieved January 15, 2008 from www.ccf-suny.org/newsroom.php?document=assembly]
15. Altbach (ed.), *The Changing Academic Workplace*, ix.
16. If you take the attribution by Steve Street of a comment to Cary Nelson, President of the American Association of University Professors that two-thirds of teaching in the US is provided by part-time faculty, then this would be about 65 percent.
17. Stevens, "Beyond Preaching to the Choir," 254–67.
18. McGuiness, "What Faculty Think," 580.

Bibliography

Altbach, Philip G., ed. *The Changing Academic Workplace: Comparative Perspectives*. Boston: Boston College, Center for International Higher Education, September 2000. www.bc.edu/bc_org/avp/soe/cihe/publications/pub_pdf/academicworkplace.pdf [retrieved December 30, 2007]

Barjak, Franz. "Research Productivity in the Internet Era." *Scientometrics* 68, no. 3 (2006): 343–60.

Belefant-Miller, Helen and Donald W. King. "How, What, and Why Science Faculty Read." *Science & Technology Libraries* 19, no. 2 (2001): 91–112.

Boyce, Peter B., Carol Tenopir, and Donald W. King. "Not All Users Are Alike: How Do Age and Productivity Affect User Behavior?" In *2003 Charleston Conference Proceedings*, 237–43. Westport, CT: Libraries Unlimited, 2004.

Budd, John M. "Faculty Publishing Productivity: Comparisons Over Time." *College & Research Libraries* 67, no. 3 (March 2006): 230–9.

Cornet, Maarten and Ben A. Vollard. *Tackling the Journal Crisis: When Authors Pay with Money instead of Copyright.* The Hague, Netherlands: Centraal Planbureau, 2000. www.cpb.nl/eng/pub/cpbreeksen/werkdoc/121/sj/2/3/3.html [retrieved April 6, 2008]

Forrest, Emily. *2004 National Study of Post-Secondary Faculty: Background Characteristics, Work Activities and Compensation of Instructional Faculty and Staff Fall 2003.* Washington, DC: United States Department of Education, Institute of Education Sciences, December 2005. http://nces.ed.gov/ pubx 2006/2006176.pdf

Jankowska, Maria Anna. "Identifying University Professors' Information Needs in the Challenging Environment of Information and Communication Technologies." *Journal of Academic Librarianship* 30, no. 1 (January 2004): 51–66. http://nces.ed.gov/pubx 2006/2006176.pdf [retrieved January 15, 2008]

Jirojwong, Sansnee and Margie Wallin. "Use of Formal and Informal Methods to Gain Information among Faculty at an Australian Regional University." *Journal of Academic Librarianship* 28, no. 1/2 (January/March 2002): 68–73.

Kinzie, Jillian. *Promoting Student Success: What Faculty Members Can Do.* Occasional Paper No. 6. Bloomington, Indiana: Indiana University Center for Postsecondary Research. http://nsse.iub.edu/institute/documents/briefs/DEEP Practice Brief 6 What Faculty Members Can Do.pdf [retrieved February 15, 2008]

Leckie, Gloria J. "Desperately Seeking Citations: Uncovering Faculty Assumptions about the Undergraduate Research Process." *Journal of Academic Librarianship* 22, no. 3 (May 1996): 201–8.

Luther, Judy. "University Investment in the Library: What's the Return? A Case Study at the University of Illinois at Urbana-Champaign." Elsevier White Paper #1 2008. San Francisco: Elsevier, February 2008. http://libraryconnect .elsevier.com/whitepapers/lcwp0101.pdf [retrieved February 26, 2008]

McGuiness, Claire. "What Faculty Think—Exploring the Barriers to Information Literacy Development in Undergraduate Education." *Journal of Academic Librarianship* 32, no. 6 (November 2006): 573–82.

Middaugh, Michael F. *Understanding Faculty Productivity: Standards and Benchmarks for Colleges and Universities.* San Francisco: Jossey-Bass, 2001.

——. "Measuring Higher Education Costs: Considerations and Cautions." In *Study of College Costs and Prices, 1988–89 to 1997–98 Volume 2: Commissioned Papers.* Washington, DC: United States Department of Education, Office of Educational Research and Improvement, December 2001. http://nces.ed.gov/pubs2002/2002158.pdf]http://nces.ed.gov/pubs 2002/2002158.pdf [retrieved April 5, 2008]

——, Rosalina Graham, and Abdus Shahid. *A Study of Higher Education Instructional Expenditures: The Delaware Study of Instructional Costs and Productivity.* Washington, DC: U.S. Department of Education, Institute of Education Sciences. NCES Research and Development Report 2003-161, June 2003. http://nces.ed.gov/pubs2003/2003161.pdf

Spanner, Don. "Border Crossings: Understanding the Cultural and Informational Dilemmas of Interdisciplinary Scholars." *Journal of Academic Librarianship* 27, no. 5 (September 2001): 352–60.

Stevens, Christy R. "Beyond Preaching to the Choir: Information Literacy, Faculty Outreach, and Disciplinary Journals." *Journal of Academic Librarianship* 33, no. 2 (March 2007): 254–67.

Vakkari, Pertti. "Perceived Influence of the Use of Electronic Information Resources on Scholarly Work and Publication Productivity." *Journal of the American Society for Information Science and Technology* 59, no. 4 (January 2008): 602–12.

Wallis, Lisa C. "Information-Seeking Behavior of Faculty in One School of Public Health." *Journal of the Medical Library Association* 9, no. 4 (October 2006): 441–6.

Weber, Michael A., and Robert Flatley. "What Do Faculty Want? A Focus Group Study of Faculty at a Mid-sized Public University." *Library Philosophy and Practice* 9, no. 1 (Fall 2006): 1–8.

7

The library's role in successful postgraduate and professional education

A framework for postgraduate and professional student success

The population of postgraduate and professional students varies with the nature and purpose of the institution, which runs the gamut from distinguished research universities and institutes producing high numbers of PhDs bound for careers in research or the professoriate, to regional or specialized universities concentrating on producing professionals to assume advanced careers in education, business, health care and other fields. These students will be the research leaders, faculty, and professional practitioners of tomorrow—the "stewards of the discipline," and as such, represent the greatest concentration of future human capital within their respective countries. Second only to faculty, postgraduate and professional students represent the largest investment of the university's academic resources. In number, they are usually two or three times greater than faculty, but many times less than undergraduate or tertiary student service populations.

The term "postgraduate and professional students" is generally used to mean Level 6 of the International Standard Classification of Education 1997 system, Cycles 2 and 3 of the Bologna Process framework and "advanced research programmes" defined by the Organisation for Economic Cooperation and Development (OECD). Like faculty, but unlike undergraduate or tertiary students, these postgraduate library users are relatively mobile and are likely to have had experience with other academic libraries. They may come with a set of expectations about the library gained from recent undergraduate experiences, or be returning to university mid-career and not know what to expect of the library. Many may be non-traditional students, older with families, and working part or full time while returning to university. In the US it is not unusual for part-time students to outnumber full-time students in advanced professional degree programs.

In general, advanced education in the US is more structured than in Europe. The US postgraduate student takes more group coursework, and may not begin to work closely with a faculty mentor/advisor until ready to begin thesis or dissertation research. Progress toward a degree is measurable in terms of specific course units awarded, whereas the European model emphasizes greater customization of study by working with a faculty teacher/mentor on a specific research project throughout the program, with less emphasis on sequenced, formal coursework.

More students than ever are seeking an advanced education. According to statistics provided by the OECD, the number of graduates of tertiary-type A and advanced research programs (roughly equivalent to master and doctoral degrees in the US) increased from 4.14 million in 1998 to 5.72 million in 2005 in the 30 countries tracked. Advanced research program students accounted for 15 percent (or 875,020) of the 2005 total.[1] According to the US National Science Foundation, 285,447 doctoral degrees were awarded by institutions in over 60 countries in 2004. A little more than half (149,601) were in science and engineering, including the social and behavioral sciences. The remainder of doctorates (135,846) were awarded in other disciplines.[2] The most productive countries outside the US, the UK and Canada in terms of postgraduate production were those with growing economies: China, India, and South Korea. Depending upon the country, an advanced education may represent a significant investment of public funds. Recruiting, retaining, and seeing that these students graduate have come to be seen as national necessities, particularly in knowledge-intensive economies.

One of the most persistent problems in US doctoral education has been the failure rate. "In the US, only about 57 percent of students who start their PhDs complete them within 10 years, though there are significant variations by discipline."[3] This statistic has varied little over the past 25 years. It is so common there is a term to describe it—ABD, or "all but dissertation." The phenomenon is largely attributable to the cost of doctoral education being borne by the student rather than by the government. Frequently, a full-time student's main support for living expenses is earned through graduate teaching or research assistantships carrying workloads equivalent to those of full-time faculty members.

Of those US students who do finish, time to degree varies by discipline, but has also remained relatively stable across time. In 2003, the average enrolled time to degree for all fields was 7.5 years. In general, science PhDs had shorter average time to degree than the social sciences, the humanities, education, health, and other professional degrees. The shortest was chemistry, at 6.0 years, and the longest anthropology, at 9.6 years.[4]

At least two major efforts have been undertaken to study and develop overall strategies to improve completion rates and shorten average time to degree. In the UK, the Quality Assurance Agency for Higher Education has released a revised edition of its *Code of Practice for the Assurance of Academic Quality and Standards in Higher Education: Postgraduate Research Programmes*, and in the US, the Council of Graduate Schools is midway through its *PhD Completion Project*. Prominent universities currently examining quality improvement factors in this area include Harvard in the US, and Imperial College, London. At Harvard, the approach began with administrative policy:

> A series of new policies in the humanities and the social sciences at Harvard University are premised on the idea that professors need the ticking clock, too. For the last two years, the university has announced that for every five graduate students in years eight or higher of a Ph.D. program, the department would lose one admissions slot for a new doctoral student. The results were immediate: In numerous departments that had for years had large clusters of Ph.D. students taking eight or more years to finish, professors reached out to students and doctorates were completed.[5]

At Imperial College, and throughout the UK, one prong of a broader approach has been to address support systems for learning "soft" skills, reflected in the Quality Assurance Agency for Higher Education's *Code of Practice*.

> Mary Ritter, pro-rector of postgraduate and international affairs at Imperial College, London, described its relatively newfound focus on teaching doctoral students and postdocs "transferable skills," with the support of a government initiative and associated funding. Imperial College now requires that all of its graduate students complete a certain number of workshops offered within seven broad skills areas: research skills and techniques, the research environment (covering topics like peer review, pressure for results, and obligation to the public), research management, personal

effectiveness, communications skills, networking and team working, and career management. The college offers more than 40 different workshops in topics like science and the media, the commercialization of research, negotiation skills, writing skills, thesis writing and stress management. Imperial College also sponsors intensive three-day residential workshops on transferable skills that each of its approximately 500 first-year Ph.D. students complete in groups of 30 to 35 at a time.[6]

Postgraduate students and the current academic environment

Advanced education has become a global marketplace. Not only has the total population of advanced students increased over the past 20 years, but so has its mobility. Despite currency fluctuations and restrictions on student visas, the US still retains the lion's share of international students, some 22 percent of internationally mobile students in 2004. The UK, Germany, and France accounted for 11 percent, 10 percent, and 9 percent, respectively. However, other countries host higher percentages of international students overall. For example, in 2004, 17 percent of students in Australian higher education were international students; in Switzerland and the UK, 13 percent; and in Austria, 11 percent, compared with only 3 percent in the US.[7]

The Bologna Process, which is a current effort of the European Higher Education Area to describe and standardize levels of advanced cycles (degrees) across 46 countries, has made, and will likely continue to make mobility even easier. The lack of "articulation," or the ability to compare and align coursework and levels of education across countries of origin hampered placement of international students in the past, but this has eased, and will likely continue to ease as the Bologna Process completes its work in 2010.[8]

The Association of Research Libraries (ARL) and the Center for Networked Information (CNI) held a forum in late 2007 to examine the implications these changes in US and world higher education might have for academic and research libraries.[9] The major trend factors for US schools, taken from a study by the Council of Graduate Schools, noted the key areas as globalization, interdisciplinarity, the expansion of professional (or practitioner as opposed to pure research) programs, broader inclusion of under-represented minorities, and general program evaluation and quality improvement.[10]

The data on globalization of and global competition for the best advanced students is in, and students appear to have a much broader array of choices for postgraduate study than in the past. Globalization of the scholarly community, fueled by the ease of electronic communication and publication, contributes to the second important factor, a rise in innovation. Interdisciplinarity is the degree to which a single researcher's or group of researchers' efforts overlap disciplinary boundaries, or connect aspects of two or more disciplines/subdisciplines to produce more broadly informed results that also might have broader applications. Interdisciplinary research is now being examined as a rich platform for creativity and innovation, and a driver of global economic competitiveness. Interdisciplinary research offers two productive approaches: mining what is already known through recombination, and the possibility of identifying entirely new fields of study altogether. Jim Teeri, Director of National Recruitment for the Integrative Graduate Education and Research Traineeship (IGERT), developed by the National Science Foundation, explains it best: "In the last 10 years, there has been a growing realization that the really big problems in science are not going to be solved within one discipline. The big complex problems, like those affecting the environment or advances in information technology, will require expertise from many areas."[11]

The implications of this for academic libraries are huge, and immediately call into question the present discovery and retrieval systems at our disposal, founded on more traditional, stable taxonomies of knowledge. Likely it will become more difficult to discover and retrieve the information needed by these world-class interdisciplinary scholars, and also more difficult to develop altogether different ways of teaching this very different brand of information literacy.

Professional, applied, or advanced programs for practitioners (sometimes referred to as "taught qualifications") have been on the rise in the US. Partly due to the trend of people working longer and having longer careers, and partly due to the shorter half-life of knowledge in professions, more specialized applied research degrees are being offered. These programs have multiplied, particularly in education, business administration, and the health sciences and allied health fields. Many professional societies have moved from bachelors (first) to masters (second) degree as the entry-level credential, and created the need for additional "transitional" or "clinical" degrees at the doctoral level that are oriented toward evidence-based rather than "pure" research. Other professions, including librarianship and business administration, have begun "executive" masters programs especially for working professionals who have extensive field experience but need theoretical retooling delivered on a fast-track schedule. These students are older, have more financial resources, and are frequent participants in e-learning programs.

For the US, and perhaps other countries with heterogeneous populations, there is the challenge of inclusiveness. Racial and ethnic minority participation in US higher education shrinks as the educational level advances, and minority groups are half as likely as their white counterparts to earn graduate degrees. Education beyond the first degree, particularly in immigrant populations, can be difficult to encourage. If there is no money or outside financial support, it may not be considered possible. If there is money from an outside source, it still may be considered too much a self-indulgence to take study time away from family responsibilities. Including all qualified citizens in advanced education is a serious matter in the US because, as the minority population has increased dramatically, the percentage of the overall population with advanced degrees will shrink further if minority participation does not keep pace. Demographic trends can have an exceptional impact on workforce replenishment and national economic success, and bear watching in every country interested in making economic progress.

By now, it should come as no surprise that the Council of Graduate Schools' report includes evaluation and quality improvement as a key assumption for the future: "The quality of graduate programs drives the success of America's higher education system. Efforts to evaluate and improve all aspects of the quality of the U.S. graduate education enterprise must be advanced and supported in order to foster innovation."[12]

Information literacy as the critical factor in postgraduate student success

Recent research on graduate students and their libraries paints a picture similar to that of faculties. Graduate students in general do not know enough about the collections and services available to them, have little facility in performing targeted searches, and rely on browsing and "trial and error" as search techniques early in their studies. They suspect they are not using the most efficient methods, but are unaware of what assistance might be available. Several recent studies across multiple countries and across general and specific graduate disciplines tend to echo these general assumptions, with particular implications for communicating with postgraduate and professional students, and for instruction in searching to develop a general capacity for information discovery, as well as to facilitate the literature review required by the dissertation process.

Sadler and Given examined the postgraduate student's library experience from the perspective of ecological psychology, which offers a holistic approach to studying the relationship between the library and the student. They engaged eight social science students (six doctoral, two masters) and three academic librarians at the University of Alberta in in-depth interviews to determine and compare what each group saw as benefits of library use. They used affordance theory as a framework. "Affordance" is the assumption that the perception of utility, opportunity, or potential usefulness is determined by the individual. An affordance can be real (a benefit intended by the library) or perceived (a benefit not intended by the library, but perceived by the student as a benefit). The basic question posed was: "What affordances do graduate students perceive in the library environment, and how might these differ from what was intended by academic librarians?"

This is a most interesting question, and critical to making quality improvements in desired library outcomes, because it puts the receiver (student) of the benefit in charge, rather than the provider of the benefit (librarian). Sadler and Given summarized their findings as:

> While many of the students' perceived affordances did not differ dramatically from those intended by librarians, it is notable that this was primarily the case for traditional library services (e.g. reference services; book browsing). There were remarkable shifts, however, between students' perceived affordances and those of librarians for newer, digital technologies and for some specific services (e.g. information literacy instruction (ILI)). Two of the most striking differences that emerged in this study, between students' and librarians' perceived affordances, were related to ILI and to communication with patrons about new library services. In this university, librarians were using ILI and the library's web site almost exclusively for their communication with graduate students, yet the participants in this study were not aware of ILI services and did not read notices on the library web site, even with repeated visits.

One of the most powerful themes to emerge in this study is that personal contact with librarians is an effective communication tool, possibly the most effective tool the academic library has at its disposal.[13]

Green and Macauley also used in-depth interviews with Australian and American doctoral students studying education to examine their research needs from a learner-centered perspective, e.g., how they developed the topic proposal, how their research ideas were changed or modified as they discovered the literature, and how they conceptualized their individual personal learning styles and processes as applied to library research.[14] Rather than taking the skills-deficit approach, they sought to discover individual student profiles, or inventories of motivations, attributes as learners, preferences for discovery, and real-life descriptions of how students went about the literature review process. The results led them to believe that many of these students, who were also mature professionals, had been engaged already as consumers of professional literature and early on in their studies were accustomed to searching familiar professional sources used to keep current in their fields. As their role shifted from consumers of knowledge to producers of knowledge, they began to use academic databases and rely on more scholarly sources, moving from secondary to primary sources and gathering alternative or conflicting results on their topics. Toward the end of their work, they reported leaving the "sanctioned" literature to discover the grey literature, technical reports, popular works, and work from fringe disciplines. If this is a typical pattern for professional program students, then information literacy approaches that begin with what the student knows already, then work outward, might be more natural and more effective. In interviews with Australian doctoral students, Nimon found the desire for personalized, point-of-need instruction by students preparing literature reviews to be sharply defined.[15] Prior to developing a compulsory course to teach the literature review process, she interviewed faculty, doctoral students, and librarians who would be teaching the course to assess their needs and gather their views:

the students were definite that what help was offered them, either as part of a course or on an ad hoc basis, needed to be provided on their terms only. Anything they undertook had to be both timely and relevant in their personal terms. Some attacked the notion of being asked to do exercises that were deemed "good for you" by someone else. Indeed, they demonstrated that they were all independent, self-motivated learners (as one would hope) and would be impatient with any course they did not judge to have immediate returns for them.[16]

Chu and Law produced two reports from library instruction research on students in their first year of doctoral study at the University of Hong Kong that further support the idea that doctoral students know best how they learn, and are exceptional learners, but haven't yet identified the best sources or searching techniques to become powerful and efficient.[17]

They worked with 12 doctoral students (6 from education, 6 from engineering) and found that initially, students were unfamiliar with database sources important to their areas of study. The barriers identified by students included: receiving no direct communication from their faculty instructors or the library about useful databases; database product names that were misleading or not descriptive; and variations in database screen displays and protocols for use. Students identified three criteria for databases they would consider useful: those with specific subject/discipline relevance to their research; those that covered high-quality academic journals; and those with full-text articles or links to the full text.

The second report followed the same group of doctoral students through a series of five instructional meetings held over the course of a year.[18] From qualitative and quantitative measures, they were able to develop a profile of how these students approached searching, and how they learned to become better researchers. The students were all novice searchers and "started from zero." Students described their process as starting with simple keyword searches to find one or several useful articles, then linking to the subject heading provided that seemed the most related. Most thought they understood subject searching, but did not understand that subject terms were formal, precise terms that were assigned by the database producer. They thought they were searching their keywords by subject headings. Many of these searches were unsuccessful, either finding no records (leading students to believe there was nothing out there on their topics) or too many records (leading students to patiently search through much unrelated material). Domain experts were better able to identify and construct search terms. As students began to find the initial body of work on their topics and become familiar with the important authors and journals, they began to use author/title searches as a preferred method of discovery. Students were then taught how to use related terms, search operators, and delimiters in database searches, and were gratified to find these techniques produced improved results. There were some discipline differences, as one might expect, given the difference in compactness of the literature between education and engineering. Chu and Law concluded that library instruction is necessary indeed for postgraduates, that being computer literate is not the same as being information literate, and that the instruction offered should be discipline specific.

A larger but more general survey of 317 graduate and professional students at the University of Iowa by Washington-Hoagland and Clougherty confirmed what we now know to expect: that students were largely satisfied by library collections and services they knew and used, but unaware of the full range of services available, and recognized their need for more information and general instruction/assistance.[19]

The notion that students will absorb library, information literacy, and search skills over the course of their studies, or during the thesis/dissertation literature review, is probably not correct. In fact, most of the research over time supports the opposite. The belief that faculty advisors or thesis/dissertation supervisors will focus on students' information needs or literature reviews is also unfounded. And perhaps most insidious, students underestimate what they need to know, overestimate search skills that might transfer from general computer use, and are largely unaware that formal instruction is critical to their success, or even available in their libraries.

From the research discussed, critical success factors for postgraduate students would appear to include personalized communication and customized information literacy support for two different purposes at two different times. The first is a need early in the program for general discovery skills; that is, to read widely within the discipline or disciplines, become familiar with important databases and journals, and become broadly cognizant of important, enduring work in the discipline. The second, later in the students' experience, is personal, individualized assistance in performing a comprehensive literature review going well beyond the general or "sanctioned" literature and deeply into the grey. From a business viewpoint, graduate and professional students would be described as "low-hanging fruit" for libraries—customers who need a product or service but are simply unaware these exist, and there is little competition for provision of the service.

Desirable outcomes of library engagement

Starting at the end of the process requires asking "What outcomes are desired by the beneficiaries of the library's collections and services?" Graduate students, their faculty supervisors, and university administrators would likely include as desirable outcomes: recruitment of high-quality students into postgraduate and professional programs; higher retention and completion rates; shorter time to degree; and successful employment and professional productivity after graduation. Librarians might add to this list the desire to equip graduates with information and research skills that will carry beyond the dissertation, and all of the desired outcomes would be predicated in part upon this "transferable" skill.

Valuation of the library's contribution toward the desirable outcomes might be centered on transitional points in the students' educational experience. For example, during recruitment, what percentage of prospective students is provided with information, or has access to information about library collections, resources, and services? Is there a link to the library's home page from graduate information pages elsewhere in the university's website? Can prospective students arrange a personal library tour prior to admission? Would library outreach to prospective students result in the recruitment of better students?

What might be the best time during the student's career to offer library and/or information literacy tutoring or instruction? Should general searching skills within the disciplines be offered during the student's first courses, as part of a "capstone" course tying together the program objectives, or prior to the comprehensive exam? When and how should personalized assistance in completing the literature review be offered? Regardless of an individual library's decisions, the best metrics will be those that express gains in time to degree and degree completion rates *for each discipline or program*, that result from a regular program of library engagement, i.e., demonstrate that greater engagement with the library improves the desired outcomes.

Postgraduate students, particularly doctoral students, are learning expert research skills that will be essential to their careers and in their role as "stewards of the discipline." Because they may be burdened in terms of financial, work, and family responsibilities during the years of advanced education, postgraduate students can be a demanding service population, requiring research assistance and personalized searching instruction entirely on their own terms. Given the high attrition rate at the point of dissertation proposal writing, the dissertation literature review may be a pivotal point for library intervention in order to reduce time to degree and improve completion rates.

Notes

1. OECD, Directorate for Education, *Online Education Database.* [Data extracted May 15, 2008 from www.oecd.org/document/54/0,3343,en_2649_39263301_38082166_1_1_1_1,00.html#4]
2. National Science Foundation, National Science Board, *Science and Engineering Indicators 2008*, Table 2-40. www.nsf.gov/statistics/seind08/c0/c0i.htm table 2-40 [retrieved May 14, 2008]
3. Jaschik, "Why and When PhD Students Finish."
4. Hoffer and Welch, "Time to Degree of US Research Doctorate Recipients," 1.
5. Jaschik, "How to Cut PhD Time to Degree."
6. Redden, "PhD Completion—and Content."
7. National Science Foundation, National Science Board, *Science and Engineering Indicators 2008*, Figure 2-38. www.nsf.gov/statistics/seind08/c2/fig02–38.htm [retrieved May 14, 2008]
8. Full information about the Bologna Process is available at www.ond.vlaanderen.be/hogeronderwijs/bologna/
9. Goldenberg-Hart, "Enhancing Graduate Education," 1–8.
10. Council of Graduate Schools, *Graduate Education.*
11. As quoted on the IGERT National Recruitment Program website. www.igert.org/faqs.asp#3 [retrieved May 17, 2008]
12. Council of Graduate Schools, *Graduate Education.*
13. Sadler and Given, "Affordance Theory," 135.
14. Green and Macauley, "Doctoral Students' Engagement with Information," 317–32.
15. Nimon. "Preparing to Teach 'The Literature Review'," 168–9.
16. *Ibid.*, 177.
17. Chu and Law, "Development of Information Search Expertise: Research Students' Knowledge of Databases," 621–42.
18. Chu and Law, "Development of Information Search Expertise: Postgraduates' Knowledge of Searching Skills," 295–316.
19. Washington-Hoagland and Clougherty, "Identifying the Resource and Service Needs of Graduate and Professional Students," 125–43.

Bibliography

Chu, Samuel Kai-Wah and Nancy Law. "Development of Information Search Expertise: Research Students' Knowledge of Databases," *Online Information Review* 29, no. 6 (2005): 621–42.

—— and ——. "Development of Information Search Expertise: Postgraduates' Knowledge of Searching Skills." *portal: Libraries and the Academy* 7, no. 3 (2007): 295–316.

Cooper, Liz, Chris Palazzolo, and Anna Van Scoyoc. "Reaching the Faculty of the Future ... Now: Marketing Instructional Services to Graduate Students." In *Proceedings of the ACRL 13th National Conference*, 237–43. Chicago: ALA-Association of College and Research Libraries, 2007.

Council of Graduate Schools. *Graduate Education: The Backbone of American Competitiveness and Innovation.* Washington, DC: Council of Graduate Schools, April 2007. www.cgsnet.org/portals/0/pdf/GR_GradEdAmComp_0407.pdf [retrieved May 15, 2008]

Goldenberg-Hart, Diane. "Enhancing Graduate Education: A Fresh Look at Library Engagement," *ARL: A Bimonthly Report,* No. 256 (February 2008): 1–8. www.arl.org/bm~doc/arl-br-256-grad.pdf [retrieved May 15, 2008]

Green, Rosemary and Peter Macauley. "Doctoral Students' Engagement with Information: An American–Australian Perspective." *portal: Libraries and the Academy* 7, no. 3 (July 2007): 317–32.

Haycock, Laurel. "Interdisciplinarity in Education Research: The Graduate Student Perspective." *Behavioral & Social Sciences Librarian* 25, no. 2 (2007): 79–92.

Hoffer, Thomas B. and Vincent Welch, Jr. "Time to Degree of US Research Doctorate Recipients." *InfoBrief* (March 2006): 1. www.nsf.gov/statistics/infbrief/nsf06312/nsf06312.pdf [retrieved May 15, 2008]

Jaschik, Scott. "Why and When PhD Students Finish." *Inside Higher Ed News,* July 17, 2008. www.insidehighered.com/news/2007/07/17/phd [retrieved May 19, 2008]

——. "How to Cut PhD Time to Degree," *Inside Higher Ed News,* December 17, 2007. www.insidehighered.com/news/2007/12/17/phd [retrieved May 18, 2008]

National Science Foundation, National Science Board. *Science and Engineering Indicators 2008.* Arlington, VA: National Science Foundation, January 2008.

Nimon, Maureen. "Preparing to Teach 'The Literature Review': Staff and Student Views of the Value of a Compulsory Course in Research Education." *Australian Academic & Research Libraries* 33, no. 3 (September 2002): 168–9.

——. "Development of Information Search Expertise: Postgraduates' Knowledge of Searching Skills." *portal: Libraries and the Academy* 7, no. 3 (July 2007): 295–316.

Redden, Elizabeth. "PhD Completion—and Content." *Inside Higher Ed News,* April 1, 2008. www.insidehighered.com/news/2008/04/01/graduate [retrieved May 19, 2008]

Sadler, Elizabeth (Bess) and Lisa M. Given. "Affordance Theory: A Framework for Graduate Students' Information Behavior." *Journal of Documentation* 63, no.1 (2007): 115–41.

Walker, George E. et al. *The Formation of Scholars: Rethinking Doctoral Education for the Twenty-First Century.* San Francisco: Jossey-Bass, 2008.

Washington-Hoagland, Carlette and Leo Clougherty. "Identifying the Resource and Service Needs of Graduate and Professional Students: The University of Iowa User Needs of Graduate Professional Series." *portal: Libraries and the Academy* 2, no. 1 (January 2002): 125–43.

8

The library's role in the success of undergraduate students

A framework for undergraduate student success

The term "undergraduate" will be used to include programs that require three or four years of study: 1st cycle programs (Bologna Process), Tertiary A and B programs that require three to five years of study (Organisation for Economic Cooperation and Development, or the OECD), and Level 5A programs (ISCED). The differences among systems are not always clear cut, but "undergraduate" will here be considered the earliest university degree or qualification that prepares students for workplace entry to a profession, e.g., nursing, teaching, accounting, engineering, etc., or for advanced theoretical study. It will not include two-year programs designed for the trades or for transfer to university, or six-year or longer preparations such as medicine. Undergraduate students will be those having their first experience of an academic library and many, but certainly not all, will be young adults in their 20s.

According to the OECD, about 38 million students in 29 countries were in Tertiary A programs during 2005, and another nine million students were in Tertiary B programs. The US accounts for one-third of Tertiary A program students, with Japan, Mexico and Poland reporting the next largest numbers of students. The US also accounts for one-third of Tertiary B program students, with the Republic of Korea, Japan and Turkey reporting the next largest numbers of students.[1] These are raw counts only and do not reflect percentages of populations or average levels of higher education obtained within countries. Using OECD averages, students graduating in 2005 were from the following grouped fields of study in rank order by size for both Type A and B programs: social sciences, business and law; humanities, arts and education;

engineering, manufacturing, and construction and health and welfare; life sciences, physical sciences and agriculture; and mathematics and computer science.[2]

Like postgraduate enrollments, tertiary enrollments have also increased, although in a slightly different pattern. UNESCO reports that "More students than ever are seeking higher education in middle-income countries, causing tertiary enrolment to skyrocket by 77 per cent over the past decade, compared to 43 per cent in rich countries ..."[3] The recent OECD policy report, *Tertiary Education for the Knowledge Society*, explains this explosive growth as a combination of diversification, inclusion, and economics.

> These days, tertiary education is much more diversified and encompasses new types of institutions such as polytechnics, university colleges, or technological institutes. These have been created for a number of reasons: to develop a closer relationship between tertiary education and the external world, including greater responsiveness to labour market needs; to enhance social and geographical access to tertiary education; to provide high-level occupational preparation in a more applied and less theoretical way; and to accommodate the growing diversity of qualifications and expectations of school graduates.[4]

In numbers, undergraduate students are overwhelmingly the largest service population of academic libraries, use more basic and resource collections than advanced students, and have distinctly different characteristics than postgraduate students. Depending upon the country, they can be considered the most important student population if they represent the pipeline for future economic growth. They are also the most-studied service population of academic libraries, and the professional literature is rich in reports on how and why these students engage with their libraries, their expectations for services, and the benefits of library use.

Undergraduate students and the current academic environment

Major policy studies of undergraduate education have been undertaken in the US and other countries, and despite cultural differences, a number of similar trends and concerns have been presented.[5] OECD enumerates the major global trends as:

- **Expansion:** Tertiary enrollment doubled between 1991 and 2004;
- **Diversification by providers:** New institution types, new offerings and new delivery modes;
- **More heterogenous student bodies:** More women, older students and students from diverse socio-economic and ethnic backgrounds;
- **New funding sources and priorities:** Increased public funding, and funding that is increasingly targeted, performance-based and competitive;
- **Changes in style of institutional governance:** Increasingly participative, with leaders seen as entrepreneurs or coalition-builders;
- **Global reach:** Internationalization, cross-border collaboration, and university–business partnerships.[6]

The trend toward "increasing focus on accountability and performance" has not been overlooked, and the OECD report notes: "The development of formal quality assurance systems is one of the most significant trends that have affected tertiary education systems during the past few decades."[7] The report makes an important distinction between quality assurance (accountability, suggested by performance indicators) and quality improvement (mechanisms to enhance quality rather than simply force compliance with a bureaucratic standard). One can think of quality assurance as the metrics themselves, and quality improvement as how an organization uses them to improve the outcomes associated with those metrics. A measure that can be replicated, tracked over time and that is meaningful in context is called a metric.

Trends in the US include grave concerns regarding the present quality of higher education, and a starkly critical Department of Education policy paper, *A Test of Leadership*, illustrates erosion of the faith the public once had in American higher education. The paper outlines the following major challenges:

- Access to higher education is being limited by inadequate secondary school [compulsory] preparation of students, lack of information about college opportunities, persistent financial barriers, especially for African-American, Native American and Latino students, increasingly expensive college costs, and a broken system of financial aid [student support].

- Decreases in the quality of learning, declining literacy rates, rising time to degree, and racial and ethnic gaps in student achievement have made a once preeminent system of higher education now 12th in the world for educational attainment.

- Accountability and transparency are lacking, to the point that there is no accurate and consistent method of collecting evidence, comparable across institutions, to determine how much students learn or whether they learn more at one college than another.

- Lack of innovation in teaching and delivery methods, difficulty in the alignment and transfer of credits between/among institutions, limits on employer-sponsored visas that discourage highly qualified international students in STEM disciplines from staying in the US, and academic structures that do not encourage interdisciplinarity have hampered the ability to find new solutions.[8]

It is likely that no country escapes criticism of its higher education system or its results, especially for provision at the entry or undergraduate level. Balancing the demand for unrestricted access, or at least optimum inclusiveness, with the demand for improved quality outcomes is difficult, and is highly resistant to the quick fix. National issues and overarching administrative policy are important for informing the missions of academic libraries, but the immediate goal must be to connect libraries to the student learning outcomes that are, in part, under our influence. According to the American Council on Education,

> Some fundamental aspects of higher education, however, do not and should not change. The most basic goals of an undergraduate education remain the ability to think, write, and speak clearly; to reason critically; to solve problems; to work collaboratively; to acquire field-specific knowledge; and to acquire the judgment, analytic capacity, and independence of thought to support continued, self-driven, lifelong learning and engaged citizenship. These critical goals of undergraduate education must endure.[9]

In addition to outcomes involving students' skills, abilities, and knowledge, broad indicators of overall institutional effectiveness also bear consideration, as they are outcomes of success. Any discussion of improvement must include completion or "survival" rates, time to degree, and second-year return rates. Completion rates for under-graduate students vary, depending on country and method of calculation, but have become a priority for improvement in the US. The OECD completion rate for all tertiary students (including advanced research programmes) averaged 70 percent in 2004.[10] Although calculated on a shorter period of time (five years) and only including students entering directly after compulsory schooling, the US survival rate for undergraduate students in 2001 appears dismal at 51 percent.[11] Even when US national figures are adjusted to other standard measures, it still appears to perform poorly by comparison. For instance, "by measures of university completion conventionally used within the US higher education community, about 66–67 per cent of US university students appear to complete their degree, a level that is measurably lower than the UK's rate of 82 per cent."[12]

This exemplifies how deeply higher education policy is rooted in culture. In US society, the assumption is that most students are capable of undergraduate study—that "all the children are above average"—and the lifetime economic benefits of an undergraduate degree have been calculated and published so frequently in the popular press that the impression may be that without one, citizens are doomed to subsistence living. Fully two-thirds of US students enroll as undergraduates immediately after completing compulsory education, but only about half of them will finish a degree within five years. No stigma is placed upon students who drop out after the first or second year, the belief being that some higher education is better than none, even if incomplete. Students are free to change their "major," or course of study at any time, or to change degree programs and/or universities entirely. In many cases, those who drop out eventually return when they are older and, perhaps, wiser. Funding a system that welcomes the majority of students is shared among the states and the institutions, with the students or their parents paying about 45 percent of the cost to attend public institutions.[13] The idea that anyone who meets the minimum qualifications and can find the money "deserves a try" at higher education may be in contrast to other countries, where the attempt may be more fully underwritten by the government.

In part, this underpins one of the greatest challenges faced by US universities, the return rate of students for the second year of the four-year course of study. About one-fourth of the US student population did not return for a second year of study in 2001, this figure being an improvement of only 1 percent over its all-time low in 1996.[14] This statistic is commonly referred to in the US as student "persistence" (in the positive) or "attrition" (in the negative), and the phenomenon has been studied widely in the US and other countries. Many universities have developed specific programs to address the problem, and the library may have a critical role to play in its solution. Given the global completion rate of 70 percent, there is probably application beyond the US to what is known about the library's role in both persistence and completion for undergraduate students.

Desirable student outcomes to which libraries can and do contribute include improvements in persistence, completion, general and specialized knowledge in a field, and overall information literacy. Five critical success factors are recurring themes in the recent literature and may provide direction for quality improvement.

Critical factors in undergraduate student success

What is known about undergraduate students as a group, about how they use libraries, what they want their libraries to provide, and how they benefit from library use? Recent findings reported in the literature have in some cases been inconclusive, contradictory, or not generalizable to other locations, but the volume of research reports certainly indicates a high level of interest in exploring the relationship between students' engagement with their libraries and the benefits in terms of positive academic outcomes.

A review of recent research supports some basic propositions for further consideration and to use as a basis for identifying meaningful directions for quality improvement. The studies range in size from longitudinal national studies with sample sizes as large as 300,000, to single institutional studies with sample sizes as small as 1,000. Key recurring findings are listed below and summarized by theme. The individual supporting studies are then discussed in detail.

Library use and patterns of undergraduate use

- High-performing undergraduates use the library more than do average or struggling undergraduates, minority students more than white students, and students who do not have the resources to purchase textbooks or personal computers more than those who do.

- Undergraduates are likely to develop a baseline frequency of library use during the first year that increases with each year they progress through a course of study, and expand their use of library services as they make progress.

- Students studying the humanities and social sciences use the library more often than students studying math, science or business, and males more than females.
- Library use patterns by undergraduate students have not changed radically in the last 15–20 years, with one exception—a dramatic increase in the use of indexes and databases.

The library as a learning environment

- Undergraduate students are most attracted to library building(s) for quiet study space, to meet with classmates to work on projects, and to use computer workstations for both academic and non-academic purposes.
- Improvements in the learning environment create a long-lasting increase in library use.

Library use and learning outcomes

- Undergraduates who use the library for non-academic purposes may benefit in terms of persistence.
- Undergraduates who use the library for academic purposes may benefit in terms of academic performance.
- Undergraduates who use the library only to socialize benefit from improved engagement with the institution and the educational experience.

Information literacy and learning outcomes

- Library instruction for library use and for developing information literacy do not appear to improve undergraduate student learning outcomes directly, but have positive and beneficial secondary effects.
- Direct assistance from librarians is considered relatively unimportant by undergraduate students in using the library.

Library funding, resource allocations and institutional outcomes

- There may be a relationship between library funding and student completion rates, and a modest relationship between library funding and student retention rates at baccalaureate colleges in the US.

- There may not be a relationship between library funding and library use by undergraduates, and library size may not be a significant factor in students' self-reported gains in critical-thinking skills—in fact, a larger library in terms of collections, complexity, and size may be a deterrent to physical use of the library by undergraduates.

- However, the size, design and condition of the library building(s) are central factors in library use by undergraduate students.

Library use and patterns of undergraduate use

How and why undergraduates use their libraries is surely one of the most studied topics in library science. The majority of universities solicit undergraduates' participation in experience, engagement, or satisfaction surveys at one or more regular points during their university experience. In most cases, the questionnaires include items about students' frequencies and reasons for using the library, along with personal perceptions of their own academic success. In many cases the library administers a separate survey to collect related information about collections and services, as well as frequency and reasons for library use. Consequently, a great deal is known about patterns of library use by undergraduates, and the results are surprisingly consistent across time and country.

In a 2003 study, Kuh and Gonyea examined the responses of more than 300,000 US undergraduate students who participated in the College Student Experiences Questionnaire (CSEQ) between 1984 and 2002.[15] The CSEQ is a "tool that assesses the quality of effort students expend in using institutional resources and opportunities provided for their learning and development" and includes questions about students' library experiences.[16] The CSEQ is not comparable, but is similar to the Course Experience Questionnaire in Australia and the National Student Survey in the UK in that all three attempt to gather information about students' learning context and experiences.

Kuh and Gonyea found that each successive year showed a significant increase in library use; that is, seniors (fourth year) use the library more than juniors (third year), who use the library more than sophomores (second year), who use the library more than freshmen (first year). A study by Omehia, Boma and Okon found significantly higher library use by fourth-year students than third-year students in a Nigerian university.[17]

The same results were also found in an earlier study by Whitmire, who looked at undergraduates' library experiences from a slightly different perspective.[18] She followed a cohort of 1,046 freshmen students selected at random from CSEQ schools and tracked the group across the 1992–95 school years. Using CSEQ items on library use, combined with data on student background characteristics collected from a second survey (National Center on Postsecondary Teaching Learning, and Assessment), she found that students used the library most frequently and consistently as a place to study across their first three years of college. However, over the three years, the frequency of use of 7 of the 11 library activities surveyed increased each year. In rank order they were: using computers, reserve and reference reading, using journal indexes, developing a bibliography, browsing book stacks, checking citations, and reading basic references. She concluded that "if students had successful library experiences during their early college years, they continued engaging in these activities over time. Good, initial academic library experiences were crucial for encouraging subsequent library use."[19] It seems plausible that students establish a baseline pattern of library use during their first year that increases in frequency and expands and diversifies in terms of services used as their years in college progress.

Kuh and Gonyea also concluded from their study that "After controlling for student and institutional characteristics, students of color [Hispanic, Latino, Asian and Pacific Islander, and black students] use the library more frequently compared with white students."[20] In a second, later study, Whitmire confirmed that students of color used the library more frequently than whites, and more often to read or study, ask a librarian for help, and read basic references.[21] This is a very interesting finding when considered alongside the study by Omehia, Boma and Okon, which surveyed third- and fourth-year students at the University of Uyo (Nigeria). They used student survey results to determine whether there were relationships between library use and academic discipline, year of study, and socio-economic background. They found significant differences between disciplines of study and year in the course of study, but also found that 64 percent of the total variance in library use could be attributed to the students' economic status. That is, students with low economic status made more use of library services than those with middle or high economic status. The authors suggest this finding reflects an earlier idea, posited by Agulou and Agulou, that "many do not have enough money to purchase even the required texts, which are unavailable in the local market, even if the students had the funds to purchase them. The Nigerian undergraduate depends heavily on library resources."[22]

Students, whatever their racial or ethnic backgrounds, who can not afford to purchase textbooks certainly need strong undergraduate collections, and may be using them to find material to substitute for basic textbooks. Students who are minorities in a country or culture may also feel more pressure to succeed, and some combination of financial need, student self-expectation and/or family expectation probably plays a role in their greater use of the library to study and discover basic materials. They may be also less likely to own a computer.

Over a long period of time, numerous studies have confirmed differences in library use by students based on academic discipline, and more recent studies serve to confirm and extend the assumption that students in the humanities and liberal arts use the library more often than students in business, math and the sciences. Kuh and Gonyea found that "students majoring in the humanities and pre-professional fields use the library more often than those majoring in business, math or science."[23] Omehia, Obi and Okon also found this to be true of students at the University of Uyo (Nigeria), finding that "Students in the social sciences and humanities use the library the most, while students in the arts use it more than those in the sciences."[24] These disciplinary differences are thought to be related to the nature of a field and discipline-specific methods and flows of scholarly communication, but they are also a function of pedagogy. The types of assignments and methods used to grade students vary by discipline, and do so in ways that affect library use. According to the *Science and Engineering Indicators 2008*,

- Most (83%) instructional faculty use lecture/discussion as the primary instructional method for undergraduate classes.

- More than half of natural sciences and engineering faculty require their undergraduate students to participate in group projects (compared with 48% of social and behavioral sciences faculty), and more than 60% require lab assignments (compared with 24% of social and behavioral sciences faculty).

- The use of term papers increased in all disciplines between 1992 and 2003. Social and behavioral sciences faculty are more likely than faculty in other S&E [science and engineering] fields to require written work of their students: 85% of social and behavioral sciences faculty require term papers of their undergraduate students compared with 76% of agricultural/biological/health sciences faculty and 57% of physical/mathematics/computer sciences/engineering faculty.[25]

Applegate cautions librarians not to rely on one-time surveys of faculties regarding their library assignments. She performed a longitudinal study of faculties' reported library assignment behaviors at a small private college, collecting data during 1996–97, 2001–2, and 2003–4, and again at a public doctoral university in 2004–5.[26] She found a good deal of variance in the data, due to changes in faculty teaching assignments, course calendaring, the mix between full-time and part-time instructors, individual year-to-year preferences, and faculty turnover. She concluded that "Discipline is important, but not entirely determinative of the use of library assignments."[27] Once again, we are reminded of the overwhelming number of intervening variables that affect library use, almost none of which are under the library's control.

Whatever the student's motivation for library use, it begs questions about how often undergraduate students use the library and how they spend their time in the library facility or on the library's website. The difference between physical and virtual library use has slightly complicated the equation over the past 15 years or so, but provides additional enlightenment about how students perceive the advantages of each milieu and express preferences for each, depending upon their academic purposes.

The Online Computer Library Center's (OCLC) report, *College Students' Perceptions of Libraries and Information Resources*, reported the responses of 396 survey respondents (about 12 percent of 3,349 total respondents in a more general study of library and bookstore patrons) who identified themselves as college students residing in Australia, Canada, Singapore, the UK, or the US in 2005.[28] Of these, 87 percent reported they had visited a college library in person, and 57 percent reported visiting an online college library (website). A further 64 percent said that they used the library at least monthly (14 percent daily, 34 percent weekly and 17 percent monthly), while 37 percent reported using the library infrequently or not at all (21 percent several times a year, 10 percent at least once a year, and 6 percent not even once a year). One of the more interesting findings was that 88 percent of all respondents said they expected their library use to increase during the next three to five years. This could be the effect of over-reporting a positive intention, or it could mean that students associate increased library use with doing better in their studies. Students reporting monthly or more frequent (daily or weekly) library use gave their purposes as:

- do homework or study (48 percent)
- use the computer/internet (45 percent)

- use online databases (44 percent)
- research specific reference books (42 percent)
- borrow print books (39 percent)
- get copies of articles/journals (32 percent).

This pattern of purpose of library use is repeated in a number of study results and provides a fairly typical profile of the in-library activities of undergraduates. Dickenson reported on the library use of over 3,000 undergraduate students from nine Colorado (US) institutions of higher education, who responded to an online questionnaire in 2005 asking about the frequency and purpose of their library use.[29] The report noted a significant level of variation in responses among the institutions, which serves as another reminder that local conditions affect everything, and there is no globally valid and reliable profile of a "typical" undergraduate library user. Even in a relatively small and coherent state university system such as Colorado's, individual school and campus differences present seemingly insurmountable challenges to the universal application of most research findings. Yet still, as to the purpose of library use among undergraduates, there do seem to be some common, almost universal patterns.

Key results of the Colorado study included a finding that undergraduates spent roughly equal amounts of time accessing library resources remotely and from computers in the library facility. The four most important reasons cited by students for using their college or university libraries were:

- quiet space for study
- availability of computers and other electronic resources
- availability of specific materials, and
- convenient location.

The most-used library services among surveyed undergraduates were:

- computer access
- electronic database/article access
- traditional printed resources, and
- meeting/study space.

Gardner and Eng surveyed 1,267 undergraduates at the University of Southern California in 2003 and saw roughly the same results in terms of undergraduate students' purposes for using the library.[30] Their particular interest was in discovering how "Generation Y" students were using the physical library. "Gen Y" or "Millennials" are those students born in or after 1982, making up the largest US generation since the post-war "baby boom." They share a set of cultural distinctions: they are the most ethnically diverse, are ambitious and optimistic, and the most technologically savvy of preceding generations, i.e., "born digital." From a list of 15 possible activities, students were asked to identify which they performed in the library. In rank order, the following activities were identified by more than 50 percent of respondents:

- study alone (80.6 percent)
- use a computer for class work (61.3 percent)
- study with a group (55.2 percent)
- use a computer for personal reasons (51.1 percent).

However, for studying alone, the library may not be the first choice of all students. Vondracek was interested in why students chose alternatives to the library at Oregon State University. In 2006 she conducted a number of focus groups and then surveyed both users and non-users of the library to learn more about their reasons for use or non-use.[31] Including non-users in the study population serves to advance the understanding of a mostly overlooked group and informs the general discussion in the literature. For frequent library users, the top choice for a place to study alone was at the domicile (private home or room in a residence hall), but the library was preferred for group study. Reasons given for the library not being the most preferred place for solitary study were that it was inconvenient, crowded, and loud. Frequent and infrequent users both preferred the library for group study because of its comfort, i.e., room to spread out books and papers, availability of group study rooms, and convenience, i.e., it provided a central location or gathering place and offered nearby opportunities to take breaks.

The library as a learning environment

The popularity of the library as a place to study, either alone or in a group, for undergraduates is one of the most replicated findings in the literature, and library use studies appear at least as early as 1933.[32] Students do need and appreciate a quiet place to study and read, a place to study and work in groups, and now, a place to use computers and access electronic resources. The return to "library as place" after years of declining library visits and reference counts began during the mid 1990s, with a wave of library building projects. Shill and Tonner identified more than 390 US and Canadian schools completing building projects in calendar years 1995–2002 and solicited their directors' participation in a survey to determine, among other things, the impact space improvements had on use of physical library features.[33] Use pre and post change was determined by four measures factored together: exit gate count, total circulation, in-house collection use, and reference transactions. Of the 171 libraries responding, 80 percent reported usage increases, with a median increase of 37.4 percent. Facility attributes most associated with post-project gains in use were the number of data ports, percentage of seats with wired network access, the number and quality of public access computers, and the quality of the library instruction lab. They concluded, "In short, *a high-quality building does make a difference*, and students continue to use an improved facility even after the novelty of a new library has worn off."[34]

Simply by providing a stable, accessible and well-equipped learning environment for undergraduate students, the library's contribution is apparent; otherwise, institutions would not support them. It may be a tautology, but *if there were no consumer demand for the library "product," it would have disappeared long ago*. The enduring value of centrality, or the library's place as "the heart of the campus," appears not to have diminished over time. But what value does the library add to undergraduate persistence beyond its role as provider of space for learning? Is library use associated with other undergraduate learning outcomes, and if so, what are those desirable outcomes and how are they related to library use?

Library use and learning outcomes

If we return to use patterns discussed earlier, there is clear evidence that library use increases in frequency, and the use of library services expands and diversifies, as students persist through successive college years, so there appears to be some longitudinal association between library use and student success. The exact nature of the relationship is less straightforward: which is the operative variable, and to what degree— the student or the library?

Returning to the Kuh and Gonyea study, additional results indicated that the level of academic challenge in the environment was positively related to library use and to higher student-reported levels of critical-thinking skills. That is, at more demanding schools with higher expectations for student effort, library use and gains in critical thinking were related. The students who reported both were also more likely to ask a librarian for help and to use indexes and databases.[35] In a 2002 study, Whitmire examined the relationship between academic library performance measures, undergraduate students' library use, and self-reported gains in critical thinking.[36] Although the results were mixed, depending upon the type of institution, one relationship was consistent at all four types of institution: undergraduates who reported behaviors associated with being an active student, i.e., participated more often in class, took notes, interacted more with faculty instructors, and did more writing, reported higher library use. Perhaps these highly engaged, high-performing students use the library because they believe it is an important component in their success "toolkit." If the student is the sole operative in the relationship between the library and student outcomes, then the *least* we can say about the library is that the better the student, the more important the library.

This knowledge is actually quite useful when applied to the other end of the curve—the students who fail to return for the second year of study. They were the least frequent library users, and least likely to use the library for more than a place to study. They may not recognize library collections and services as operative factors for academic success, or may simply not have enough experience to judge their relative importance. We could posit that their failure to recognize and exploit the library during that first year of study contributed to their overall academic failure, and that some intervention by the library might have been beneficial. Kuh, Boruff-Jones, and Mark recommend the following:

> Librarians would do well to connect with students in the early days of their first academic term to help them in the initial development of the research and information literacy skills and competencies they need to succeed in college ... They [librarians] must collaborate with classroom faculty to design assignments that require students to become familiar with information technology and with student affairs colleagues who have ongoing contact with students outside the classroom.[37]

The NSSE Documenting Effective Educational Practices (DEEP) study, which examined schools with higher than expected graduation rates, provided an outline of what faculty could do to improve student success, and was discussed in Chapter 6. The DEEP study also had import for what librarians could do to improve student success and ways the library could promote student engagement. The authors suggested:

> First, they [schools with higher than expected graduation rates] teach students early on how to take advantage of institutional resources for their learning. Second, they make available to students *what* they need *when* they need it.
>
> Involvement in classroom instruction gives librarians visibility and helps them connect to students ... DEEP colleges take advantage of librarians' expertise by sewing them into redundant safety nets that help enrich the student experience and promote student success. [E.g., DEEP colleges worked to identify at-risk students who could benefit from library instruction to reduce library anxiety, involved librarians during the freshman year to help prepare students for senior-level capstone projects, provided the opportunity for job rotation between librarians and teaching faculty, and ensured that their libraries worked closely with their writing centers.]
>
> One of the more effective ways to teach information literacy skills systematically to large numbers of students early in their college careers is to include librarians on the instruction team for first-year seminars.
>
> Librarians can help students adjust to college life by orienting them to the library and library resources or just from personal contacts and close cooperation with faculty members ... Spending time with students ... is essential.
>
> For librarians to engage students more effectively, they must not only concentrate on content but also become familiar with and use instructional design concepts and pedagogies that take students' different learning styles into account.
>
> To engage Gen Y or Next Gen students more effectively, librarians should focus on how these students learn. [E.g., offer technologies on a par with students' preferences, design web pages that are more exploratory and discovery-oriented than a "table of contents" approach, embed library features into course management systems.][38]

Toda and Nagata conducted a study of the relationship between library use, the benefits of library use, and learning outcomes by surveying former students of Bunkyo University (Japan) in 2003.[39] Their questionnaire was returned by 304 students, who reflected upon their earlier student experiences. "Use" variables included such activities as using the library catalog, using periodical databases, consulting librarians, browsing through stacks (stocks), reading materials unrelated to a class, and studying alone or in groups. "Benefit" variables included finding information, gaining new perspectives or ideas, encountering books they would not have found elsewhere, gaining a sense of fulfillment from reading interesting books, spending time in an intellectually stimulating ambience, access to information systems not otherwise available, and improving search skills and knowledge. "Learning outcome" variables included general knowledge, specialized knowledge, information searching and utilization skills, and skills for investigation and reflection. There were high positive correlations between 23 of the 64 possible combinations of use and benefit variables, and between 13 of the 40 possible combinations of benefit and outcome variables. In addition, those who rated "benefits" highly also rated highly the "degree of library contribution" toward their learning outcomes. Discovering a basis for linkage between library use, benefits of library use, and learning outcomes, and confirming that the library contributed to the linkage, the authors devised a second study to learn more about what specific library uses or patterns of use were most associated with positive learning outcomes.

For this study, Nagata, Todo, and Kytomaki used the results of two focus groups to develop a paper questionnaire which was administered at different times to students at three Japanese universities and one Finnish university.[40] When responses from the first university were analyzed, four different clusters or types of users were revealed. "Learners," who were 66 percent of the total, used the library primarily to study, to use resources and materials, and to do research. "Strollers," who were 7.6 percent of the total, used the library primarily to browse for interesting books. "Extended users," who were 6.4 percent of the total, used the library primarily as a place to socialize and secondarily to use computers. "Place and PC users," who were 15.6 percent of the total, used the library primarily to use computers. Subsequent survey administrations at the three other universities revealed that not all user types were present, i.e., "strollers"; and that other types appeared, for example, a "resource users" type, separate from the "learners" type and composed of students who had high interest in overall library resources.

Three groups were present, although in different percentages, at all four universities: learners, extended users (social users), and place and PC users.

Survey respondents were also asked what they thought they had gained from their use of the library and were given a list of eight outcomes from which to choose. The outcomes were improvement in 1) technical or specialist knowledge in main subject of study, 2) general knowledge, 3) new ideas or perspectives, 4) emotional satisfaction, 5) critical thinking, 6) information literacy, 7) fun of study and learning, and 8) developing the habit of learning by themselves (self-efficacy).

The strongest correlation coefficients (between 0.403 and 0.543) at three universities were between library use for resources and research and the acquisition of technical or specialist knowledge. Results from the fourth university were eventually dropped because they were taken from students in new academic fields who had used only a branch library, as opposed to the three retained sets of results for universities where students used a main library. "Strollers" were present as a separate user type in only one university, but "strolling" as an activity was recognized by students at all three universities, and was highly correlated with the acquisition of general knowledge, new ideas and perspectives, and emotional satisfaction.

The authors concluded that "Using the library for its materials or [for] research purposes is the most likely usage that has a direct connection to students' achievement of educational outcomes."[41] Hardly a surprising revelation for many academic librarians, but few other studies have actually confirmed what has been suspected—that use of the library as a place to study and work in groups is a *convenience* benefit, but use of library collections and materials is a *learning* benefit. Bringing materials and collections together with students is the highest function of academic libraries, and this inevitably leads to a discussion of the relationship between information literacy programs and learning outcomes.

Information literacy and learning outcomes

The search for evidence that students' overall frequency and fluency in using library materials and resources were somehow connected to positive critical thinking and learning gain (as measured by student self-report), coupled with increasing pressure for accountability, has resulted in a fair explosion of research reports on information literacy programs and projects. During the 2000s, reports of single university and national studies to test connections between library offerings and the development of students' information literacy skills, and to discover best practices for optimizing student success became increasingly complex, fragmented, and in some cases contradictory. However, a discussion of the most promising results will inform all academic libraries in their attempts to discover and maximize their contributions toward student and institutional success through providing information literacy instruction.[42] Is there hard data to support the idea that information literacy instruction has a positive effect on the development of critical-thinking skills, student grade point averages, student persistence, or student completion rates? Although it seems intuitively so, the present answer would be no, at least not yet.

Developing students' specific skills in finding, interpreting, evaluating, and using information is unquestionably a worthy effort and resonant with the enduring goals of undergraduate education: to produce graduates who can think critically, find and use information, analyze and solve problems, write and speak clearly, and who develop a capacity for lifelong learning. The desirable outcomes seem to be clearly and consistently agreed upon by all the stakeholders in higher education, but the best ways to achieve those outcomes, how to distribute the efforts, and how to measure progress are less clear. The following are key issues discussed in the literature.

How best to define information literacy and produce an inventory of observable, measurable, and meaningful learning outcomes

In 2000 the Association of College and Research Libraries (ACRL) developed the document "Information Literacy Competency Standards for Higher Education,"[43] which has influenced some US regional accrediting agencies to include information literacy in their standards for accreditation,[44] and no doubt influenced the recent development of instruments to measure students' information literacy competency levels.[45] ACRL's efforts have been criticized because the standards were specified according to the librarian's concept of information literacy and may have excluded the ideas of other stakeholders (students and faculties), and they have been seen by some as the librarian's attempt to create "instructional turf," but they nonetheless generated a great deal of interest and momentum.

How best to design instruction in terms of pedagogy and placement within curricula

There is debate about the effectiveness of the method, e.g., one-shot group presentations to students enrolled in specific classes; mandatory or voluntary for-credit courses; scheduled sessions open to any interested student; instruction and assistance by appointment; self-directed learning modules (online or paper). Koufogiannakis and Wiebe provide an excellent review and meta-analysis of the literature on the methods and effectiveness of information literacy delivery mechanisms for undergraduate students.[46] They successively filtered 257 articles down to 122 unique studies that met their topic inclusion criteria, 55 that met their quality criteria, and 16 that further met the criteria of including a cognitive assessment of instruction, i.e., pre- and post-tests, production of a bibliography, or grades received on a specific assignment. They concluded that the analysis pointed to three key factors that could affect practice:

- Computer assisted instruction is as effective as traditional instruction.
- Traditional instruction is more effective than no instruction.
- Self-directed, independent learning is more effective than no instruction.[47]

It seems clear that one of the reasons we have so little hard evidence that library or information literacy instruction contribute to students' academic success is because institutions and their librarians simply have not collected the data to prove it. Of the 122 studies meeting Koufogiannakis and Wiebe's criteria for topic and quality, only 16 used any form of assessment. However, their conclusions about these 16 studies support a contention that both traditional (face-to-face) instruction by library staff and computer-assisted instruction produced better results than no instruction at all.

Who should teach these skills and at what point(s) in the course of study?

This discussion is difficult, because each institution and each library may have either fragmented the instructional effort between teaching faculty along departmental or program lines, or left it to individual faculty members to sort out, or assigned part of it to librarians without any real awareness of who is doing or not doing what in terms of attention to information literacy. Many institutions have made a consolidated effort in the first-year instructional program, embedding instruction by librarians and/or teaching faculty into writing courses, courses identified as "writing intensive," or entire general education programs.[48] Others have placed a secondary effort on discipline-specific instruction later in the course of study, when the student is immersed in specialized or technical study. Both points of intervention would seem to be useful—early on to improve persistence, and later to improve completion. Whatever decisions are made about information literacy requirements, instructional content, delivery method, position in curricular sequence, and responsibility are not as important as adopting an institution-wide, systematic, and coherent plan. This returns us to a much earlier theme of the book: quality improvement on any institution-wide scale is a long process and requires commitment of time and resources. The library can not be an independent operator in the process, or can not silo itself off from the rest of the participants and expect transformational results.

How should information literacy skills be measured and evaluated?

If there is any recommendation that seems beneficial to the discussion, it would be to eliminate students' self-reported gains in information literacy as the sole measure and to institute multiple measures, particularly those involving demonstration of skills. In general, assessment should match instruction. That is, whatever scheme is used for instruction (embedded in specific courses or sequences of courses; taught for performance-based assignments, for general education or discipline-specific skills; or one-off, stand-alone instruction provided by librarians) complementary and proportional measurements of information literacy gains should be included. At best, measurements for each instructional activity will be designed to produce an overall, summative indicator. This allows for a great deal of customization by the individual institution and by individual disciplines and avoids the expense of a one-size-fits-all indicator such as average scores on national tests or exams. But again, customization based on an individual institution's mission and purpose requires a long-term commitment to transformational change that many institutions have been either unable or unwilling to make.

Library funding, resource allocations and institutional outcomes

Are there relationships between total library funding, internal library resource allocations and positive student and institutional outcomes? If money does matter, how does it matter, and to what end? Like so many other questions, the answer is elusive and the relatively few large and broad studies have not discovered universal results. Beginning with broad, large-population studies, and then examining studies that are more specifically about library expenditures, illuminates the role libraries and their use of resources might play in the large picture of student success.

US research examines institutional expenditures using a set of national, standardized accounting categories. Library expenditures are included in the category of "academic support," which also contains expenditures for museums, galleries, audio/video services, academic computing support, academic administration, personnel development, and course and curriculum development. The other standard categories are: instruction, research, public service, student services and institutional support. At one time or another, research has found that all these categories of expenditures have been related to student engagement and/or positive student outcomes. Pike, Smart, Kuh, and Hayek posited that the relationship between expenditures (including library expenditures) and educational outcomes are indirect, due to the mediating effect of student engagement.

> We hypothesize that the inconsistent findings in studies of college expenditures and student learning may be in part a function of indirect and contingent effects of expenditures on educational outcomes. Specifically, we believe that the effects of expenditures on student outcomes are indirect because they are mediated by levels of student engagement. We also believe that the relationships are contingent on a variety of institutional and individual characteristics ...[49]

Student engagement is a somewhat loose term to describe the behaviors or dispositions students bring to their educational experiences, or that are stimulated within the educational environment. In the positive, student engagement is demonstrated through higher interest in academic program content, higher effort exerted, and higher involvement in social and academic activities offered by the school. In the negative, it is demonstrated by uninterested or disaffected behaviors such as skipping class, not studying, not turning in assignments, and failure to participate fully in either the academic or social aspects of the educational experience. Interest in student engagement as an important operator in student success has not been limited to the US.

"Engagement" has emerged as a cornerstone of the higher education lexicon over the last decade. It has become a catch-all term most commonly used to describe a compendium of behaviours characterising students who are said to be more involved with their university community than their less engaged peers. Engagement refers to the time, energy and resources students devote to activities designed to enhance learning at university. These activities typically range from a simple measure of time spent on campus or studying, to in- and out-of-class learning experiences that connect students to their peers in educationally purposeful and meaningful ways.[50]

Student use of the library to study alone or in groups, to use library materials and services, and to socialize, discussed at length earlier in this chapter, would seem to be a plausible indicator of students' level of engagement. In the simplest terms, Pike and his co-authors found that money does matter, but only indirectly, and matters more (or less) depending upon the type and purpose of the institution and the level of the student. Their study examined 2001 data from what is the "gold standard" for measurement of student engagement in the US, *The National Survey of Student Engagement* (NSSE); expenditure figures reported to the US federal government through the Integrated Postsecondary Education Data System (IPEDS); and, as a variable of selectivity in admissions, data from the *US News* ratings. During the 2001 administration of NSSE, 177,103 first-year and senior (fourth-year) students attending 321 universities participated in data collection.

For first-year students at public institutions, expenditures for academic support (which includes library expenditures) had the highest association of any expenditure category, with five of the six student engagement factors. The five student engagement factors associated with academic support expenditures, as grouped from questionnaire items on the NSSE, were: level of academic challenge, active and collaborative learning, student interaction with faculty members, and enriching educational experiences. Expenditures for institutional support (general administrative services, executive direction and planning, legal and fiscal operations, public relations, and development) had the next highest correlations, with five of the six student engagement factors. Neither of these findings held true for first-year students at private institutions, or for seniors attending public or private institutions. Given what we know from earlier studies of the library use patterns of first-year students, these findings hint at a possible connection between total library expenditures and the level of student engagement of first-year students, which then would affect their success and/or persistence.

A slightly older study examined institutional expenditures by public universities in the US by the standardized expenditure reporting categories, but also separated library expenditures from total "academic support" expenditures for analysis both within the academic support budget and independently. Hamrick, Schuh, and Shelley analyzed 1998 data reported by 444 US public universities of all Carnegie types. They found library expenditures not only to be positively associated with completion rates, but to offer the best return on investment for improving completion rates.

> Of the institutional expenditures categories included in the model, instructional, library and academic support minus library expenditures were significantly related to graduation rates in the full model. These variables also had the greatest independent effects on graduation, and each explained between 21% and 34% of the variance in graduation rates when analyzed as sole predictors.[51]

> Based on these results [bivariate regression of independent variables upon the dependent variable] the best "payoffs" in higher graduation rates from strategically targeted institutional budgetary enhancements would seem to come from increase per student expenditures for instruction (+1.99 percentage points), followed closely by library (+1.77) and more distantly by physical plant (+1.07) and nonlibrary academic (+0.98) ... In the full model, for the same benchmark 10% per student headcount increase in any one expenditure category ... the greatest "payoff" is attributable to enhanced expenditures on library (+0.92) and instruction (+0.80) ...[52]

This means for every 10 percent per student headcount increase in library expenditures (10 percent of the per-student library expenditure equaled an average of US$36.05 in 1998) an additional 1.77 percentage points of graduation rate would result. The increase of 10 percent per student headcount in instructional expenditures (10 percent of the per-student expenditure equaled an average of US$428.29 in 1998) would result in an increase of 1.99 percentage points of graduation rate. The authors indicate they had no way of knowing exactly how library expenditures would have broken down during 1998. For instance, if resources were expended disproportionately on technology and access infrastructure rather than collections, there would be no way to separate the effect. Still, it certainly makes libraries look like a great bargain in terms of institutional expenditures of all types.

Another study posed the question more directly as, "Is there a direct connection between campus-wide retention and the academic library?"[53] Mezick examined data on academic libraries at four-year or higher schools collected by the Association of Research Libraries (ARL) and the Association of College and Research Libraries (ACRL) to compare specific library expenditures with fall-to-fall retention rates at US universities that report these data as part of the IPEDS process. Academic libraries reported data to the library professional associations for the fiscal year 2002–3, but Canadian libraries were deleted from the study because their data on retention would not have been included in IPEDS. The universities were grouped into simplified Carnegie-based categories of bachelor of arts, master of arts, and doctoral institutions for comparison. Mezick's results included two important findings that associate different types of library expenditures with retention.

> Moderate relationships with student retention were indicated between total library expenditures (r =+.505), total library materials (r =+.569), and serials (r =+.597) for those institutions categorized within the Carnegie Classification System as baccalaureate colleges. The positive signs of all correlations calculated indicate that expenditure and retention variables are directly related ... Costs incurred in each of these three expenditure categories explain 26 percent, 32 percent, and 36 percent of the total variation in student retention, respectively.[54]

In undergraduate colleges, library "money," particularly for collections, does appear to "matter" in terms of student retention. There were lower, but significant, correlations between the number of professional library staff employed and retention. These correlations were 0.210 at bachelors-granting institutions, 0.054 at masters-granting institutions, and the highest, 0.287, at doctorate-granting institutions.

So, if money spent on the academic library *does* matter in terms of student engagement, and retention and completion rates, is library funding a formative or summative indicator—a leading or lagging indicator—of quality? It probably has value as both. That is, a single year's data can be summative, reflecting the past, but longitudinal funding trends within the academic library could have some predictive value about future student and institutional success.

Desirable outcomes of library engagement

There is enough evidence to say that use of the library—its collections, staff, and physical facility—provides benefits to undergraduates that however indirect, improve student engagement, general and specific knowledge, and progress toward completion. Not only does the library tend to support the university's best undergraduate students, it supports students who may be socially or financially disadvantaged. Intuitively we may believe that information literacy instruction by librarians improves overall critical-thinking skills, but unless libraries begin to collect the data to demonstrate a relationship, the extent of any effect will remain unknown.

Libraries have traditionally relied upon measures of volume to support their contributions toward improved student outcomes, e.g., circulation, door count, use of electronic resources, numbers of student instruction sessions, etc., but these measures have no meaning unless they can be provided in the context of improvement in student outcomes. Library budget increases are often proposed as a library need rather than as a student benefit, even though they appear to be associated with faculty research productivity and student completion rates. It would be truly courageous if libraries would select and use promising traditional measures and tie them to measures of university-wide student outcomes over a long period of time, say five to ten years. Would fluctuations in student use of the library appear as fluctuations in student outcomes? We can never hold all things equal in an environment as large and complex as a university, but unless the best possibilities for converting volume measures into metrics are tested, we will never know our value.

Colleges and universities all over the world are facing new challenges and new realities for undergraduate education—increasing enrollment, more competition among national and global providers, meeting workforce demands for the twenty-first century, increasing costs, and a renewed call for accountability. Academic libraries have begun to respond to these challenges by searching for metrics to value their contributions toward the outcomes desired by enterprise stakeholders, including improved academic performance outcomes, retention, and completion. Research performed in the last decade suggests five recurring themes, or ways in which libraries forward those desired outcomes and provide return on investment to their institutions. Studying undergraduate library use patterns across time and countries indicates that academic libraries remain central to the provision of an adequate learning environment, and that this learning environment benefits students through improved student engagement and, for some, improved academic performance. The widespread improvement of undergraduates' information literacy skills through library engagement is in an early period of development, and is likely to remain so until it becomes a priority within institutions. However, as an investment of institutional capital, the library returns enormous value for money and library expenditures tend to improve retention and completion.

Notes

1. OECD, Directorate for Education, *Online Education Database*. [Data extracted May 22, 2008 from www.oecd.org/document/54/0,3343,en_ 2649_39263301_38082166_1_1_1_1,00.html#4]
2. OECD, *Education at a Glance 2007*: 69.
3. UNESCO Institute for Statistics, *Education Trends in Perspective*.
4. OECD, *Tertiary Education for the Knowledge Society*, 2.
5. Examples of national policy statements on higher education that address trends similar to those in the OECD report include: *The Organic Law on Universities Bill*, passed in Spain in 2001 and published by the Agencia Nacional de Evaluacion de la Calidad y Acreditacion [retrieved June 6, 2008 from www.aneca.es/ingles/docs/lou_eng.pdf]; New Zealand Ministry of Education, *Tertiary Education Strategy 2007–12* [retrieved May 22, 2008 from www.minedu.govt.nz/web/downloadable/dl11727_v1/tes-2007–12-incorp-step-2008–10.pdf]; Higher Education Funding Council for England, *Strategic Plan 2006–2011* [retrieved June 6, 2008 from www.hefce.ac.uk/pubs/hefce/2008/08_15/]
6. Summarized from OECD, *Tertiary Education for the Knowledge Society*, 3–4.
7. *Ibid.*, 4.
8. Summarized from U.S. Department of Education, *A Test of Leadership*.
9. American Council on Education. *Addressing the Challenges*.
10. OECD, *Education at a Glance 2007*, 72.
11. ACT, "More First-Year College Students Return for Second Year," *ACT News*, April 26, 2001.
12. Weko, "Executive Summary, New Dogs and Old Tricks," 4.
13. An estimate of 45 percent was made by the authors from the graph, *Share of Cost From Tuition*, in "Issue Brief #1: Who Pays for Higher Education? Changing Patterns in Cost, Price, and Subsidies," published by The Delta Project on Postsecondary Education Costs, Productivity, and Accountability. It is used to indicate the approximate percentage of educational cost recovered from tuition payments by public institutions in the US in 2005, and 45 percent would reflect the student's portion of cost if the student paid the full tuition amount out of pocket. www.deltacostproject.org/resources/pdf/issuebrief_01.pdf [retrieved May 25, 2008]
14. ACT, "More First-Year College Students Return for Second Year."
15. Kuh and Gonyea, "The Role of the Academic Library," 256–82.

16. *The College Student Experiences Questionnaire* is available for viewing and printing. http://cseq.iub.edu/pdf/cseq_whole.pdf [retrieved May 28, 2008]
17. Omehia et al., "Student Characteristics and Use of Library Services."
18. Whitmire, "A Longitudinal Study," 379–85.
19. *Ibid.*, 384.
20. Kuh and Gonyea, "The Role of the Academic Library," 265.
21. Whitmire, "Cultural Diversity," 148–61.
22. Omehia et al., "Student Characteristics and Use of Library Services," 3.
23. Kuh and Gonyea, "The Role of the Academic Library," 265.
24. Omehia et al., "Student Characteristics and Use of Library Services," 6.
25. National Science Foundation, "Higher Education in Science and Engineering," 2.4.
26. Applegate, "Faculty Information Assignments," 355–63.
27. *Ibid.*, 361.
28. OCLC, *College Students' Perceptions of Libraries.*
29. Dickenson, *How Academic Libraries Help Faculty Teach.*
30. Gardner and Eng, "What Students Want," 405–20.
31. Vondracek, "Comfort and Convenience?" 277–93.
32. Eurich, "Students' Use of the Library," 421–4.
33. Shill and Tonner, "Does the Building Still Matter?" 123–50.
34. *Ibid.*, 149 (italics in original).
35. Kuh and Gonyea, "The Role of the Academic Library," 267.
36. Whitmire, "Academic Library Performance Measures," 107–28.
37. Kuh et al., "Engaging Students in the First College Year," 25.
38. *Ibid.*, 20–4.
39. Toda and Nagata, "Students' Library Use and Their Learning Outcomes." This article was not available to the authors, but Toda and Nagata provide a thorough description of the study in a paper included in the conference proceedings noted below.
40. Nagata et al., "Students' Patterns of Library Use."
41. *Ibid.*, 9.
42. Two excellent literature reviews include Hannelore B. Rader's "Information Literacy 1973–2002"; and Christine Susan Bruce's "Information Literacy Programs and Research."
43. Association of College and Research Libraries, "Information Literacy Competency Standards."
44. Gratch-Lindauer, "Comparing the Regional Accreditation Standards," 14–25.
45. These would include tests used nationally in the US, including the Educational Testing Service iSkills test of information and communications technology literacy; Kent State University's Project SAILS, or the Standardized Assessment of Information Literacy Skills test, and James Madison University's ILT, or information literacy test. Examples of single-institution tests developed by US universities are linked from the ACRL page www.ala.org/ala/acrl/acrlissues/acrlinfolit/infolitresources/infolitinaction/iltestssurveys.cfm.
46. Koufogiannakis and Wiebe, "Effective Methods for Teaching Information Literacy Skills," 3–43.

47. *Ibid.*, 19.
48. Ilene F. Rockman provides an excellent and detailed discussion of such programs in "Strengthening Connections," 185–98.
49. Pike et al., "Educational Expenditures and Students Engagement," 850.
50. Krause, "Understanding and Promoting Student Engagement."
51. Hamrick et al., "Predicting Higher Education Graduation Rates."
52. *Ibid.*
53. Mezick, "Return on Investment," 561–6.
54. *Ibid.*, 564.

Bibliography

ACT. "More First-Year College Students Return for Second Year; Fewer Students Graduate in Five Years." *ACT News*, April 26, 2001. www.act.org/news/releases/2001/04-26-01.html [retrieved May 20, 2008]

American Council on Education. *Addressing the Challenges Facing American Undergraduate Education, A Letter to Our Members: Next Steps*, September 21, 2006. Washington, DC: American Council on Education, 2006. www.aau.edu/education/ACE_Attachment_9-21-06.pdf [retrieved May 23, 2008]

Applegate, Rachel. "Faculty Information Assignments: A Longitudinal Examination of Variations in Survey Results." *Journal of Academic Librarianship* 32, no. 4 (July 2006): 355–63.

Association of College and Research Libraries. "Information Literacy Competency Standards for Higher Education." Chicago: American Library Association, 2000. www.ala.org/ala/acrl/acrlstandards/standards.pdf [retrieved June 9, 2008]

Bruce, Christine Susan. "Information Literacy Programs and Research: An International Review." *Australian Library Journal* 49, no. 3 (August 2000): 209–18.

Dickenson, Don. *How Academic Libraries Help Faculty Teach and Students Learn: The Colorado Library Impact Study*. Denver CO: Library Research Service, Colorado State University and University of Denver, February 2006. www.LRS.org [retrieved June 27, 2007]

Eurich, Alvin C. "Students' Use of the Library: Seasonal Variation in the Use of a University Library." *Journal of Higher Education* 4, no. 8 (November 1933): 421–4.

Foster, Nancy Fried and Susan Gibbons, eds. *Studying Students: The Undergraduate Research Project at the University of Rochester*. Chicago: ALA-Association of College and Research Libraries, 2007.

Gardner, Susan, and Susanna Eng. "What Students Want: Generation Y and the Changing Function of the Academic Library." *portal: Libraries and the Academy* 5, no. 3 (July 2005): 405–20.

Gratch-Lindauer, Bonnie. "Comparing the Regional Accreditation Standards: Outcomes Assessment and Other Trends." *Journal of Academic Librarianship* 28, no. 1 (January–March 2002): 14–25.

Hamrick, Florence A., John H. Schuh, and Mack C. Shelley. "Predicting Higher Education Graduation Rates from Institutional Characteristics and Resource Allocation." *Education Policy Analysis Archives* 12, no. 19 (May 2004). http://epaa.asu.edu/epaa/v12n19/ [retrieved May 24, 2008]

Koufogiannakis, Denise and Natasha Wiebe. "Effective Methods for Teaching Information Literacy Skills to Undergraduate Students: A Systematic Review and Meta-Analysis." *Evidence Based Library and Information Practice* 1, no. 3 (2006): 3–43. http://ejournals.library.ualberta.ca/index.php/EBLIP/article/view/76/153 [retrieved June 9, 2008]

Krause, Kerri Lee. "Understanding and Promoting Student Engagement in University Learning Communities," keynote address presented at the James Cook University Symposium *Sharing Scholarship in Learning and Teaching: Engaging Students* held in Townsville/Cairns, Queensland (Australia) September 21–22, 2005. www.cshe.unimelb.edu.au/pdfs/Stud_eng.pdf [retrieved June 9, 2008]

Kuh, George D. and Robert M. Gonyea. "The Role of the Academic Library in Promoting Student Engagement in Learning." *College & Research Libraries* 64, no. 4 (April 2003): 256–82.

——, Polly D. Boruff-Jones, and Amy E. Mark. "Engaging Students in the First College Year: Why Academic Librarians Matter," in *The Role of the Library in the First College Year*, edited by Larry L. Hardesty. Columbia, SC: University of South Carolina, National Resource Center for the First-Year Experience and Students in Transition, 2007.

Mezick, Elizabeth M. "Return on Investment: Libraries and Student Retention." *Journal of Academic Librarianship* 33, no. 5 (September 2007): 561–6.

Nagata, Haruki, Akira Toda, and Paivi Kytomaki. "Students' Patterns of Library Use and Their Learning Outcomes." In *Proceedings of the 4th International Evidence Based Library & Information Practice Conference*. Chapel Hill, NC: University of North Carolina, 2007. www.eblip4.unc.edu/papers/Nagata.pdf [retrieved June 7, 2008]

National Science Foundation, "Higher Education in Science and Engineering." In *Science & Engineering Indicators 2008, Volume* 1 (2008): 2.4. www.nsf.gov/ statistics/seind08/pdf/c02.pdf [retrieved May 15, 2008]

OCLC, Inc. *College Students' Perceptions of Libraries and Information Resources*. Dublin, OH, 2006. www.oclc.org/reports/perceptionscollege.htm [retrieved February 6, 2008]

OECD. *Education at a Glance 2007*. Paris: OECD Directorate for Education, 2007. www.oecd.org/document/30/0,3343,en_2649_201185_39251550_1_1_1_1,00.html [retrieved May 22, 2008]

——. *Tertiary Education for the Knowledge Society*. Paris: OECD Directorate for Education April 2008. www.oecd.org/dataoecd/20/4/40345176.pdf [retrieved May 22, 2008]

Omehia, Anthonia E., Boma B. Obi, and Henry Itohowo Okon. "Student Characteristics and Use of Library Services in the University of Uyo." *Library Philosophy and Practice*, March 2008. www.webpages.uidaho.edu/~mbolin/omehia-obi-okon.htm [retrieved June 2, 2008]

Pike, Gary R. et al. "Educational Expenditures and Students Engagement: When Does Money Matter?" *Research in Higher Education* 47, no. 7 (November 2006): 847–72.

Rader, Hannelore B. "Information Literacy 1973–2002: A Selected Literature Review." *Library Trends* 71, no. 2 (Fall 2002): 242–59.

Rockman, Ilene F. "Strengthening Connections Between Information Literacy, General Education, and Assessment Efforts." *Library Trends* 51, no. 2 (Fall 2002): 185–98.

Shill, Harold B., and Shawn Tonner. "Does the Building Still Matter? Usage Patterns in New, Expanded and Renovated Libraries, 1995–2002." *College & Research Libraries* 65, no. 2 (March 2004):123–50.

Toda, Akira and Haruki Nagata, "Students' Library Use and Their Learning Outcomes: A Study on Outcomes Assessment in College and University Library," *Journal of the Japan Society of Library and Information Science* 53, no. 1 (2007): 17–34.

UNESCO Institute for Statistics. *Education Trends in Perspective—Analysis of the World Education Indicators*. Montreal: UNESCO Institute for Statistics, 2005. www.uis.unesco.org/ev.php?ID=6292_201&ID2=DO_TOPIC [retrieved May 22, 2008]

U.S. Department of Education. *A Test of Leadership: Charting the Future of U.S. Higher Education*. Washington, DC: September 2006. www.ed.gov/about/bdscomm/list/hiedfuture/reports/final-report.pdf [retrieved May 22, 2008]

Vondracek, Ruth. "Comfort and Convenience? Why Students Choose Alternatives to the Library." *portal: Libraries and the Academy* 7, no. 3 (July 2005): 277–93.

Weko, Thomas. "Executive Summary, New Dogs and Old Tricks: What Can the UK Teach the US about University Education?" Oxford: Higher Education Policy Institute, March 2004. www.hepi.ac.uk/pubdetail.asp?ID=123&DOC=Reports [retrieved May 24, 2008]

Whitmire, Ethelene. "A Longitudinal Study of Undergraduates' Academic Library Experiences." *Journal of Academic Librarianship* 27, no. 5 (September 2001): 379–85.

——. "The Relationship between Undergraduates' Background Characteristics and College Experiences and Their Academic Library Use." *College & Research Libraries* 62, no. 6 (November 2001): 528–40.

——. "Academic Library Performance Measures and Undergraduates' Library Use and Educational Outcomes." *Library & Information Science Research* 24, no. 2 (2002):107–28.

——. "Cultural Diversity and Undergraduates' Academic Library Use." *Journal of Academic Librarianship* 29, no. 3 (May 2003): 148–61.

Zhong, Ying and Johanna Alexander. "Academic Success: How Library Services Make a Difference." In *Proceedings of the ACRL 13th National Conference*, 141–8. Chicago: ALA-Association of College and Research Libraries, 2007.

9

User satisfaction as a quality indicator

Customer satisfaction has been extensively researched in the business environment since at least the 1950s, and in academic libraries since the mid 1980s. There is no single, agreed-upon definition of user or customer satisfaction in either the business or library literatures, and no agreed-upon standards for library user satisfaction. Satisfaction with a product or service is defined internally by individuals, and is a construct based upon sensory experience, personal perception, memory, personality, comparisons with similar past experiences, and shifting expectations. It seems simple at first—a library user is either satisfied or not—but becomes complicated when trying to measure a person's level of satisfaction, and even more complicated when trying to predict future behaviors based on a user's present level of satisfaction. Satisfaction is a temporary state, and may last only until the next need or desire presents itself. Being satisfied during one service encounter tends to increase the expectations for future encounters, and expectations ratchet upward whenever a competitor introduces a "new and improved" product or service, or one that is just as good, but more convenient or easier to use.

Is user satisfaction even important for academic libraries? Does it affect retention, time to degree, completion rates, faculty productivity or any of the other desirable faculty and student outcomes discussed earlier? Satisfaction with the library's collections, services, and facilities is the basis of use, and without users, the library will not survive. Satisfied library users are more likely to exhibit the same customer loyalty behaviors that business organizations rely upon for success: higher repeat business, faster acceptance of new services and products, and user recommendations to non-users. High satisfaction among users creates goodwill, credibility, and institutional capital for the library to draw upon in a competitive academic environment. It can also contribute to "brand" loyalty and commitment to the institution by faculty, current students, and alumni. In short, it is something every library wishes for its service operation.

Despite the slippery nature of satisfaction, an unavoidable fact is that no one can know a library user's level of satisfaction except that user, and there is no way to find out other than by asking directly. Thus, the research on satisfaction is based almost entirely on collecting information directly from users through survey, focus group and interview methods.

Approaches to satisfaction research

There are a number of approaches to determining customer satisfaction levels as market intelligence, and each offers a different insight into and purpose for collecting and using data about customer satisfaction, and by extension, into the related constructs of customer loyalty (repeat business, ready acceptance of new products, recommending products to others) and commitment (integrating the organization into other parts of a customer's life, e.g., making a donation of money, attending library events or programs, joining a Friends of the Library group, etc.). Satisfaction is part of the "Customer" perspective of the Balanced Scorecard system of strategic planning and management discussed in detail in an earlier chapter. Customer Relationship Management (CRM) is a set of methodologies, software, and internet and/or telephone capabilities that permit organizations to record and analyze business transactions at the individual customer level. Examples of industries where CRM is prevalent would include personal financial management, banking, or other enterprises that collect data, usually online, about individual user needs and past buying behaviors to predict future needs and buying behaviors, to selectively offer new products, and to encourage long-term relationships. Because the customer has many choices among competing businesses, these organizations rely upon long-term customer loyalty to stay in business, and typically operate in market sectors that have higher costs for capturing new customers. Simultaneous Multi Attribute Level Trade Offs (SIMALTO) is a well-developed survey methodology that offers customers all possible combinations of benefits and costs, allowing organizations to make logical decisions on products and services on the basis of exact customer preferences, and to identify "tipping points" between the costs and benefits of specific features.

Certainly the most familiar and widely used model in academic libraries is based on SERVQUAL, which uses the disconfirmation theory of satisfaction. That is, the measure of satisfaction is the mathematical result of the difference between a user's perception of actual service received, minus the user's incoming expectation for service. Disconfirmation theory proposes the resulting number, whether negative or positive, represents the gap between expectation and experience, i.e.

perception of service – expectation for service = satisfaction (+ *or* – *gap score*)

This concept is the basis of the LibQUAL+® service quality survey, developed by the Association for Research Libraries (ARL), and which has been used by numerous academic libraries in the United States, Canada, Australia, New Zealand, the United Kingdom, France, Ireland, the Netherlands, Switzerland, Germany, Denmark, Finland, Norway, Sweden, Egypt, the United Arab Emirates, and South Africa. A shorter version of the original 22-item questionnaire, LibQUAL+® Lite, is currently in development. Although LibQUAL+® identifies itself as a survey of users' perceptions of service quality rather than a satisfaction survey, it is popularly taken to be a satisfaction measurement tool. So much has been written about LibQUAL+®, and in such great detail, that interested readers are referred to the chapter bibliography for direction to the recent literature.

Because user satisfaction, however it is measured, is temporary and malleable, it should not be isolated to a single measurement tool, such as the results of an annual survey. It is useful to note that all types of customer satisfaction surveys reveal between 65 and 85 percent of customers as satisfied customers, and this result has been found across thousands of trials in all business sectors. Despite these relatively high reported levels of satisfaction, business organizations continue to experience some level of complaint and customer loss. This tendency for people to report higher levels of satisfaction than they actually experience is what the gap score between perceived and expected satisfaction attempts to correct. It also begs the use of additional measures to support user reports of satisfaction. There are multiple measures to support user assessments of satisfaction, and these include some of the familiar performance indicators, e.g., door count, circulation count, service use counts, etc. These related performance measures can serve as proxy or confirming measures of satisfaction. That is, they would be expected to co-vary positively with satisfaction. For example, if users indicated that they were well satisfied with collections, use data for collections would be better than average or better than expected, and should increase or decrease along with user reports of satisfaction. Some service quality experts say user satisfaction is the only thing that matters and that nothing else is relevant, but traditional performance indicators can provide supporting evidence to confirm users' reported levels of satisfaction. If there are disconnects between what users say about their level of satisfaction and their actual behaviors, further investigation would be required to determine the source of the discrepancy. Using traditional performance indicators to support satisfaction measures has some advantages and disadvantages. They are more objective because they are observable behaviors, are easier to quantify, and are easier to define and compare with other libraries. However, when used alone, they are not valid measures of satisfaction because satisfaction can only be imputed to them.

User-centered research

Attempts to explore user satisfaction, regardless of the method selected, begin with interacting with users, and perhaps the greatest challenge is defining the purpose of the research and deciding exactly what it is the library wishes to know.

Does satisfaction mean how happy a user is at the end of a specific transaction? Does it mean how happy a user is with a particular library service or product? Does it mean how happy a user is with his/her overall experience in the library? Does it mean happiness with the eventual outcome of the service? Does it mean usefulness of the library resources discovered by the user? Does it mean a user completely and totally satisfied, or just satisfied enough not to complain? Does satisfaction mean that an agreed-upon objective standard has been met?

User-centered measures of satisfaction in academic libraries have typically been derived from three methodologies: unmediated survey (paper or online), focus group, and key informant interview. Other common methods include soliciting comments and complaints online or on-site and collecting spontaneous or prepared testimonials from faculty and students. These can be insightful, but are not descriptive of entire service populations. There are disadvantages to user-centered data collection as a gauge of satisfaction. Responses will be entirely subjective perceptions, are dependent upon the willingness of users to take part and the accuracy of the sample, and usually leave out non-users. But again, there is no way to know the mind of the user otherwise, and user opinions are the only ones that matter according to service quality experts. The customer is always right. The challenge is to select the most appropriate method for collecting data, clearly define the library's purpose and objectives for the research, and design a set of effective questions.

Survey research

In survey research, the tendency of those genuinely curious to learn about user satisfaction is to rush into questionnaire development, which should be instead the final task prior to implementation. Before questionnaire development, the surveyors must determine the objectives of the survey, decide exactly what they wish to learn and from whom, make decisions about how much data will be collected and for how long, plan how the results will be tabulated and interpreted, and how and to whom the results will be disseminated. A key decision prior to questionnaire development is to determine whether the survey will be a one-off administration, or repeated over time, such as annually. If the survey is to be administered annually, for how many years should it be planned? If the survey will be administered repeatedly over a period of time, what environmental changes might the surveyors reasonably predict during that period, e.g., opening a new facility, improvements in technology that become available, etc.? Equally important to determining the interval between survey administrations is to consider the library's reasonable capacity for action to improve quality during the intervening periods. If a source of dissatisfaction is suspected, or actually identified in survey results, is it actionable during the interval period? Are sources of suspected dissatisfaction under the library's control? If not, then questionnaire items are wasted on the issue and may even imply to users that the library can and will do something to alleviate the problem once it has been identified. There is no advantage to including survey questions asked out of curiosity, or to surveying users repeatedly if no corrective action is taken as a result of survey findings. *There is no intrinsic value in measurement isolated from action.* Or, as the farmers' saying has it, "You can weigh a cow every day, but that doesn't make her any fatter."

There are two common approaches to satisfaction surveys: transaction surveys, which are administered at the point of service to individual users, and total quality surveys, which are administered to a sample of, or to the entire user population.

Transaction surveys ask directly about the users' immediate experiences before they can forget them and before they can generalize their responses to previous library transactions or to their entire history of library use. Transaction, or point-of-service surveys are most often used to determine satisfaction with a particular department or departmental service, e.g., reference, circulation, computer use, etc., but can also be delivered as the user exits the library. They capture only users of the service during a specific period, but are useful in pinpointing local quality issues such as staffing levels, staff performance, or adequacy of computer workstations. Some suggestions for transaction survey development include:

- Limit the survey to no more than three or four questions about a specific transaction or library experience. If there are more questions, consider using multiple versions of the survey and rotate versions.

- Depending upon the volume of transactions, determine whether you will survey all users or a sample, e.g., every third or fourth user.

- Survey multiple days and multiple times until you reach a previously determined participant volume. Do not stop the survey if the early results seem conclusive, e.g., the first 25 or 50 users report similar a level of satisfaction.

- Set up a parallel complaint-handling process during the survey period and address specific complaints as soon as possible after receipt.

Below are general suggestions for all types of surveys.

- **Be brief:** Avoid long, introductory explanations and explain the purpose of the survey in simple sentences. Ask the most important questions first, before the user has the opportunity to become impatient and rush through the survey. The first question should be intriguing and easy to answer. It should make the respondents feel they are knowledgeable and have something worthwhile to contribute, e.g., "As a graduate student who uses the book collection, how satisfied are you with the collection in your area of study?" Do not offer too many choices for item responses, as there is a bias for respondents to choose the last answer from a long list.

- **Be clear:** Use common terms and avoid library jargon entirely. If you must use an unusual term, define it for the user. Avoid hypothetical questions, e.g., "If the library were open longer, would you use it more often?" Ask for opinions rather than facts, e.g., "I think the library staff are discourteous to faculty," rather than, "The library staff are not courteous to faculty."

- **Be direct:** If several response choices are offered, they should be mutually exclusive and distinct, e.g., "too difficult" and "too complicated" mean the same thing in the minds of many. Avoid questions that can be answered "don't know" or "does not apply." Do not combine multiple questions into one, e.g., "Estimate your level of satisfaction with the online catalog and the ease with which you are able to find books in the library."

- **Be respectful:** Do not phrase questions in a manner that implies suspicion of a user's motives or introduces a negative concept, e.g., "Would you use computers more frequently if you had more instruction on their use?" Avoid offering a response choice such as "because I wait until the last minute to do library assignments." Do not ask for demographic information such as age or gender unless it has a bearing on the ability to improve the library's performance. If it is useful to let respondents know how long it will take to complete the survey, simply say "This survey takes approximately 10 minutes to complete," rather than "This survey will only take 10 minutes of your time." No one has so much time that its value should be minimized or diminished. Thank all respondents for their participation and accept turn-downs gracefully.

Focus group research

Focus groups are face-to-face interviews with a group of potential or actual users. Discussions are led by a single facilitator and documented either by recording the session (with permission) or by a note-taker. Focus groups are generally used for one of two purposes—to explore the participants' beliefs or opinions about the library, or to follow up on information revealed by a previous survey. Exploratory focus groups can be used to test responses to new initiatives or the acceptability of policy or service changes, to identify barriers to user satisfaction, or to understand the strength and character of user dissatisfaction. Follow-up focus groups seek deeper understanding of an issue or problem, usually identified in a survey, by clarifying or interpreting meaning from the users' point of view, discovering misunderstandings, and asking additional questions. Focus groups can be particularly useful in understanding or interpreting conflicting results from survey questions. For example, it would not be shocking for an undergraduate survey to reveal that 50 percent of respondents think the library is too noisy and 50 percent think they should be able to talk loudly and use their cell phones wherever they like in the library. A focus group could provide some insight into what types of user prefer quiet, for what purpose, and when and where quiet is especially important. Participants might even be able to make acceptable suggestions for resolving the conflict between the two "camps" of users.

Below are some considerations and suggestions for planning focus group discussions.

- The group should include no more than six to ten participants, involve no more than five or six questions, and last no longer than 90 minutes.

- Participants should be people with similarities (e.g. graduate students) or who are members of the same group (e.g. all members of the same department or school), but who do not know one another well. Eliminate participants whom you know to have an ax to grind, or whose concerns and ideas are already known.

- The facilitator should not be a member of the library staff. Library staff members have an ingrained service response, i.e., to offer explanations and rationales, to provide additional information and examples, and to answer questions directly. If participants have questions about library practices or policies the facilitator should ask the note-taker to write them down for referral to the appropriate library authority. The note-taker should not sit at the table with the group or speak to the group and should remain as unobtrusive as possible.

- Whenever possible, do not wait more than five minutes for latecomers. Get the group involved in the interview as quickly as possible. Begin with factual questions before moving on to questions of opinion or feeling and ask questions about the present before asking about the past or the future. These techniques help anchor the group, provide a structure, and get the participants on task before unrelated conversations begin.

- The skilled facilitator often prearranges a brief interruption, e.g., to take a phone call, and leaves the room for a few minutes at some point late in the discussion. This action anticipates that during those few minutes alone, participants are more likely to express their truest beliefs or feelings, which might otherwise be held back out of politeness or respect.

- The session should close by giving participants a final opportunity to comment on the topic, or on any other library topic of their choice.

Key informant interviews

Personal, one-on-one interviews are directed toward understanding a person's knowledge, motivations, or the basis of their opinions and deep beliefs. The key informant approach involves identifying and selecting persons of some stature and influence; persons who have special knowledge, experience or perspective, and who are in a position to accurately articulate the needs of an entire service population or an institution. Examples of key informant pools for library operations research would include faculty curriculum committees, deans, department chairs, groups of distinguished research faculty members, higher-level IT staff, student library employees, library department heads, etc. Key informant interviews are useful for discovering what the most influential members of service populations or key administrators think about the library, determining the strength of their support for library initiatives or changes, understanding what faculty across an institution might believe, or learning how key informants make decisions external to the library, but that affect the library.

There are a number of advantages to conducting key informant interviews. They are relatively quick and inexpensive and do not require the development of a complex questionnaire. It is much easier to schedule a single informant at his or her convenience than to schedule a group meeting, and interviews can be conducted over the phone. Key informants are limited in number, so the selection or sampling process is easier. Conducting key informant interviews can provide legitimacy and credibility not always associated with larger population surveys. Being able to share with others the results of key informant interviews can be impressive, e.g., "The most distinguished researchers in the university believe our collections need to be strengthened by the inclusion of ...," "Based on their career histories, deans of the university believe services provided by our library to be outstanding."

Key informant interviews can also have disadvantages, and interview results are not scientific in the statistical sense. Information gathered is often general and impressionistic, and does not represent a cross-section of the population. The key informant perspective can be colored by bias against the institution and completely unrelated to library operations. The number of key informants interviewed may be too small to make meaningful within-group comparisons or across-group statements, and because they are busy people, key informants can be difficult to schedule during a short interval of time, e.g., the same week. However, key informant interviews can be more useful and yield more significant information than other methods, particularly when exploring how library policy affects larger service populations, or when external support, collaboration, or partnerships are required to plan and implement new library initiatives.

Analyzing qualitative data from user-centered research

Qualitative data must be analyzed even though statistical tests and measures are not appropriate, and there are some basic steps for analyzing qualitative information. These can be applied to respondents' oral comments or statements during focus group or interview sessions, written comments offered at the end of survey questionnaires, and "suggestion box" or web-based comments offered by library users. The basic steps are to gather the text of the responses and read, organize, label, and count them, identify patterns, and write a written summary. A small group, i.e., three or four people, should read the comments or transcripts at one sitting, and read them again at a further sitting a few days later. This small group will perform the analysis and at its first meeting will organize the comments into similar categories, e.g., concerns, complaints, praise, suggestions, strengths, weaknesses, similar experiences, etc. At a subsequent meeting the group will label the categories by theme, e.g., collections, noise, staff issues, service desks, hours of library operations, etc. Comments can be additionally coded as positive, negative or neutral. If there are enough responses and/or partial responses, comments in labeled categories can be counted and rank-ordered to identify priority issues. In addition to identifying priority issues, there may be patterns in the comments that are associated with certain conditions, e.g., all who used the library in the evenings made similar comments, newer faculty or students were unaware of a library service, graduate students misunderstood a basic policy, etc. One member of the group should summarize the results by category, theme, priority and pattern, with the rest of the group serving as readers and drawing conclusions. Regardless of the results, the report should be distributed as widely as possible.

User satisfaction is an elusive concept, and satisfaction can be difficult to measure accurately, but satisfaction constitutes the basis of continued library use. If library users are dissatisfied, they are disinclined to return, to expand their own library use, or to explore the library, and they may share their dissatisfaction with others. Satisfied library users are more likely to exhibit the same customer loyalty behaviors that business organizations rely upon for success: higher repeat business, faster acceptance of new services and products, and user recommendations to non-users. High satisfaction among users creates goodwill, credibility, and institutional capital for the library to draw upon. Information on satisfaction can be used for strategic planning and evaluation, to develop long-term relationships with customers, and to develop a competitive edge. The most widely used standardized tool for gauging satisfaction among academic library service populations is currently the LibQUAL+® survey, which is based on the disconfirmation theory of satisfaction. Other user-centered approaches to gauging user satisfaction include transactional and general surveys, focus groups and key informant interviews.

Bibliography

Andaleeb, Syed Saad and Patience L. Simmonds. "Explaining User Satisfaction with Academic Libraries: Strategic Implications." *College & Research Libraries* 59, no. 2 (March 1998): 156–67.

Becher, Melissa L. and Janice L. Flug. "Using Student Focus Groups to Inform Library Planning and Marketing." *College & Undergraduate Libraries* 12, no. 1/2 (2005): 1–18.

Calvert, Philip J. "A Different Time, A Different Country: An Instrument for Measuring Service Quality in Singapore's Polytechnic Libraries." *Journal of Academic Librarianship* 24, no. 4 (July 1998): 296–303.

——, and Peter Hernon. "Surveying Service Quality within University Libraries." *Journal of Academic Librarianship* 23, no. 5 (September 1997): 408–15.

Creaser, Claire. "User Surveys in Academic Libraries." *New Review of Academic Librarianship* 12, no. 1 (2006): 1–15.

——. "One Size Does Not Fit All: User Surveys in Academic Libraries." *Performance Measurement and Metrics* 7, no. 3 (2006): 153–62.

Cullen, Rowena. "Perspectives on User Satisfaction Surveys." *Library Trends* 49, no. 4 (Spring 2001): 662–86.

—— and Philip J. Calvert. "Stakeholder Perceptions of University Library Effectiveness." *Journal of Academic Librarianship* 21, no. 6 (November 1995): 438–48.

Franklin, Brinley and Terry Plum. "Successful Web Survey Methodologies for Measuring the Impact of Networked Electronic Services (MINES for Libraries)." *IFLA Journal* 32, no. 1 (2006): 28–40.

Hernon, Peter, Danuta A. Nitecki, and Ellen Altman. "Service Quality and Customer Satisfaction: An Assessment and Future Directions." *Journal of Academic Librarianship* 25, no. 1 (January 1999): 9–17.

—— and John R. Whitman. *Delivering Satisfaction and Service Quality: A Customer-Based Approach for Libraries.* Chicago: American Library Association, 2001.

Jeng, Judy. "Usability Assessment of Academic Digital Libraries: Effectiveness, Efficiency, Satisfaction, and Learnability." *Libri* 55, no. 2/3 (June/September 2005): 96–115.

Lynch, Beverly P., Catherine Murray-Rust, and Susan E. Parker. "Attitudes of Presidents and Provosts on the University Library." *College & Research Libraries* 68, no. 3 (May 2007): 213–27.

McGregor, Felicity. "Exploring the Mystery of Service Satisfaction." Paper presented at the 6th Northumbria International Conference on Performance Measurement in Libraries and Information Services. Durham, England, August 22–25, 2005. Author version at http://ro.uow.edu.au/asdpapers/29

Miller, Lynette. "User Satisfaction Surveys." *Australasian Public Libraries and Information Services* 17, no. 3 (September 2004): 125–33.

Parasuraman, A. "Assessing and Improving Service Performance for Maximum Impact: Insights from a Two-Decade-Long Research Journey." *Performance Measurement and Metrics* 5, no. 2 (2004): 45–55.

Saw, Grace and Nicole Clark. "Reading Rodski: User Surveys Revisited." In *Proceedings of the 25th Conference of the International Association of Technological University Libraries.* Auckland: International Association of Technological University Libraries, 2004. http://iatul.org/conference/pastconferences/2004conferences.asp

Shi, Xi and Sarah Levy. "A Theory-Guided Approach to Library Services Assessment." *College & Research Libraries* 66, no. 2 (May 2005): 266–77.

10

Using group norms and peer comparisons as contexts for quality

It seems intuitive to seek quality assurance by determining an institution's status and comparing it to the relative status of its institutional peers. Collection of data on standardized measures for comparison across institutional members of a group is a long-standing and widespread practice in higher education. Lists of standards and rankings abound, and are becoming more competitive than ever. In the minds of many, status ratings and rankings are indicative of the relative, if not absolute, quality of institutions in higher education.

Some ranking or rating systems have become popular as consumer guides (sometimes referred to as "league tables") to help potential students select the best college or university "fit." Since 1983, *US News & World Report* has released grouped rankings of "American's Best Colleges."[1] Since 1998, The Princeton Review has periodically released a report, "The Best ... Colleges," selecting somewhere around 300 of the "best" US colleges based on the results of student surveys.[2] *The Times* (UK) releases a similar report, the "Good University Guide."[3]

More recently, national and world university ranking systems have been established and have drawn enough attention to become the topic of a series of annual international symposia held at the University of Leiden, which also publishes a ranked list of the best 100 European universities based entirely on faculty productivity bibliometrics.[4] One of the more interesting and controversial efforts to devise a rubric for world university rankings was launched in 2003 by Shanghai Jiao Tong University, the "Academic World Ranking of Universities" or ARWU.[5] The "Shanghai Rankings" were developed for the purpose of Chinese universities to determine their position among world-class universities and identify and work toward improvement, but quickly provoked curiosity and some criticism on an international scale. The Shanghai

Rankings cover approximately 500 universities and are heavily based on faculty productivity bibliometrics in the sciences. One year later, in 2004, The *Times Higher Education Supplement* published its first list of "World University Rankings."[6] *The Times*'s annual lists also include about 500 universities, and rankings are based on peer review, faculty productivity bibliometrics, and the proportion of international faculty and students at each institution. Somewhat more flexible than the Shanghai Rankings, the World University Rankings are subdivided into national and regional rankings and broad fields of study, e.g., arts and humanities, life science and biomedicine, social sciences, etc. Many influential stakeholder groups in higher education, and at individual universities, have become strongly attached to comparative indicators as evidence of the relative quality of individual institutions. Although many may doubt their real meaning and usefulness, an equal number seem addicted to size and status rankings as evidence of quality, and academic libraries have not been immune to the lure of creating their own rating and ranking systems.

Gathering and reporting data on standardized performance measures across academic libraries is a common practice. Once large national or association data sets are collected, normative statistics such as averages, percentiles, and rankings can be calculated or extrapolated in any number of ways. Performance indicators such as those developed and/or used by IFLA (international), OIS (international), ARL (large libraries in the US and Canada), CAUL (Australia and New Zealand), SCONUL (UK and Ireland), NCES (US), BIX (Germany) and ASIBU (France) can be shared among academic libraries, and some of the agencies maintain searchable interfaces to their databases. The varieties and uses of standardized performance indicators for academic libraries are discussed at length in Chapter 4, and perhaps the best single access point to complete information about national standards, guidelines, performance indicators, and comparative tools is a web page created and maintained by IFLA.[7]

Why compare your library to other libraries?

Despite their debatable usefulness as absolute evidence of quality, statistical norms for grouped libraries and one-on-one library comparisons serve some very practical purposes. Internally, they can help libraries to set actual and target benchmarks, identify or confirm library strengths and weaknesses, and help set future goals. When shared externally, they can help library cohort groups to identify common problems and spur collaborative problem-solving efforts, communicate goals and needs to library staff and university administrators, and communicate their special assets or distinctions. In some cases, library statistics are used as a basis for peer-equity funding by government agencies. In many cases, tracking library statistics and contributing them to the designated collection agency is mandatory for receipt of federal, state, or regional funding, or is regularly reported in some form to an accrediting or auditing body. The practice also ensures transparency for public institutions and encourages the free exchange of information. In short, the tradition of collecting performance indicators and resource inputs/outputs and using them to compare across groups is firmly embedded in the culture of higher education and not likely to disappear anytime soon.

Peer and cohort comparisons

A higher and perhaps more meaningful purpose for systems of classification, rating, and ranking is to identify institutions similar to one's own, and compare overall institutional and library statistics. Institutions identified for general comparison are referred to as "peer institutions" or "peer group institutions." Comparison peer institutions can be either "actual" peers or "aspiration" peers. Actual peers are institutions that have been grouped by an agency on the basis of similarities of purpose and mission, level and number of degrees offered, full-time equivalent enrollments, and other gross measures. "Aspiration" peers are selected by an individual institution to represent a model, or what the institution might strive to become in the future. Lists of designated peer groups have been generated by jurisdictional and funding agencies, but may not always represent the best peer groups for library comparisons. Such lists have usually been developed from highly statistical, multivariate, cluster or factor analyses that compare gross institutional characteristics, but not fine programmatic distinctions that would be important for making academic library comparisons. Most institutions have unique features or situations, such as their academic libraries, and prefer a panel approach to identifying individual peers and peer groups for libraries. The panel approach is non-statistical and relies on the informed judgment of a group with specialized knowledge about an institutional program or function. Academic libraries will frequently choose library peers outside their institution's designated peer group because of library considerations not included in the institution's classification methodology, e.g., specialized collections, similarities in the intensity of library technology used, strength of information literacy programs, seating capacity, character of student body, etc.

In general, institutional classifications are based on gross features such as mission and purpose; full-time equivalent enrollment; number of faculty members; number, level, and type of degrees offered and degrees awarded; and funding from all sources, including grants and contracts. Gross indicators are useful to establish a pool from which libraries can refine a smaller list of library peers for comparison. Important library characteristics for consideration in refining peer groups might include the age of the institution, which affects print collection size and depth. The oldest established libraries have been collecting so much longer and have such large print volume collections that newer institutions, whatever their current funding levels, would never be likely to catch up in terms of size alone. Total library materials expenditures from all sources and total staff size may be more important factors to consider in selecting peers than collection size. Setting may have a profound effect on library use patterns, and the residential or urban nature of the institution, as well as the number of branch libraries, would be important considerations for selecting peer libraries.

Accreditation and quality audits

As a rule, accrediting bodies do not compare institutions or their libraries to one another, but compare the assets, activities, and outcomes of the institution under review to a pre-determined set of qualitative standards. Requirements for data and supporting evidence about the library vary by accrediting body, but in general, the institution must demonstrate maintenance and access to "adequate" library collections and provide library services "adequate" to achieve its mission, goals, and objectives. In addition to information about how the institution meets a set of pre-determined standards, accrediting bodies have begun to request either as a separate document, or combined with the standard report, a quality audit and plan for quality improvement. Evidence of quality improvement, discussed at length in Chapter 3 of this book, is based largely on outcome data, reversing the past practice of using resource or efficiency-based measures, and has changed the emphasis for academic library reporting. In the US, the trend has been toward integrating library impacts, particularly information literacy, into broad student outcomes and measures of student engagement, and away from reporting data on traditional library performance indicators. In some cases, a formerly required separate reporting section on library services and resources has been eliminated altogether, with the library's contribution evidenced throughout in other relevant sections of the report.

Communicating the results

Regardless of the intended purpose or application of information collected about the library, comparative or otherwise, and evidence gathered to demonstrate its contributions on an institutional level, some type of report(s) will be produced. When the results are dismaying to the library, or in some way or other suspect, the practice too often has been to simply disregard them or soften the reporting. This is a bad practice and should be avoided. If libraries truly wish to improve, then all information is valuable. Unless there are gross errors in methodology or rigor, or the object of the measurement is something no one cares about anyway, bad news can be a tangible payoff and provide an essential basis for planning quality improvements. This key conviction differentiates the fruitless exercise in measurement from finding the truest direction to make lasting improvements in quality. All valid findings should be reported as widely as possible within the library and the institution, and to interested external stakeholders. Widely used venues for publication of library study results have included a dean or director's "state of the library" address to library staff, articles in student newspapers, library internal and external newsletters, the library's website, faculty and staff newsletters, library conference presentations, and presentations to groups of institutional deans and directors, and presentations to teaching faculty.

Notes

1. Owens, ed., *America's Best Colleges 2008*.
2. Franek, *The 366 Best Colleges*.
3. Times Higher Education Supplement, *Good University Guide*.
4. Leiden University, Center for Science and Technology Studies, *The Leiden Ranking*.

5. Shanghai Jiao Tong University, Institute of Higher Education, *Academic Ranking of World Universities*. [Retrieved June 24, 2008 from http://ed.sjtu.edu.cn/ranking.htm]
6. Times Higher Education—QS, *World University Rankings*. [Retrieved July 7, 2008 from www.topuniversities.com/worlduniversityrankings/]
7. IFLA, *Information Resources on Library Statistics and Performance Measures*.

Bibliography

Dalrymple, Prudence. "Understanding Accreditation: The Librarian's Role in Educational Evaluation." *portal: Libraries and the Academy* 1, no. 1 (January 2001): 23–32.

Franek, Robert et al. *The 366 Best Colleges*. New York: The Princeton Review, 2008.

Gatten, Jeffrey N. "Academic Quality Improvement Project (AQIP) and Accreditation: When Assessment is not Optional." In *Proceedings of the 4th Northumbria International Conference on Performance Measurement in Library and Information Services*, 113–17. Washington, DC: Association of Research Libraries, 2002.

Gratch-Lindauer, Bonnie. "Comparing the Regional Accreditation Standards: Outcomes Assessment and Other Trends." *Journal of Academic Librarianship* 28, no. 1 (January/March 2002): 14–25.

Hurley, Rodney G. "Identification and Assessment of Community College Peer Institution Selection Systems." *Community College Review* 29, no. 4 (Spring 2002): 1–16.

IFLA, *Information Resources on Library Statistics and Performance Measures*. www.ifla.org/VII/s22/statlinks.htm#IRL [retrieved June 24, 2008]

Owens, Eric, ed. *America's Best Colleges 2008*. New York: US News & World Report, 2007. http://colleges.usnews.rankingsandreviews.com/usnews/edu/college/rankings/rankindex_brief.php [retrieved July 7, 2008]

Leiden University, Center for Science and Technology Studies, *The Leiden Ranking*. www.cwts.nl/cwts/LeidenRankingWebSite.html [retrieved July 7, 2008]

Schwarz, Stefanie, and Don F. Westerheijden, eds. *Accreditation and Evaluation in the European Higher Education Area*. Dordrecht: Kluwer Academic Publishers, 2004.

Shanghai Jiao Tong University. *Academic Ranking of World Universities*. Shanghai: Jiao Tong University, Institute of Higher Education, 2007. http://ed.sjtu.edu.cn/ranking.htm

Times Higher Education—QS. *World University Rankings*. London: Times Higher Education, 2007. www.topuniversities.com/worlduniversityrankings/

Times Higher Education Supplement. *Good University Guide*. London: The Times Online, August 13, 2008. www.timesonline.co.uk/tol/life_and_style/education/good_university_guide/ [retrieved July 7, 2008]

Windham, Patricia. "Using Centralized Data Systems for Institutional Assessment." *Assessment Update* 12, no 6 (November 2000): 4.

11

Toward surviving the future

Left to their own devices, most academicians and academic librarians would ignore changes in their world and continue the familiar practices of the past. Considerable anxiety over assessment, evaluation, accountability, and quality control has been raised during the past quarter-century, and this anxiety has often risen to the level of fear—of losing control of daily operation of the library; of a forced abandonment of the notion of the library's role in scholarship, replaced by expectations from the business world; and of being marginalized within a marginal parent institution. These fears reflect very real fears of the parent institution. Politicians, policy makers and funding authorities have their own sets of expectations for the future. In order to survive the future intact, academic libraries must face the uncertain and commit to accountability, quality control and quality improvement. Failure to do so may result in suspicion on the part of decision makers and funding authorities that academics believe they should be exempt from accountability. One might also wonder how much of the reluctance to embrace a future grounded in accountability might be rooted in librarians' own self-doubts about the contribution of the academic library to faculty, student, and institutional success.

Making a commitment to quality would have several beneficial effects, one of which would be to establish the academic library as a model for the rest of its parent institution. Such a commitment will not be easy and will require fundamental changes in the operations of most academic libraries. Most of all, it will take time—time to alter the way in which academic libraries have organized themselves, delivered services, managed resources, made decisions, and planned for the future.

Several management tools are available to academic librarians that can facilitate their commitment to accountability and assessment for quality improvement. Most of these have been developed outside the academic world, but have been adapted or modified to apply to academe. Globally, only a handful of academic libraries have employed some of these tools, and they appear to have done so in isolation. Library directors must determine for themselves whether they are prepared to make the leadership commitment to ensure the successful integration of assessment and accountability into the fabric of the library. Such leadership cannot be delegated.

All academic librarians should make the commitment to conduct Lakos's "Culture of Assessment" survey to understand their library's current organizational position in terms of assessment. The results of the survey will provide them with the beginnings of an understanding of the work that lies before them. Library directors need to confront the cultural reality of the library before any progress can begin and the library staff can start their education in assessment. Moving too quickly toward a commitment to assessment and accountability, or taking action prior to developing a culture of assessment, may do more long-term harm than good.

When a library is ready to move forward from this point, there are quality excellence frameworks that can be utilized to gain a thorough understanding of the library organization. Global regional frameworks, such as the Malcolm Baldrige National Quality Award, the European Framework for Quality Management, the Australian Business Excellence Framework, or any of the various national quality frameworks are available to academic libraries. All require a commitment of scarce library resources—time and money—to be of long-term value. The results of these framework assessments will be sobering because they will no doubt expose any deficiencies in the library's operations and organizational structure. Library directors must take the key leadership role in such analyses so the results can be used carefully and in a manner that is positive and non-threatening. This is a very difficult leadership goal to accomplish.

The results of a quality framework analysis provide information for strategic planning that is more than just a "make-work" exercise or the basis of yet another annual report. The usual library approach to strategic planning stops at the identification of goals and objectives, and omits performance targets, action plans, benchmarks or milestones, and statements of desired outcomes with their companion metrics.

The Balanced Scorecard approach to measurement complements strategic planning as a tool to measure change. One advantage to the scorecard is its forced choice of a small number of critical metrics. Few libraries have adopted the scorecard approach and integrated it with management activities, let alone into their decision-making processes.

Until such a vital connection between assessment and improvement is made, it remains unlikely that academic libraries will be successful in long-term assessment of anything they do. The Balanced Scorecard requires librarians to think critically about those activities, services, and collections that are most important to the library's success. The scorecard requires librarians to acknowledge and understand the relationships between the financial, customer, internal processes, and learning and growth perspectives of the library, and to develop the rigor in evaluation and assessment so often avoided in the past.

One singular advantage of the Balanced Scorecard is that it requires the identification of a limited number of indicators for monitoring. This goes against the grain of academic librarians, who historically have collected masses of data regardless of their meaningful value even to themselves, much less to external stakeholders. If academic librarians are going to be successful in demonstrating their contribution to institutional outcomes, they will have to engage in thoughtful consideration of the indicators that will provide the most accurate assessment of their value. We might prefer to avoid this activity, for it is the ultimate measure of accountability.

Standardized library performance indicators are extremely useful for peer and cohort comparisons, and collecting data for comparison to institutional peers is a long-standing and widespread practice in higher education. In the minds of many administrators and some potential students, status ratings and rankings are indicative of the relative, if not absolute, quality of institutions in higher education. However, they are not outcome-based measures, and say little about the perceived value or actual benefits imparted to faculty and students' success.

Value should be determined by the receivers of the benefits, not by the provider. Most standardized indicators are based on amounts of resources expended or measure the efficiency of library operations and can be useful for librarians and administrators, but they are not transformative activities that improve library quality. In order to plan quality improvements, the essential and first task is to ask broad questions of faculty and students, and to listen to the answers.

Too often, we tend to think of the efforts undertaken in data collection as the end instead of the means, and our facilities, collections, and services as a banquet laid out for diners. We wait for them to partake, and then count what they have eaten. There is no intrinsic value in data collection and comparison. However, there is value in data collection as part of a program of transformational assessment when the results are directed toward making the quality improvements that have a direct relationship with student and faculty success.

Large studies of faculty in many countries indicate that the library's most significant contribution to their research, publication, and grant-writing success has been in saving them time at critical and self-determined points in these processes; almost as if they prefer calling the ambulance when critically ill to seeing a physician regularly. Being expert learners, they want a relationship with the library only when it has an immediate benefit for them. This is counter to the way the academic library has done business in the past, but is also counter to reality. The library must change its approach and develop metrics to capture the outcome in terms of transactional success in helping faculty meet their research goals.

As to faculty teaching goals, they may view information literacy instruction more appropriately as a general responsibility of students—a choice to be made by learners. This leaves one to wonder whether the large information literacy message should be directed toward individual faculty members, or whether it is better directed toward curriculum planners in the general education core. Libraries have done little serious outreach to part-time faculty members who, as a group, teach a disproportionate number of students; something between 25 and 65 percent of all classes. In order to impact teaching across a university, this oversight cries out for correction.

In contrast to faculty members, research on how graduate students use their libraries indicates that this group needs and wants personal contact with a librarian. Graduate students may attribute different benefits to library use than librarians intend, but customized assistance at the point of need is especially desired during the dissertation-writing period, and the more interdisciplinary their topics, the greater their need. Because they are becoming expert learners in their disciplines, they are far more likely than undergraduates to take responsibility for acquiring the information literacy skills necessary for their individual academic success, and later, their career success. One fertile approach may be to reach these students at transitional points in time—during recruitment, at orientation, or at the beginning of the proposal-writing process.

Studies of undergraduate library-use patterns across time and countries indicate that academic libraries remain central to the provision of an adequate learning environment, and that this learning environment benefits students through improved student engagement, and for some, improved academic performance. The widespread improvement of undergraduates' information literacy skills through library engagement is in an early period of development, and is likely to remain so until it becomes a priority within institutions. However, as an investment of institutional capital, the library does return enormous value for money, and library expenditures may tend to improve retention and completion.

User satisfaction is an elusive concept, and satisfaction can be difficult to measure accurately, but satisfaction constitutes a user's basis for continued library use. If library users are dissatisfied, they are disinclined to return, to expand their own library use, to explore the library, and they may share their dissatisfaction with others. High satisfaction among users creates goodwill, credibility, and institutional capital for the library to draw upon. Information on satisfaction can be used for strategic planning and evaluation, to develop long-term relationships with customers, and to develop a competitive edge.

If academic librarians can persuade themselves to use the available assessment tools discussed in the early chapters of this book, and in their proper sequence, they may establish themselves as leaders in the assessment process at the institutional level. Demonstrating a willingness to take the initiative in assessment will reduce the possibility that external and inappropriate processes will be imposed by institutional or governmental authorities. Librarians who are able to position themselves as institutional leaders in assessment, evaluation, accountability, and quality will strengthen the library's position within the political structure of the institution and possibly improve its share of institutional resources. Academic librarians who choose not to step forward run the risk of allowing others to control the assessment process and ultimately determine the institutional future of the library. This is an unacceptable alternative and threatens the very survival of academic libraries.

Index

ABEF, 31, 45–8, 192
Academic Quality Improvement
    Project – *see* AQIP
Academic World Ranking of
    Universities – *see* ARWU
accountability, 3, 8, 21, 55, 143–4,
    191
accreditation, 36, 159, 188–9
ACRL, 99, 102–3, 159, 165
affordance theory, 133
Annuaire Statistique Interactif des
    Bibliothèques Universitaires –
    see ASIBU
Applegate, Rachel, 151
AQIP, 37–9
ARL, 114, 130, 165, 175, 186
ARWU, 186
ASIBU, 186
assessment, definitions of, 8–9, 31
    – *see also* self-assessment, culture
    of assessment
Association for College and Research
    Libraries – *see* ACRL
Association of Research Libraries –
    see ARL
Australian Business Excellence
    Framework – *see* ABEF

Balanced Scorecard, 59–63, 72, 174
    adapted to academic libraries,
    63–7, 84, 87–91, 192

Barrionuevo, Miguel Duarte, 4
Beck, Susan, 10–11
benchmarking, 68–9
    barriers to, 71–2
    benefits of, 67
    considerations for, 70–1, 87
    types of, 69
Bertot, John Carlos, 98
best practices, 68, 117–18
Bibliotheksindex – *see* BIX
BIX, 87, 186
Blixrud, Julia C., 27–8
Bologna Process, 127, 130,
    141
Boruff-Jones, Polly D., 155
Brophy, Peter, 4, 99
Budd, John M., 114–15
Bunkyo University, 157

Cameron, Kim S., 32
CAUL, 186
Center for Networked Information –
    see CNI
Ceynowa, Klaus, 87
Chu, Samuel Kai-Wah, 135–6
Clougherty, Leo, 136
CNI, 130
College Student Experiences
    Questionnaire – *see* CSEQ
Council of Australian University
    Librarians – *see* CAUL

Covey, Denise – *see* Troll Covey, Denise
Cram, Jennifer, 97, 100
CSEQ, 148–9
Cullen, Rowena, 20–1, 96
culture of assessment, 20–1, 96
  – *see also* assessment, self-assessment
  barriers to, 21
  evaluation of, 22–3, 33
  prerequisites for, 27
customer relationship management, 174

Dalton, Pete, 99–100
data collection, 6–7, 10, 44, 68, 71, 160, 176, 193
  – *see also* focus group research, interview research, survey research
de Jager, Karin, 86
degree completion rates, 129, 137, 144–6
Derfert-Wolf, Lidia, 85–6
Dew, John Robert, 38, 57
Dickenson, Don, 152
Dow, Ronald E., 8
Dugan, Robert E., 8

EFQM, 31, 39–45
Eng, Susanna, 152
European Foundation for Quality Management – *see* EFQM
Evans, Margaret Kinnell, 9, 72

faculty, 111
  – *see also* outcomes, faculty
  productivity, 113–14
  library use profile, 116, 150–1
  part-time, 118–19
focus group research, 179–80

frameworks for quality improvement, 192–3
Fraser, Bruce T., 96–8
Frye, Richard, 8

gap score, 175
Gardner, Susan, 152
Garrod, Penny, 72
German Library Association, 87
Given, Lisa M., 133–4
goals and goal setting, 7, 11, 22, 27, 45, 56, 61–2, 70, 82, 98
  SMART goals and objectives, 56–7
Gonyea, Robert M., 148–50, 154–5
Gratch-Lindauer, Bonnie, 98, 100
Gray, Chris, 19
Green, Diana, 2
Green, Rosemary, 134

Hamrick, Florence A., 164
Harvard University, 129
HEFCE, 40
Henczel, Sue, 71–2
Hides, Michael Trevor, 39
Higher Education Funding Council for England – *see* HEFCE
Hiller, Steve, 3, 9
Hseih, Ling-Feng, 95

IFLA, 1, 81–2, 85–7, 89–91, 95, 186
impacts, 20, 96, 99–100, 188–9
Imperial College, 129–30
information literacy, 120, 132–6, 147, 156–61, 194
Integrated Postsecondary Education Data System – *see* IPEDS
interdisciplinarity, 130–1
International Federation of Library Associations and Institutions – *see* IFLA

International Organization for
    Standardization – *see* OIS
international students, 130, 144
interview research, 181
IPEDS, 163, 165
ISO – *see* OIS

Jackson, Sue, 39
Jacobson, Alvin L., 59
Jankowska, Maria Anna, 117
Jilovsky, Cathie, 3

Kaplan, Robert S., 61–3
Kinnell, Margaret – *see* Evans,
    Margaret Kinnell
Koufogiannakis, Denise, 160
Kuh, George D., 148–50, 154–5
Kuldvee, Birgit, 40–1
Kyrillidou, Martha, 9

Lakos, Amos, 19–23, 26, 192
Law, Nancy, 135–6
leadership role in quality
    improvement, 26, 33, 35, 37–8,
    40–1, 45–6, 192
Leahy, Emily H., 96–8
learning environment (library as),
    147, 153–4, 166, 194
Leiden University, 185
LibQUAL+™, 175, 183
library funding, 3, 55, 113–16, 121,
    143, 145, 147–8, 161

Macauley, Peter, 134
Malcolm Baldrige National Quality
    Award, 31–7
Mark, Amy E., 155
Markless, Sharon, 57–8
Matthews, Joseph R., 11, 20–1, 23,
    28, 59, 83
McClure, Charles R., 96–8

McGuiness, Claire, 119
measurement, 6
  – *see also* metric
  of information literacy, 166
  systems of measurement, 59, 65–6,
    83
Melo, Luiza Baptista, 86–7
metric, definition of, 143
Mezick, Elizabeth M., 165
minority participation in higher
    education, 132, 143, 150
Monash University, 2, 66

Nagata, Haruki, 157
National Center for Education
    Statistics – *see* NCES
National Science Foundation, 128,
    131
National Survey of Student
    Engagement – *see* NSSE
NCES, 113, 186
Nearing, Molly McGowan, 38, 57
Niederer, Ulrich, 86
Nimon, Maureen, 134–5
Niven, Paul R., 66–7
Norton, David P., 61–3
NSSE, 117, 155–6, 163
Nuut, Anu, 85

Obi, Boma B., 148–50
OCLC, 151
OECD, 127–8, 141–4
OIS, 1, 85, 87, 92–5
Okon, Henry Itohowo, 148–50
Omehia, Anthonia E., 148–50
O'Neil, Jr., Harold F., 65
Online Computer Library Center –
    see OCLC
Organisation for Economic
    Cooperation and Development –
    see OECD

organizational climate, 41, 67, 86
organizational culture, 19, 25, 45–6,
    62, 96
outcomes, 96–7, 101–2
    definitions of, 97–9
    faculty, 121–2
    graduate student, 137–8
    undergraduate student, 147,
        154–8, 166–7

peer library comparison, 187–8
Peischl, Thomas M., 70
performance indicators, 72, 82, 111,
    186, 193
performance measurement, 7, 62, 69,
    81–3
Pernat, Marie, 2
Phipps, Shelley, 21–2
Pike, Gary R., 162–3
Pires, Cestalina, 86–7
Poll, Roswitha, 4, 63–4, 72, 84,
    99–100, 102
Porter, Leslie, 31
Powell, Ronald R., 102

quality assurance, 86, 129, 143, 185
quality criterion, 5, 33–4
quality, definitions of, 1–2, 4

return on investment (ROI), 114–15,
    164–5

Sadler, Elizabeth, 133–4
satisfaction (user), 173, 185
Schuh, John H., 164
SCONUL, 186
Seissl, Maria, 87
self-assessment, 3, 7, 10–11, 33
    – see also assessment, culture of
        assessment

benefits of, 48–9
    stages of, 9, 39, 44
Self, James, 9, 65
SERVQUAL, 175
Shanghai Jiao Tong University, 185
Shanghai Rankings, 185–6
    – see also ARWU
Shaughnessy, Thomas W., 67
Sheffield Hallam University, 40
Shelley, Mack C., 164
Shill, Harold B., 154
SIMALTO, 174
Society of College, National and
    University Librarians – see
    SCONUL
Sparks, JoAnne L., 59
staff involvement in quality
    improvement, 20–2, 59–60,
    86–7
stakeholders, 4, 25–6, 38, 159
Stevens, Christy R., 119
strategic planning, 55–9
    action plans, 57–8
    barriers to, 60
Streatfield, David, 57–8
students:
    – see also degree completion rates,
        international students, minority
        participation in higher
        education, outcomes
    engagement, 162–3
    freshman year, 145, 155, 160,
        163
    graduate library use profiles, 134,
        194
    production of graduate students,
        128
    undergraduate library use profiles,
        146–53, 194
survey research, 177–9

Tanner, S.J., 31
Tavelra, Anna, 86–7
te Boekhorst, Peter, 85
Thebridge, Stella, 99–100
Toda, Akira, 157
Tonner, Shawn, 154
Troll Covey, Denise, 9, 21, 97

University of Illinois at Champaign-
    Urbana, 115
University of Southern California,
    64
University of Virginia, 65–6

University of Wisconsin-Stout, 32
University of Wollongong, 49

Vakkari, Pertti, 115
value (to users), 100
Vondracek, Ruth, 152

Washington-Hoagland, Carlette, 136
White, Lynda S., 67–8
Whitmire, Ethelene, 149, 155
Wiebe, Natasha, 160
Wilson, Anne, 70–1
Winn, Bradley A., 32